Green Justice

SECOND EDITION

Green
Justice

The Environment
and the Courts

Thomas More Hoban
Richard Oliver Brooks

WestviewPress
A Division of HarperCollins*Publishers*

Copyright © 1987, 1996 by Westview Press, A Division of HarperCollins Publishers, Inc.

Published in 1996 in the United States of America by Westview Press, 5500 Central Avenue, Boulder,
Colorado 80301-2877, and in the United Kingdom by Westview Press, 12 Hid's Copse Road, Cumnor
Hill, Oxford OX2 9JJ

Library of Congress Cataloging-in-Publication Data
Hoban, Thomas More.
    Green justice : the environment and the courts / Thomas More Hoban
and Richard Oliver Brooks.—2nd ed.
        p.   cm.
    Includes bibliographical references and index.
    ISBN 0-8133-2603-6
    1. Environmental law—United States—Cases.   2. Pollution—Law and
legislation—United States—Cases.   I. Brooks, Richard Oliver.
II. Title.
KF3775.A7H63   1996
344.73′046—dc20
[347.30446]   96-19731
                                                                                    CIP

The paper used in this publication meets the requirements of the American National Standard for
Permanence of Paper for Printed Library Materials Z39.48-1984.

10   9   8   7   6   5   4   3   2   1

Contents

Part Four
Law as a Means of Attaining Environmental Ideals   153

judge decide either way? Did the judge really decide *this* case, or was he or she enunciating principles that, although never stated in the arguments by either side, were assumed by all parties to be the most significant? Was the judge more concerned about how the decision would look in fifteen years than with the individuals and arguments actually before the court? If so, is this necessarily either right or wrong? It is no coincidence that courtroom dramas have consistently provided, generation after generation, some of our most compelling movies. Strip all the principles, all the jurisprudence, all the high-minded posturing away from a hard-fought case and you've got magnificent drama, opera on a grand scale, farce for the ages.

We believe that, like the common law that underlies it, the second edition of *Green Justice* has been able to retain its identity and to incorporate the significant changes in the field that appear so wrenching as we live through them on a day-to-day basis. We have retained five of the cases from the first edition (*Just v. Marinette, Boomer v. Atlantic Cement Company, Tanner v. Armco, Audubon v. Los Angeles,* and *Sierra Club v. Morton*), which we believe continue best to illustrate both the more lasting principles and the more intractable problems to be confronted. We have reluctantly dropped such classic cases as *Scenic Hudson, TVA v. Hill, Reserve Mining, Calvert Cliffs,* and *Village of Wilsonville v. SCA,* although we have retained discussions of them in the commentary on related cases. The nine cases we have added have been chosen not merely because they are more recent (indeed, one, *du Pont v. Train,* is an older decision) but because we believe that they best illustrate new ways of thinking about the conflicts we have seen before in environmental or other contexts.

T.M.H.
R.O.B.

Introduction

The Environmental Movement

"Environment," "environmental," "environmentalists"—in today's social and political climate, few terms are likely to generate as much controversy. Our use of them is bizarre, almost surreal: talismanic terms we strew about in wildly contradictory ways. An industrialist touts a new factory as environmentally responsible at the same time a neighborhood environmental group seeks to close it down because of its unacceptable environmental impact; off-road vehicle users speak of their environmentalism even as a local environmental group fights to restrict or outlaw their use of off-road vehicles, dirt bikes, and dune buggies in environmentally sensitive areas. Recently, we have added entire new categories of environmentally charged words to our vocabularies: One pressure group fights to "preserve biodiversity" as another advocates "sustainable development."

The attitudes of Americans toward the environment—our conflicting desires to raise our standard of living by developing natural resources while enhancing our quality of life by preserving nature—reflect traditions dating back to the discovery of the New World. These traditions, themselves a continuation of an earlier European tradition dating back at least as far as ancient Greece, have not always remained consistent, have been evolving throughout European and American intellectual history. From the sixteenth century on, as Europeans—the English, French, Spanish, Portuguese, and others—explored and settled ever deeper into the newly discovered Americas, their relationship to the land and peoples they discovered was never clear cut. To many Europeans, the land was a source of wealth, an inexhaustible mine from which they hoped silver, gold, tobacco, and furs would stream in endless rivers back to Europe. To others, the Americas were a wilderness to be subdued, rationalized, planted, and made fruitful; its people, savages to be civilized and Christianized for their own material and spiritual well-being. To still others, the continents were an Edenic paradise peopled with noble savages whose encounters with corrupt Europeans demeaned them.

1

These ambivalent attitudes toward the New World and its peoples have indelibly stamped religion, philosophy, literature, and even daily attitudes in the United States. The Puritans regarded Nature as God's "Second Book" in which they could espy Him and His works. The Transcendentalists imagined that somewhere behind the mask of Nature, the Spirit animating it could be found. That Spirit was not always benign: Whereas Emerson and Whitman found solace in the natural processes around them, Hawthorne uncovered a post-Edenic Nature rich in hereditary sin and evil; whereas Thoreau confidently asserted goodness, Melville puzzled out riddles, contradictions, and endless ambiguities.

By the middle of the nineteenth century, the original boundless wilderness had shrunk as the flood of Europeans cascaded Westward. At least some Americans had become aware that Nature was not an infinite resource and that certain areas should be set aside for parks and preserves. As early as 1864 Vermont's George Perkins Marsh published his *Man and Nature,* arguably the first modern ecological treatise, in which he reasoned that our profligate attitude toward Nature was the equivalent of "breaking up the floor and wainscotting and doors and window frames of our dwelling for fuel to warm our bodies and seethe our potage." Although Marsh's prophetic warning was all but forgotten during the next 100 years, other conservationists did work both individually and in organized groups on projects more limited than the wholesale alteration of mankind's behavior, which heeding Marsh would most likely require. In the American West, the spectacle of Nature was hard to ignore. On March 1, 1872, President Ulysses S. Grant signed legislation creating Yellowstone National Park. The Appalachian Mountain Club was founded in 1876, in 1892 it was joined by a west coast version, the Sierra Club, founded by the great Scottish born, U.S. naturalist, John Muir. In 1894, an amendment to the New York State Constitution set aside a huge region in upstate New York to be kept "forever wild" as the Adirondack Wilderness. Recent detailed studies of the history of U.S. conservation and environmentalism include Joseph Petulla, *American Environmentalism: Values, Tactics, Priorities* (College Station: Texas A&M University Press, 1980); Roderick Nash, *Wilderness and the American Mind* (New Haven, Yale University Press, 1973); and Frank Graham, *The Adirondack Park: A Political History* (New York: Knopf, distributed by Random House, 1978). Clarence J. Glacken's *Traces on the Rhodian Shore: Nature and Culture in Western Thought from Ancient Times to the End of the 18th Century* (Berkeley: University of California Press, 1976) covers the beginning of environmental thought.

From today's vantage point we could easily regard these early conservationists and preservationists as fortunate, as if all they had to do was select a magnificent piece of land (there certainly was enough of it. Still is.), carve it out, and protect it from development by getting a few laws passed. Egocentric, we assume willy-nilly that we have it tougher than anyone; that life today is more complex and difficult than ever before; that those who lived in "simpler" times did not encounter the hard choices we face today; that they did not have to strike the balance we must strike today between housing and resource development; that they were granted immunity from considering the various offsets between the generation of manufacturing wastes and continued production, between a growing population's need for housing and the desire of landowners not to give up their property or their rights to do with it what they want. Yet historical periods were never as easy to live through as they seem to later generations. The debates between preservationists and conservationists, advocates of controlled and uncontrolled development, respectively, raged within the ranks of nineteenth- and early twentieth-century conservationists much as they do today. On one side were those like John Muir, who favored preservationism and advocated as little development of the then undeveloped resources as possible; on the other side were those like Gifford Pinchot, who saw forests and lakes as natural resources to be developed and utilized for the best and noblest ends of an ever-expanding population. Remnants of this nineteenth-century dispute can still be seen today in the different policies and programs among the agencies of the federal bureaucracy.

Between 1850 and 1970 the preservationist-conservationist debate smoldered out of sight of the majority of Americans. Working long hours in mines, mills, and mercantiles, most Americans, especially recent immigrants, were swept up in the momentous events of the times—the Industrial Revolution, World War I, the Great Depression, and World War II. Before the development and widespread availability of inexpensive automobiles, even the most affluent Americans lived in circumscribed neighborhoods, their travel limited to established (though far more extensive than we are often aware of today) streetcar, bus, and train lines.

By the late 1950s and mid-1960s circumstances had changed. Economically as well as militarily, the United States had "won" World War II. Unprecedented affluence, widespread education, and the increase in leisure time available for travel now brought the Gospel of Nature to more novices than ever before. The two-week vacation had now become the occasion for an automobile trip, frequently a camping trip to a national, regional, or state park. The newly constructed interstate highway system, ostensibly constructed for national defense, became far more significant as a way of increasing the mobility of an already mobile public. The interstate system opened huge areas of the country to leisure travel for a public that had previously traveled mainly, if at all, out of necessity. Along with the knowledge that the great outdoors was there to enjoy came a desire to preserve it for both present and future generations.

Throughout the 1960s, starting with Rachel Carson's *Silent Spring* in 1962, a gradual awareness was building in the public consciousness (or, more precisely, in the consciousness of those portions of the populace with the educational, economic, social, and political influence to be heard) that all was not right with the world, that the country was now facing a wholly different type of pollution problem than it had faced ever before in its history. Some newly discovered horror was mentioned almost daily: The Food and Drug Administration was forced to prevent over 28,000 pounds of Lake Michigan salmon from going to market because of excessively high levels of DDT and dieldrin; the Great Lakes were widely reported to be dying, choked to death in large part by phosphates that encouraged the growth of plant life; the Apollo astronauts had no trouble picking out the cloud of smog over Los Angeles from space; the unforeseen consequences of one of history's great engineering projects—the Aswan High Dam—threatened to destroy the ecological balance of the entire Nile River and topple the fishery of the Eastern Mediterranean; as Americans congratulated themselves on their generally high living standards and levels of health, reports also showed that breast milk from American mothers contained four times the level of DDT the federal government considered safe for human consumption.

The importance of environmental issues came to the forefront of public consciousness in such well-publicized events as the oil spill off Santa Barbara in January 1969. Earth Day, April 22, 1970, focused attention on the entire complex of environmental problems with lectures and demonstrations on college campuses across the country advocating cleaning up the environment and halting the degradation that modern-day society seemed to bring with it.

Newly perceived environmental imperatives sometimes took on ominous, even apocalyptic, colors. That the lack of conservation and environmental control could pose serious threats to present and future generations was the thesis of Paul Ehrlich, a noted demographer in what until then had been an obscure field. Ehrlich seized the popular imagination in *The Population Bomb* (New York: Ballantine Books, 1968), purporting to show that the current rate of population growth inevitably spelled disaster for humankind. If Ehrlich and other popular ecological doomsayers were right, hard choices lay ahead not only for Americans but for all of humankind. The pending crisis knew no geographical, ideological, or linguistic barriers. In one of the more influential, dramatic, and controversial studies of the period, *The Limits to Growth* (New York: Universe Books, 1972), Donella Meadows and Dennis Meadows demonstrated through the use of impressive mathematical models (later criticized by Mihajlo Mesarovic in *Mankind at the Turning Point* [New York: New American Library, 1974] as well as by others) that the affluence attained by the Western world and Japan could not be extended to the Second or Third World and, more ominous still, could not be sustained at current levels beyond the year 2000. Perhaps the most sophisticated of the new prophets was Barry Commoner, arguing in *The Closing Circle* (1971) that corporations, by using reductive chemical processes, failed to respect nature's cycling process.

By the mid-1970s the name and image of conservationists had changed. Only a few years before, many people had considered conservationists oddities; at best a small band of quirky elitists tromping harmlessly through the woods in khaki shirts and hobnailed boots, at worst, out and out obstructionists. Now, calling themselves environmentalists and enlisting support from the findings of the new study of ecology (modern ecology is generally dated from the 1942 work of R. L. Lindeman, who examined the dynamics of energy flow through ecosystems), they cast themselves in the role of saviors. No longer mere nature lovers or bird-watchers, environmentalists saw themselves as having taken on a social, almost divine, mission: to save our species and the planet as well from the consequences of our self-indulgent development past. Knights in shining armor, environmentalists tilted at bulldozers, championing clean air, pure water, and Mom's pesticide-free apple pie. At first their enemy was easy to identify: The polluters were everywhere; sooty symbols of U.S. industry and agribusiness, like caricatures sprung from Thomas Nast, they were obese moneybags made rich by the diseases they spread far and wide.

By the end of the 1970s and into the early 1980s, the environmentalists' shining mantle had begun to cling suspiciously like a burden. Glib generalities had given way to the realization that absolute villains, pasteboard caricatures, and comic book conflicts could not stand up to scrutiny or even to reality for long. As defenders of pure air and clean water, the environmentalists sooner or later had to face the hard fact that in some ways the absolutes they sought with such clarity of vision were amenities and that such amenities don't come cheap. The bulldozer that makes so fine a target was made by (and is probably being driven by) someone who needs a job to support a family: Take that job away—for any reason—and you may have made an enemy, one who will turn a deaf ear to your claims that there are broader reasons why the society will be better off for his or her discomfort. For factories to operate at near-zero pollution the final cost of their products would have to be greatly increased; in turn, higher final costs would reduce sales, force cutbacks in production, and lead inexorably to job losses. Although some studies have demonstrated that environmental responsibility will ultimately pay off, ultimate payoffs and turnarounds take time; the "temporary dislocation" glibly spoken of by some environmental apologists may in reality be the loss of some worker's livelihood, food, or clothes, or some child's well-being. We might well ask environmentalists why such brutal facts as recession, unemployment, and reduced living standards—all prices we may be forced to pay for cleaner air and water—should not be considered "environmental issues." Perhaps our social goals of higher employment rates and an ever-increasing standard of living *do* conflict with our newly enunciated goals of maintaining and protecting a clean environment. Two cases in the first edition of *Green Justice*, *International Harvester Company v. William D. Ruckelshaus* and *Reserve Mining v. Environmental Protection Agency*, illustrated this perfectly. In the first, the future of the automobile industry appeared to be threatened, in the second, the continued existence of the major employer of the region.

Over the past eight years, as in the decades of the 1960s and 1970s, the only constant in the environmental field has been change. In 1993, Congress passed the new Clean Air Act, intended to make more stringent the standards that industries and automobiles are required to meet. Recently we have seen the growth of a market-based approach to pollution, in which industries are allowed to buy and sell pollution "rights." Even its most ardent supporters have come to acknowledge that whatever else Superfund may be accomplishing, it is blotting up immense amounts of money with frustratingly little to show for it other than a class of wealthy engineers and lawyers. There has been an expansion of the uses to which risk assessment has been and will be put in the future. Business and the public have begun to recognize the importance of recycling and to expand its use. More broadly, we have also seen the importance of international law in dealing with environmental issues become more widely recognized. In one of the more significant changes in the public utilities area, the ten years between 1985 and 1995 saw the gradual eclipse of the domestic nuclear industry along with the shrinking importance of discussions of energy. Disputes between and among states and the federal government over the long-term storage of nuclear wastes have grown with the passing years, as stockpiled wastes approach and exceed storage capacities. Finally, the current controversy over the Endangered Species Act promises to be a central issue in the coming years.

Contemporary Environmental Law

The Legal System and the Ecosystem

The ecosystem is the pattern of relationships between all biotic (living) and abiotic (nonliving) entities within a defined boundary of space and time. Let's assume for a moment that we were able to look into a drop of pond water. We'd see minerals, plants, animals, sunlight, life, and death in much the same way we see the same objects and processes in an ocean, a field, a forest, or a city. Although the players change, the plot remains the same, governed by an endless number of infinitely complex scripts. In our drop of pond water—technically not an "ecosystem" but about as simple as we can get—the complexity is so great that the sum total of the relationships, the entire pattern, remains beyond our knowledge. The slightest change in any one element of an ecosystem produces changes in the other elements: Some we consider minor; others, major; many, totally unforeseen. Take away, reduce, or increase a mineral, and the plant life is affected; alter the plant life, and the animals are affected.

Specific ecosystems include the oceans, estuaries and seashores, mangroves and coral reefs, streams and rivers, lakes and ponds, freshwater marshes, forested wetlands, deserts, grasslands, tundra and forests. In discussions of specific ecosystems, humankind may be treated in either of two ways: as just another organism or as the dominant life-form. Discussions of agro-ecosystems and urban industrial techno-systems provide one example of this phenomenon.

Although the ecosystem is a real part of nature, the way we understand the system is part of the science of ecology and related disciplines. Ecology views nature as a self-regulating system of interrelated parts having emergent characteristics; they may change over time, depending upon other changes in the system. In short, the system is, itself, dynamic rather than static. Describing such a dynamic system in traditional categories has proven difficult, and ecology has adopted an entire vocabulary: "energetics" (tracing energy flow through the biosphere); "material cycles" (the cycling of chemical constituents); "population ecology" (the growth and decline of populations of communities within systems as well as competition within and among communities); and many other terms. The discipline known as applied ecology seeks to understand the intervention of humans into these systems.

Which is where law comes in. The Greeks may or may not have been right about man being a rational animal, but, rational or not, we sure like to judge. We evaluate not only our own actions but those of other people, political systems, and other cultures. Not even animals, the weather, and volcanoes ("Mount Pinatubo had a disastrous effect on the equatorial ozone layer."), natural forces acting as they have acted since long before humanity's arrival, can escape our rage to evaluate. Invariably, our judgments are anthropocentric, based upon whether or not we like the results. We evaluate nature, its changes, and their effects in a peculiarly human way, not guided by ecosystems or an ecology that evaluates impacts upon nature but by measuring them against a yardstick that includes economics, politics, morality, aesthetics, and law. Mount Pinatubo distressed us because of its effect on the ozone layer and what we saw as the danger this presented to living creatures. But, of course, similar, and many far larger volcanoes have been erupting in just this way for millions of years, every now and then sizzling off the ozone layer with whatever effects on living things that may have. It is neither good nor bad; benign nor disastrous.

Infinitely more difficult for us to evaluate is the relationship between a "natural" and a "man-made" event when the two have similar consequences: Mount Pinatubo, for example, and the release of chlorofluorocarbons (CFC) from manufacturing. The mere existence of volcanoes does not somehow absolve manufacturing sources of CFCs from their responsibilities for ozone depletion. But it does point out that there may be multiple causes or even multiple effects: Whereas manufacturing sources may be responsible for a certain percentage of some effects (a larger percentage of the Antarctic ozone hole), natural sources may account for a larger share of other effects (the equatorial stratospheric ozone hole).

Perhaps "global warming" provides another example: It is one thing to say that there is evidence that the temperature is rising, quite another to say that this phenomenon has been caused by humans, another still to say that because it has been caused by humans it is qualitatively different from other warming cycles the earth has gone through both before and since the appearance of humans. We all seem to have a tendency to assume that a given phenomenon through which we are living is not only a certain sign of a long-term trend, but also that it is manufactured or caused by humans and, therefore, somehow unnatural.

When a concern for nature enters into our deliberations, it is frequently just one more weapon we use to advance another agenda. And we need not be dealing with entire ecosystems at all. Virtually everything we do has both environmental and economic consequences. The farmer who has drained the marsh at the low end of her farm and planted a new corn hybrid that grows well in the damp soil looks at it and sees that it is good. Not so the plants, insects, birds, amphibians, and reptiles that once lived in the marsh. And not so the farmer downhill, who once got drinking water from an aquifer charged by water purified by the marsh. Maybe not this year, maybe not next, but soon the once pure water on the downhill farm may exhibit increased levels of fertilizer, pesticides, herbicides, or salts, and the soil may show erosion from the runoff that was once soaked up by the marsh.

Now, taking into account the environmental effects of the uphill farmer's good—a few extra dollars a year in increased yield—it may not look as beneficial. In fact, not only has the marsh paid for these benefits in environmental terms, but the downhill farmer may also have to pay more in monetary terms to correct the new problems than the uphill farmer has profited from the changes. Should we shut the uphill farmer down? Maybe force her to reengineer the marsh? Perhaps the few extra dollars that the uphill farmer makes this year will mean a slightly better education for her child or a better diet for the entire family. Surely, in human terms, we might be tempted to say that the increased opportunity for the child's education is a good and that the good to the uphill farmer outweighs the harm to the downhill farmer. Would we say the same if the extra money went to a ski trip or a more expensive car rather than to education? And what of an ecological evaluation? In trying to come to grips with these changes, shouldn't we also consider the damage the farmer has done to the environment? Of course we should, but just how do we balance the harms done to some life-forms against the benefits to others? And why stop there? What of the damage done to the soil by *all* farming, particularly farming supported by politically expedient subsidies that encourage overproduction?

Suppose we had been able to step in beforehand (just as zoning and other land-use regulations allow us to do) and not permitted the uphill farmer to drain the marsh. Sounds good at first, but look again: Wouldn't this restriction have resulted in a windfall—a free benefit—to the downhill farmer, who would not ever have to spend money on improving his or her water supply? This approach would inevitably raise the question of whether we should protect the downhill farmer's investment in this way and thus increase the value of the farm. Now it appears as if our land-use regulations have created a subsidy for one to the detriment of the other. Would our edict against draining the marsh extend to all uphill farms or only this one? Perhaps we should decide on a case-by-case basis. And, while we are asking questions, just who are we to be deciding what is best for others in the first place? Does our education or our knowledge of the environment or the law give us that right? Isn't it the farmers' land and wouldn't they be perfectly within their legal rights to ignore us, to tell us to get off their land and out of their lives? One of the central questions, raised time and again in *Green Justice,* is "Just who gets to make these decisions that are disruptive to some lives and beneficial to others?"

Whether ecosystem changes are caused by human or nonhuman action, as the uphill-downhill example illustrates, the consequences of those changes affect us unequally. Some prosper, others fail; some make vast amounts of money from changes that force others to buy their drinking water at the local supermarket. The legal system becomes important in dealing with these consequences of change and in avoiding or rectifying any perceived wrongs; this is where environmental law, as reflected in this text, begins.

The legal statements of our society's goals—whether social, political, or environmental—are enunciated in common-law court decisions and in the statutes or laws passed by local, state, or federal legislatures. Under our system of representative democracy, statutes passed by elected representatives are presumed to reflect our will as a sovereign people. Occasionally, however, that will, as reflected in one statute, conflicts with our will, as reflected in other statutes. As we will see in the cases in this text, the goal of economic development may conflict with the goal of preserving endangered species (*Palila v. Hawaii Department of Land and Natural Resources*); that of a healthy manufacturing sector and the continued existence of the automobile industry may conflict with the goal of maintaining and improving air quality (*Ethyl Corporation v. Environmental Protection Agency*); and the goal of wetlands protection may conflict with the rights of property owners to do what they want with their own land (*Just v. Marinette County*).

As will become clearer in Part 1 of the text, the traditional way of dealing with the issues we now call environmental was local, primarily through the common-law categories of nuisance, trespass, and negligence. The difficulty we now face is that our new environmental and ecological awareness has forced us to recognize that although these mechanisms worked admirably well for localized, individual disputes, they collapse when confronted with the sorts of problems we now call upon the law to protect, and they make imperative a reexamination of these traditional legal institutions and mechanisms. Today's environmental crises differ from the isolated pollution scares of the past, such as the London killer fogs of the 1950s or the Minamata, Japan, mercury poisonings; given our current perception of the environment as global, even these large-scale events were "local"; it is now our perception that individual instances of pollution are not unrelated and that no environmental issue arises or is resolved in a vacuum. Today we understand, or believe we understand (which is much the same thing), that no area of the country is immune from events elsewhere. Air, water, thermal, and other forms of pollution are all interrelated. Pluck at any one point in the intricate fabric of our ecosystem, and the web of relationships changes shape, disrupting the previous equilibrium so that further changes must be made to offset both intended and unintended effects. This new perception of the world in which we live, one in which human beings are merely another component of an immensely complex ecosystem, makes us more fully aware of the magnitude of the environmental problems we face. Complicating matters further, environmental problems are not confined by national boundaries; the recent friction between the United States and Canada over acid rain presages more and deeper international environmental disputes.

The American Legal System

Unlike the ecosystem, which appears to operate by specific, natural rules and thus has an internal consistency or logic of its own, the legal system is a human creation, a regulator of social behavior developed long before our ecological awareness arose. If the ecosystem at any one moment is the manifestation of an infinite number of rules, the legal system is the end result of an infinite number of practical social compromises reached between and among individuals in the past: concessions made by one neighbor to another; gradually agreed-upon and accepted codes of conduct by which the society constrains individuals to benefit the common good; compacts between neighboring communities; the intricate agreements between states and nations; and, in the United States, the agreements by which fifty sovereign states gave up much of their power to a federal government that was initially as alien and suspect as the one the colonists had rebelled against just a few years previous.

Because from the start each state had its own legal system, its own legislature, executive, and judiciary, the United States legal system is made up of fifty-five geographical jurisdictions (that is, the area—either geographic or conceptual—over which a court can exercise its power): the fifty states, the territories, the federal court system, and a number of overlapping, non-geographic jurisdictions, such as admiralty, military justice, and bankruptcy (which do not concern us here). The legal systems of the individual states and of the federal courts operate largely independent of each other although they overlap, most significantly in two areas: The U.S. Supreme Court may review a state supreme court decision if it involves a significant federal issue (but not if the state court based its decision on an independent reason under state law), and the federal district courts can hear a case based upon state law if it is between citizens of different states.

Common Law and Statutory Law

Courts in the United States, whether state, federal, or local, hear cases or disputes that arise from three general sources: constitutions (the federal constitution or those of the individual states), common law, and statutory law. Statutes are bills passed by the legislature, signed into law by the executive (typically the governor or president), enforced by the executive, and interpreted by the judiciary. Typically, environmental statutes are enforced either by governmental agencies or by citizens who are authorized by the statute to bring so-called citizens' suits to enforce its terms if the agency charged with enforcement has neglected to do so. The common law is more amorphous, having developed over successive centuries as the decisions of individual judges, independent of statutes. A common law proceeding typically has at its heart one citizen's bringing a complaint, that is, com-

approach to environmental problems be to leave these technical decisions to experts in the field? Shouldn't biologists decide about endangered species, chemists about levels of hazardous wastes, meteorologists about airborne pollution, and planners about zoning?

Part of the joy of studying environmental law comes from the study of environmental policy—the specific objectives of environmental law, such as protecting a wilderness or saving an endangered species. Policies may be buried in environmental regulation, boldly set forth in statutes and invoked by courts. But unexceptional general policies (who wouldn't want to save the whales) are tested not only in the crucible of politics but also in court battles. To study how legally mandated policies are tested in court cases is to learn the cost of policies and the difficulty of applying those policies in specific situations. The study of law doesn't just teach one how to question policies, it does so by means of concrete facts and angry plaintiffs!

Cases and Their Citations

The cases compiled for *Green Justice* have been selected from both lower level and appellate courts. A lower court (one in which the legally significant facts are determined and legal principles are first applied to those facts) renders its decision based upon the facts and, if one of the parties has objected to that decision, it may be appealed to the next highest court. In its objection the party raises one or more legal (as opposed to factual) issues that it maintains were decided incorrectly in the court below and that, if corrected, would result in a more favorable decision—either to reverse, to modify, or to remand the decision for reconsideration. The judge in an appellate decision usually limits the discussion to those legal issues raised in the appeal and does not directly evaluate the merits of the case or its facts—these were thoroughly discussed in the lower court. Appellate judges give a great deal of deference to lower court decisions and to the facts as determined by the lower court. An appellate court's function is easily stated: Given the facts as found by the court below, was the correct rule of law applied correctly?

One of the most forbidding aspects of legal study, at least at first, is its system of citation. The examples in this text are intended to assist in unraveling this seemingly complex, but in reality straightforward, system. Legal decisions in print are not official court documents. They are published by private companies (referred to as reporters) in bound volumes. There are nine regional reporters, which reprint the written decisions of state appellate courts, and three major federal reporters, one each for the U.S. Supreme Court (called *U. S. Reports*, abbreviated U.S.), for the federal circuit courts of appeal (collected in the *Federal Reporter*, either "F" for earlier cases, "F.2d" or "F.3d" for more recent decisions), and for the federal district courts (*Federal Supplement*, or "FSupp"). Citations to these reporters are always given in precisely the same order: volume number, the title of the reporter, the page on which the decision begins, the page on which the relevant or quoted passage can be found, and, in parentheses, the court identification and the year. Citations to U.S. Supreme Court cases do not name the court because only Supreme Court decisions appear in *U.S. Reports*. Four examples of legal citations for cases included in this text are

> *Sierra Club v. Morton*, 405 U.S. 727 (1972).
> *Ethyl Corp. v. United States Environmental Protection Agency*, 541 F.2d 1, 15 (D.C. Cir. 1976).
> *Tanner v. Armco Steel*, 340 F. Supp. 532 (S.D. Tx. 1972).
> *Just v. Marinette County*, 56 *Wis.2d* 7, 201 *N.W.2d* 761 (Wis. 1972).

The first decision was written in 1972 and can be found on page 727 of volume 405 of *U.S. Reports*. Because it is in *U.S. Reports*, we automatically know that the decision must have been handed down by the United States Supreme Court. The second decision was written by the federal circuit court of appeals for the District of Columbia; the quoted passage is on page 15 of a decision that begins on page 1 of volume 541 of *Federal Reporter, Second*. The third decision was made by a United States district court, here, the U.S. District Court for the Southern District of Texas. It begins on page 532 of Volume 340 of *Federal Supplement* (most federal district courts are in this reporter). Finally, the last decision was by a state court, the Wisconsin Supreme Court. It can be found in two reporters, either in volume 56 of *Wisconsin, Second*, or in volume 201 of *Northwest Reporter, Second*.

What This Text Is—and Is Not

This book presents some of the more significant legal decisions in the history of environmental protection as carried out by the legal system of the United States. The selection focuses primarily, but not exclusively, on the period between 1970 and 1990, what the authors have come to call the "environmental decades." Severely edited versions of fourteen cases from a twenty-year period can provide only the briefest possible introduction to the richness of the legal material that has developed over this time. The student must be sensitive to the historical context of the cases and is encouraged to reach beyond the text to understand how each case fits within broader historical patterns. The cases resulting in these decisions arose from the clash between those seeking environmental protection—for health, wealth, safety, aesthetic, even philosophical, reasons—and those advancing competing values (frequently also based upon health, wealth, safety, aesthetic, or philosophical reasons). The resulting opinions are sometimes plodding, sometimes flashing, but always reflect the responses of experienced judges attempting to fashion a proper application of law to cope with a new environmental conflict.

In format this book is a casebook rather than a textbook. Properly used, a casebook fulfills a function opposite to that of a textbook: A text presents historical or factual material in detail, whereas a casebook forces the reader to come to grips with the conflicting views and principles underlying the decisions. Casebooks have been the standard means of instruction in law schools for over ninety years and have recently gained increasing acceptance in graduate schools of business administration. One reason for their widespread acceptance is that they enable both professor and class to focus their discussion on the conflicting policy and ethical issues underlying individual decisions rather than on background material more readily obtained from the class, the professor, or outside reading.

The decisions in this casebook illustrate the complex relationships between the competing, and at times conflicting, values that characterize environmental law and the ways in which individual judges have been forced to confront these values—by bringing to bear their own backgrounds, talents, abilities, even their own biases, in addressing the issues and in writing the decisions. As will quickly become apparent, a legal decision is often the record of a conscientious judge trying to feel the way through a thicket of logical and policy snares, not simply the dry-as-dust application of a few sterile legal formulas. Like the legal briefs that led to them, the decisions are often exercises in rhetoric, designed to convince the reader at least as much as they are designed to get at the "truth." The student should be sensitive to the dimensions of rhetoric in these opinions. We believe that the casebook approach is ideal to illustrate the tentative, exploratory nature of environmental law decisions precisely because it forces the reader to examine the principles underlying these seminal environmental decisions.

Analogous conflicts and resolutions arise in other fields of law: What the reader brings away from these cases will prove useful in other law and policy courses. Environmental law is too important to limit to lawyers. It affects all of us, and the issues raised in these decisions have a far greater application and effect than merely to the individuals involved in a particular case. Whether the reader's primary concern is history, literature, philosophy, or natural science, this casebook should provide ample occasion to understand the relevance of these disciplines to decisionmaking within the law. Appended to each case are notes that seek to link it to related questions arising in other disciplines. If the two sides of these disputes were not almost equally strong, these cases would not have reached the courts. It is our hope that after studying the cases collected here, our readers cannot easily voice oversimplified environmental shibboleths or uninformed attacks against "polluters" any more than they will be able to defend equally simplistic "environmental" positions. As a society and as individuals we must become aware that to a large extent it is our own values that have created our environmental problems; perhaps we will recognize that we cherish these values too much to give them up. In this melodrama we all wear gray hats: It is our own values, our desire for economic success, our demands for food, for clothing, for shelter, and for luxuries, and our desire to leave our children a little better off—that create environmental problems. Perhaps by studying the courts' efforts to resolve these problems, we can begin to resolve them ourselves. In short, we must study these cases not as outside observers but as actual or potential participants in the legal process of our nation.

Part 1

Environmental, Personal, and Property Rights

For the first Edition of *Green Justice*, eight years ago, we identified a number of "severe, identifiable ecological or environmental problems: Acid rain falls on the Northeast; the prodigal fishery of Puget Sound is threatened by pollution; the Monument Valley sky is smeared by smoke from the coal-burning power plant at Four Corners, the once ferocious Colorado River evaporated in a fertilizer-encrusted salt pan miles inland from its original delta" (p. 17). Not one of these environmental concerns has been remedied, or even significantly abated: Acid rain continues to fall; the salmon, symbol of the Northwest fisheries, has become sufficiently threatened to warrant the partial suspension of fishing, an entire industry incapacitated; Monument Valley and the Colorado River continue as before. In the brief period between this and the first edition, our attention as a society has become riveted upon new environmental issues, threats, and causes: the spotted owl and the effect its preservation may or may not have upon the timber industry of the Northwest; the "hole in the ozone" over the Antarctic and the consequent worldwide ban imposed on chlorofluorocarbons (CFCs), an entire family of industrial chemicals; the continued cutting of the tropical rainforests. Of these, only rainforest harvesting had been identified as a significant issue when the first edition of this text was published.

Not only have our original ecological problems remained, they may be getting worse. As the list above demonstrates, most of our identifiable environmental problems fall into two broad general categories: pollution problems or a reduction in natural resources. By far the most dramatic are the pollution problems; the environmental issues besieging us daily in the newspapers or over the radio or television are almost always related to pollution. Ecological disasters make good copy and most of us have come uncritically to accept the too-simple equation of environmental law with antipollution law. But there is a great deal more to environmental law than that. As we hope you will come to recognize, these rights is-

sues are directly related to pollution: If a party has the right to use his or her property as he or she wants, with no restrictions, from where does another's right not
to have his or her life disrupted by pollution from that property arise?

Like the environment itself, environmental problems are interrelated: Pollution
problems arise in conjunction with other, natural resource, problems. Two of the
three cases we have chosen to begin our casebook (*Boomer* is the exception) have
little or nothing to do with pollution as conventionally defined. They deal instead
with our rights as citizens: the rights we have to use the property we own in the
manner we choose; the right we have to enjoy our own property without unreasonable trouble from our neighbors; and, finally, the right we have (or think we
may have) to a decent environment in which to live. The discussions preceding the
cases seek to determine just what these rights may be and, perhaps a more intriguing question, just from whence they may come.

As to the *Just* case, we must consider whether our rights to use our property as
we wish (a right for which we have expended good money) can be limited for generalized social or environmental good or whether, in attempting to limit or restrict that use, our society is actually taking away a definable good we have purchased. If a society (in this case, the county) passes a regulation for the greater
good, must an individual landowner bear the burden and expense of that regulation? The more significant questions raised by the *Just* case go far beyond narrowly defined environmental issues: What property, specifically, is being regulated? And, assuming that our use of our property is subject to some social limits
or control, just which citizens or groups of citizens get to decide whose property
is subject to whose constraints?

A somewhat different issue, but still dealing with our rights to the use and enjoyment of our own property, is the *Boomer* case. Here we confront the relationship between property rights and pollution directly. At issue is whether our neighbor can use his own property in such a way as to destroy or negatively affect our
use of our own property. The further question raised by *Boomer* is, of course, if
so, should the neighbor (or the government, which allows him to use his property
that way) pay us for the use or enjoyment he or it has taken?

Finally, in *Tanner*, we deal with the claim that, as citizens of the United States,
we all have a right to a "decent environment." Brave words. They certainly sound
fine enough, but if such a right exists, just where would it come from? Since there
is no statute providing it, and since no common law precedent exists on which to
base such a claim, it can only come from the United States Constitution. This is
what Mr. Tanner thought; as we will see, the court was not as sure. To relate it back
to our discussion of mutual rights and responsibilities, if the court had found that
Mr. Tanner did have such a right, would he then be able to sue his neighbors for
violating that right when they used their backyard barbecue?

1
Property Rights
"Natural" and "Unnatural" Uses of Property

Case Study:
Just v. Marinette County

We've all been told not to use clichés. But there has always been someone willing to argue that clichés become clichés precisely because they contain more than just a smattering of truth. And although aphorisms may lose their sparkle when their social setting changes, Pierre–Joseph Proudohn's "Property is theft" can still turn heads a century and a half after it was written. It is certainly true that property ownership prevents others from possessing the same thing at the same time, but is this theft? If so, from whom, specifically, has the thief taken the property in the first place? How can my property belong to my neighbor? How can it *not?* The first case in this text addresses what we mean by "property" and what we can and can't do with it; in this case the type of property we call real (real estate, house lots) to distinguish it from personalty.

What does it mean to say that we own something? We all own (or think we own—which may be the same thing) our clothes, books, CDs, computers, pencils, and toothbrushes. These are all physical objects: We can put them aside; lock them up; shut them inside other things we own to protect them; and decide just who, if anyone, we will allow to use them and under which circumstances. Some of us are fortunate enough to own other, intangible, things that can be bought and sold as if they were concrete: stocks representing portions of corporations or other organizations; rights to the interest on loans not yet made, much less paid; objects not manufactured, under contracts not to be performed for years. Others of us, inventors and writers, can own ideas, words, or concepts: so-called intellectual property, owned through patent and copyright mechanisms. To those of us living in the late twentieth century, ownership is like breathing: so perfectly natural that we hardly ever think about it. We assume that if we want, we can just throw away our clothes, burn our books, sell our CDs and computers, and license our patents.

But we don't live alone, we live in a society and all of our so-called rights have some relationship to (may even originate in the rules of) that society. So it is with property rights. Their boundaries or limits are defined by the society within which we live: the getting (Proudohn's point—what we own can't be owned by anyone else); the keeping (a large portion of our societies' tax expenditures go toward paying the police to protect that property); the spending (the Food and Drug Administration and other governmental agencies decide that there are certain classes of goods you simply cannot purchase); and the parting with property (many capitalists believe, with many socialists, that inheritance should be done away with because it institutionalizes inequities, thereby blocking individual initiative) all have social consequences far beyond mere ownership. There is no aspect of property ownership that could not be argued endlessly.

Before looking at the *Just* case, let's examine a few of those social dimensions of property ownership. The social restrictions are most obvious with certain personalty. Although you can burn your books and throw away your clothes, there are some things that society just doesn't let you do with the things you own: You can own and play your CD, but not so loudly that it bothers your neighbors; you can drive your car, but only so fast in certain areas; you can own a handgun, but its use is strictly regulated, to the point of requiring a permit.

Personalty is not the only form of property subject to governmental constraints. There are currently restrictions on the types of renovations and extent of remodeling that the owners of buildings on the National Register of Historic Buildings can do to their real property. The theory is that the scarcity of these objects has resulted in their becoming museum pieces, "belonging" not just to those who happen to have paid for and live in them but in some sense to those of us who can see them as well. The argument is that once historical buildings are torn down, disappear, or get remodeled beyond recognition, we all lose something. Assuming that this is a reasonable restriction, would the same restriction make equal sense in the case of antique automobiles or airplanes? Should the owners of Bugattis or Sopwith Camels be prevented from driving, racing, or flying their own property lest these historical cultural objects also be destroyed? A good exercise might be to go through a list of your personal property items and examine the ways in which their uses are limited by social conventions and laws. You might also ask how you would react to a new statute preventing you from the commercial use of a building you own in a historic district. In what ways would the Justs' lakefront property be different from the commercial building? (See case excerpt later in this chapter.)

Social Restrictions on the Use of Real Property

In the 1990s when we speak of environmental law most people probably assume that we are referring to the complex federal and state network of statutes regulating air and water pollution and hazardous waste disposal, including the Clean Air Act, the Water Pollution Control Act or Clean Water Act, the Resource Conservation and Recovery Act, and the Comprehensive Environmental Response, Compensation, and Liability Act (CERCLA or Superfund). But environmental law as conceived of by a practicing attorney or planner has many more facets and a far more familiar face than the mere rumblings of some far off legislative machine in Washington, D.C., or our state capital that we become aware of every month or so on the nightly news.

More immediate and with a much more direct impact on us all are the land-use regulations imposed by our state and local governments. Most Americans, certainly most landowners, are aware that the majority of localities in the United States are zoned. The notable exceptions are Houston, Texas, which did not have conventional zoning until very recently, and Hawaii, which has what amounts to statewide zoning. By and large the United States is zoned village by village, city by city, or county by county.

Understanding the *Just* decision requires a theoretical background extending beyond traditional zoning. The two basic concepts behind zoning are that some land is more appropriately used for some purposes than is other land and that compatible uses are best kept together and incompatible uses best kept separate. To accomplish these goals, the state gives local governments the authority to enact legislation (local statutes called ordinances) setting up zones. Under a typical zoning scheme the local government would divide the land under its jurisdiction into areas, some of which would be labeled "residential"; others, "commercial"; still others, "industrial." Obviously, these schemes would vary in scope and complexity depending upon the locality. Within each zone there might be smaller zones. In residential areas, for example, there might be zones where the minimum lot size might be one acre, two acres, or some other predetermined size. At least one locality in the United States has a zone requiring a 50-acre minimum lot size. Other residential areas might permit multiple residences such as two- or three-family apartments but not allow four-family residences. Still others might allow professional offices or only residences of two stories or less.

Similar restrictions would also be applied within commercial or industrial zones in an attempt to establish and maintain a degree of homogeneity and to reduce conflicting uses within and between zones. Certain commercial zones might allow a heavy concentration of stores, restaurants, and service stations, whereas others might limit these commercial establishments to only a handful. A small commercial area might be allowed in residential zones for convenience stores, which could provide milk, bread, and newspapers to people living in those zones. Industrial zones might be limited as to the amount of heavy industry allowed in them, and provisions might be made requiring the industry to be near similar uses, thus keeping down the dust, noise, and dirt levels.

In the abstract, and in a general discussion such as this one, all of this is intuitively consistent; it just makes sense. Because most of us have lived with zoning of this sort for most of our lives, the system seems natural, almost inevitable. But, like all concepts, zoning has a history, and in the United States that history is usually dated from the U.S. Supreme Court decision in *Village of Euclid v. Ambler Realty Co,* 272 U.S. 365 (1926). Because of the *Euclid* case, zoning in the United States is even today referred to as Euclidean.

When the Ambler Realty Company attacked the zoning ordinance of the Village of Euclid, Ohio, a suburb of Cleveland, zoning had been used in the United States for about twenty-five years, but its constitutionality had not been directly addressed by the Supreme Court. Although the facts in the *Euclid* case were fairly complex, it all came down to a bottom-line question for Ambler, which owned a piece of property located on the fringe of an industrial area. Without zoning in force, the parcels would have been worth about $10,000 per acre or $150.00 per running foot of frontage as industrial property. Unfortunately for Ambler, however, the property was zoned residential. As residential property, the value was much lower: $2,500 per acre or $50.00 per running foot of frontage. Zoning was costing Ambler a lot of money, and they didn't like it one bit. The company went to court claiming that zoning was effecting an unconstitutional deprivation of property (the difference in value that they could not now recover) without due process of law in violation of the Fifth and Fourteenth Amendments to the United States Constitution. The Supreme Court rejected Ambler's challenge to the ordinance, holding that such laws were constitutional exercises of governmental police power: "Under these circumstances, therefore, it is enough for us to determine, as we do, that the ordinance in its general scope and dominant features, so far as its provisions are here involved, is a valid exercise of authority, leaving other provisions to be dealt with as cases arise directly involving them" (*Village of Euclid v. Ambler Realty Co.,* 272 U.S. 365, 397 [1926]).

To understand the court's decision—and zoning—more fully we must begin by understanding that local governments in the United States have no independent legal power. The states, which were originally independent and possessed all the political and legal power, gave up some of their power to the central government to permit smoother functioning. Within the states themselves, however, the county, town, or municipal governments are creatures of the state: Legally, they are merely administrative units having only the powers specifically granted them by the state. What the state gives, the state can take away. In land-use and zoning matters the state grants this legal authority to local governments through what is called enabling legislation, and one of the traditional tasks of local governments is to plan the ways that land use will be regulated within the boundaries of the localities. A locality's powers are limited; it can do no more than the state has allowed it to do. If a local ordinance is challenged as being unconstitutional or too restrictive, a court will look very closely to determine whether the locality has overstepped its bounds by asserting a control over the use of private property that is more stringent than that which the state has allowed it to do in the enabling legislation. If so, the court will declare the local action void for the simple reason that the locality has attempted to do what it cannot. Zoning is one area about which you can fight city hall and win; the arena is the courts.

What the localities are enabled to do generally falls within the bounds of the state's police power. (The police power is the power to enact legislation to further the general health and public welfare.) Part of the independent power of each state, subject to certain constitutional limits, is the power to regulate individuals' lives so as to promote the general welfare. The state delegates part of this power to the municipalities.

Land-use regulation is perhaps the most highly developed example of police power delegation. In most states, each town, municipality, county, or other local governmental unit has a planning commission (the name of this group will vary from state to state) whose function it is to plan for growth and land use in the locality. This planning commission will typically develop some sort of comprehensive plan, frequently embodied in a map with specific land-use areas delineated. A person wishing to build must consult this map and the specific requirements for the zone in which the proposed development will go. If the proposed use conforms to the requirements, the developer will receive a permit; if the proposed use does not conform, a permit will probably be refused. The developer will usually have the opportunity to appeal the refusal of the permit to a zoning board of appeals. If that board refuses the permit as well, the developer may proceed to court to ask that this refusal be reversed, usually (as in *Euclid*) on the grounds that the refusal has unconstitutionally deprived him or her of an allowable use of the property.

The municipality will typically argue that its denial of the permit was a legitimate exercise of police power. In *Euclid* the village argued that the zoning scheme was necessary for the well-being of most citizens even if Ambler Realty did lose money; the Supreme Court agreed: "If it be a proper exercise of the police power to relegate industrial establishments to localities separated from residential sections, it is not easy to find a sufficient reason for denying the power because the effect of its exercise is to divert an industrial flow from the course which it would follow, to the injury of the residential public if left alone, to another course where such injury will be obviated" (*Euclid*, at 390).

In legal shorthand or jargon, the issue in *Euclid*, the same one that arises in most land-use regulation cases, is called the "taking issue." A "taking" occurs when the government (which could be the state or federal government as well as the local one) acts in such a way or passes a law or regulation that requires a property owner to give up property rights without adequate monetary compensation; in effect, it "takes" rights with financial value from the real-estate taxpaying landowner without paying for them and then confers those rights upon the general public without charging them for the benefit. The government could simply appropriate and pay for the land by exercising its power of condemnation or eminent domain. But this approach has two significant drawbacks for any elected official: First, it makes people angry; second, and far more important, the land must be paid for—a significant consideration because it leads to higher taxes (the angry people again) and, as a result, fewer votes in the next election. An easier and far less painful approach than purchasing the land is simply to regulate the uses to which it can be put. Most property owners benefit from these regulations and find land-use restrictions bearable aggravations that go with the territory like mowing the lawn and paying property taxes. At times, however, these restrictions become too onerous, and the property owner would rather sell the land to the municipality than continue to own property that he or she cannot use as desired. If the locality refuses to purchase or condemn the land, an owner could wind up with a useless piece of property on which taxes must still be paid.

Precisely how far should a locality go in regulating development to bring about environmentally sound land-use practices? Not many years ago, the highest and best use anyone could imagine for marshes, swamps, and bottomlands was to fill them in (frequently as uncontrolled dumps) and build on them. Now these areas are called wetlands and the common wisdom is that their continued existence and even health is essential to the well-being of our waterways, aquifers, countless species of birds and animals, even humankind. Since 1970, an entire new field of environmental land-use protection has arisen. The statute at issue in *Just v. Marinette County* regulates land use in what many would consider an ecologically sensible manner in order to promote the general public health, safety, and welfare. The county shoreland zoning ordinance is well thought out and thorough, its mechanisms for designating wetlands both reasonable and consistently applied. Under current thinking, the *Just* decision is a clear victory for the environment and for the community as a whole.

But what about the Justs? They had purchased a tract of Wisconsin lakeside property intending to build on it themselves, subdivide it, and sell those parts to others to build on. Presumably the price they paid for the land reflected these potential uses. From their perspective, the county simply stepped in and took away these uses, reducing the amount that the Justs could get for their property when they could sell it. The Justs can no longer make full use of the land they originally purchased. And no one is likely to purchase the land for a price sufficient for the Justs to recoup their initial investment on terms close to their original intent. As far as the Justs are concerned, the county has donated their property—which they purchased and on which they must still pay taxes—to a public purpose without compensating them. Part of its value has been taken.

The *Just v. Marinette County* opinion identifies several theories about taking. According to the court, a taking is found where "too much" value is taken; where no uses are left in the land; where the regulations don't actually prevent the harm they ostensibly exist to prevent or remedy, existing merely to provide a mechanism whereby a locality may acquire land for public use; where the property is not held in trust; where the property is not an inextricable part of a complex ecosystem; or where the regulation takes "the natural aspect" of the land.

In reading this opinion, you might try to determine which of those tests makes sense to you first in the abstract and second as applied to the Justs' property. You might also try to sort out who really wins a case like this: the county? the residents? the future purchasers of the Justs' lot? Also, how might Justice Hallows or anyone else go about deciding what the natural character of a piece of land is?

Ronald JUST and Kathryn JUST, his wife, Appellants

v.

MARINETTE COUNTY, Respondent

Supreme Court of Wisconsin
October 31, 1972
[201 N.W.2d 761]

HALLOWS, Chief Justice.

Marinette county's Shoreland Zoning Ordinance Number 24 was adopted September 19, 1967, became effective October 9, 1967, and follows a model ordinance published by the Wisconsin Department of Resource Development in July of 1967. See Kusler, Water Quality Protection For Inland Lakes in Wisconsin: A Comprehensive Approach to Water Pollution, 1970 Wis.L.Rev. 35, 62–63. The ordinance was designed to meet standards and criteria for shoreland regulation which the legislature required to be promulgated by the department of natural resources under sec. 144.26, Stats. These standards are found in 6 Wis. Adm. Code, sec. NR 115.03, May, 1971, Register No. 185. The legislation, secs. 59.971 and 144.26, Stats., authorizing the ordinance was enacted as a part of the Water Quality Act of 1965 by ch. 614, Laws of 1965.

Shorelands for the purpose of ordinances are defined in sec. 59.971(1), Stats., as lands within 1,000 feet of the normal high-water elevation of navigable lakes, ponds, or flowages and 300 feet from a navigable river or stream or to the landward side of the flood plain, whichever distance is greater. The state shoreland program is unique. All county shoreland zoning ordinances must be approved by the department of natural resources prior to their becoming effective. 6 Wis. Adm. Code, sec. NR 115.04, May, 1971, Register No. 185. If a county does not enact a shoreland zoning ordinance which complies with the state's standards the department of natural resources may enact such an ordinance for the county. Sec. 59.971(6), Stats.

There can be no disagreement over the public purpose sought to be obtained by the ordinance. Its basic purpose is to protect navigable waters and the public rights therein from the degradation and deterioration which results from uncontrolled use and development of shorelands. In the Navigable Waters Protection Act, sec. 144.26, the purpose of the state's shoreland regulation program is stated as being to "aid in the fulfillment of the state's role as trustee of its navigable waters and to promote public health, safety, convenience, and general welfare." In sec. 59.971(1), which grants authority for shoreland zoning to counties, the same purposes are reaffirmed. The Marinette county shoreland zoning ordinance in sec. 1.2

and 1.3 states the uncontrolled use of shorelands and pollution of navigable waters of Marinette county adversely affect public health, safety, convenience, and general welfare and impair the tax base.

The shoreland zoning ordinance divides the shorelands of Marinette county into general purpose districts, general recreation districts, and conservancy districts. A "conservancy" district is required by the statutory minimum standards and is defined in sec. 3.4 of the ordinance to include "all shorelands designated as swamps or marshes on the United States Geological Survey maps which have been designated as the Shoreland Zoning Map of Marinette County, Wisconsin or on the detailed Insert Shoreland Zoning Maps." The ordinance provides for permitted uses and conditional uses. One of the conditional uses requiring a permit under sec. 3.42(4) is the filling, drainage or dredging of wetlands according to the provisions of sec. 5 of the ordinance. "Wetlands" are defined in sec. 2.29 ... "(a)reas where ground water is at or near the surface much of the year or where any segment of plant cover is deemed an aquatic according to N. C. Fassett's "Manual of Aquatic Plants." Section 5.42(2) of the ordinance requires a conditional-use permit for any filling or grading "Of any area which is within three hundred feet horizontal distance of a navigable water and which has surface drainage toward the water and on which there is: (a) Filling of more than five hundred square feet of any wetland which is contiguous to the water ... (d) Filling or grading of more than 2,000 square feet on slopes of twelve per cent or less."

In April of 1961, several years prior to the passage of this ordinance, the Justs purchased 36.4 acres of land in the town of Lake along the south shore of Lake Noquebay, a navigable lake in Marinette county. This land had a frontage of 1,266.7 feet on the lake and was purchased partially for personal use and partially for resale. During the years 1964, 1966, and 1967, the Justs made five sales of parcels having frontage and extending back from the lake some 600 feet, leaving the property involved in these suits. This property has a frontage of 366.7 feet and the south one half contains a stand of cedar, pine, various hard woods, birch and red maple. The north one half, closer to the lake, is barren of trees except immediately along the shore. The south three fourths of this north one half is populated with various plant grasses and vegetation including some plants which N. C. Fassett in his manual of aquatic plants has classified as "aquatic." There are also non-aquatic plants which grow upon the land. Along the shoreline there is a belt of trees. The shoreline is from one foot to 3.2 feet higher than the lake level and there is a narrow belt of higher land along the shore known as a "pressure ridge" or "ice heave," varying in width from one to three feet. South of this point, the natural level of the land ranges one to two feet above lake level. The land slopes generally toward the lake but has a slope less than twelve per cent. No water flows onto the land from the lake, but there is some surface water which collects on land and stands in pools.

The land owned by the Justs is designated as swamps or marshes on the United States Geological Survey Map and is located within 1,000 feet of the normal high-water elevation of the lake. Thus, the property is included in a conservancy district and, by sec. 2.29 of the ordinance, classified as "wetlands." Consequently, in order to place more than 500 square feet of fill on this property, the Justs were required to obtain a conditional-use permit from the zoning administrator of the county and pay a fee of $20 or incur a forfeiture of $10 to $200 for each day of violation.

In February and March of 1968, six months after the ordinance became effective, Ronald Just, without securing a conditional-use permit, hauled 1,040 square yards of sand onto this property and filled an area approximately 20 feet wide commencing at the southwest corner and extending almost 600 feet north to the northwest corner near the shoreline, then easterly along the shoreline almost to the lot line. He stayed back from the pressure ridge about 20 feet. More than 500 square feet of this fill was upon wetlands located contiguous to the water and which had surface drainage toward the lake. The fill within 300 feet of the lake also was more than 2,000 square feet on a slope less than 12 percent. It is not seriously contended that the Justs did not violate the ordinance and the trial court correctly found a violation.

The real issue is whether the conservancy district provisions and the wetlands filling restrictions are unconstitutional because they amount to a constructive taking of the Justs' land without compensation. Marinette county and the State of Wisconsin argue the restrictions of the conservancy district and wetlands provisions constitute a proper exercise of the police power of the state and do not so severely limit the use or depreciate the value of the land as to constitute a taking without compensation.

To state the issue in more meaningful terms, it is a conflict between the public interest in stopping the despoliation of natural resources, which our citizens until recently have taken as inevitable and for granted, and an owner's asserted right to use his property as he wishes. The protection of public rights may be accomplished by the exercise of the police power unless the damage to the property owner is too great and amounts to a confiscation. The securing or taking of a benefit not presently enjoyed by the public for its use is obtained by the government through its power of eminent domain. The distinction between the exercise of the police power and condemnation has been said to be a matter of degree of damage to the property owner. In the valid exercise of the police power reasonably restricting the use of property, the damage suffered by the owner is said to be incidental. However, where the restriction is so great the landowner ought not to bear such a burden for the public good, the restriction has been held to be a constructive taking even though the actual use or forbidden use has not been transferred to the government so as to be a taking in the traditional sense. . . . Whether a taking has occurred depends upon whether "the restriction practically or substantially renders the land useless for all reasonable purposes," *Buhler v. Racine County.* The loss caused the individual must be weighed to determine if it is more than he should bear. As this court stated in Stefan, at pp. 369–370, 124 N.W.2d

319, p. 323, ". . . if the damage is such as to be suffered by many similarly situated and is in the nature of a restriction on the use to which land may be put and ought to be borne by the individual as a member of society for the good of the public safety, health or general welfare, it is said to be a reasonable exercise of the police power, but if the damage is so great to the individual that he ought not to bear it under contemporary standards, then courts are inclined to treat it as a 'taking' of the property or an unreasonable exercise of the police power."

Many years ago, Professor Freund stated in his work on The Police Power, sec. 511, at 546–547, "It may be said that the state takes property by eminent domain because it is useful to the public, and under the police power because it is harmful. . . . From this results the difference between the power of eminent domain and the police power, that the former recognizes a right to compensation, while the latter on principle does not." Thus the necessity for monetary compensation for loss suffered to an owner by police power restriction arises when restrictions are placed on property in order to create a public benefit rather than to prevent a public harm. Rathkopf, The Law of Zoning and Planning, Vol. 1, ch. 6, pp. 6–7.

This case causes us to reexamine the concepts of public benefit in contrast to public harm and the scope of an owner's right to use of his property. In the instant case we have a restriction on the use of a citizens' property, not to secure a benefit for the public, but to prevent a harm from the change in the natural character of the citizens' property. We start with the premise that lakes and rivers in their natural state are unpolluted and the pollution which now exists is man made. The state of Wisconsin under the trust doctrine has a duty to eradicate the present pollution and to prevent further pollution in its navigable waters. This is not, in a legal sense, a gain or a securing of a benefit by the maintaining of the natural status quo of the environment. What makes this case different from most condemnation or police power zoning cases is the interrelationship of the wetlands, the swamps and the natural environment of shorelands to the purity of the water and to such natural resources as navigation, fishing, and scenic beauty. Swamps and wetlands were once considered wasteland, undesirable, and not picturesque. But as the people became more sophisticated, an appreciation was acquired that swamps and wetlands serve a vital role in nature, are part of the balance of nature and are essential to the purity of the water in our lakes and streams. Swamps and wetlands are a necessary part of the ecological creation and now, even to the uninitiated, possess their own beauty in nature.

Is the ownership of a parcel of land so absolute that man can change its nature to suit any of his purposes? The great forests of our state were stripped on the theory man's ownership was unlimited. But in forestry, the land at least was used naturally, only the natural fruit of the land (the trees) were taken. The despoilage was in the failure to look to the future and provide for the reforestation of the land. An owner of land has no absolute and unlimited right to change the essential natural character of his land so as to use it for a purpose for which it was unsuited in its natural state and which injures the rights of others. The exercise of the police power in zoning must be reasonable and we think it is not an unreasonable exercise of that power to prevent harm to public rights by limiting the use of private property to its natural uses.

This is not a case where an owner is prevented from using his land for natural and indigenous uses. The uses consistent with the nature of the land are allowed and other uses recognized and still others permitted by special permit. The shoreland zoning ordinance prevents to some extent the changing of the natural character of the land within 1,000 feet of a navigable lake and 300 feet of a navigable river because of such land's interrelation to the contiguous water. The changing of wetlands and swamps to the damage of the general public by upsetting the natural environment and the natural relationship is not a reasonable use of that land which is protected from police power regulation. Changes and filling to some extent are permitted because the extent of such changes and fillings does not cause harm. We realize no case in Wisconsin has yet dealt with shoreland regulations and there are several cases in other states which seem to hold such regulations unconstitutional; but nothing this court has said or held in prior cases indicate that destroying the natural character of a swamp or a wetland so as to make that location available for human habitation is a reasonable use of that land when the new use, although of a more economical value to the owner, causes a harm to the general public.

Wisconsin has long held that laws and regulations to prevent pollution and to protect the waters of this state from degradation are valid police-power enactments. . . . The active public trust duty of the state of Wisconsin in respect to navigable waters requires the state not only to promote navigation but also to protect and preserve those waters for fishing, recreation, and scenic beauty. . . .

This is not a case of an isolated swamp unrelated to a navigable lake or stream, the change of which would cause no harm to public rights. Lands adjacent to or near navigable waters exist in a special relationship to the state. . . . The restrictions in the Marinette county ordinance upon wetlands within 1,000 feet of Lake Noquebay which prevent the placing of excess fill upon such land without a permit is not confiscatory or unreasonable.

. . .

It seems to us that filling a swamp not otherwise commercially usable is not in and of itself an existing use, which is prevented, but rather is the preparation for some future use which is not indigenous to a swamp. Too much stress is laid on the right of an owner to change commercially valueless land when that change does damage to the rights of the public. It is observed that a use of special permits is a means of control and accomplishing the purpose of the zoning ordinance as distinguished from the old concept of providing for variances. The special permit technique is now common practice and has met with judicial approval, and we think it is of some significance in considering whether or not a particular zoning ordinance is reasonable.

A recent case sustaining the validity of a zoning ordinance establishing a flood plain district is Turnpike Realty Company v. Town of Dedham (June, 1972), 72 Mass. 1303, 284 N.E.2d 891. The court held the validity of the ordinance was supported by valid considerations of public welfare, the conservation of "natural conditions, wildlife and open spaces." The ordinance provided that lands which were subject to seasonal or periodic flooding could not be used for residences or other purposes in such a manner as to endanger the health, safety or occupancy thereof and prohibited the erection of structures or buildings which required land to be filled. This case is analogous to the instant facts. The ordinance had a public purpose to preserve the natural condition of the area. No change was allowed which would injure the purposes sought to be preserved and through the special-permit technique, particular land within the zoning district could be excepted from the restrictions.

The Justs argue their property has been severely depreciated in value. But this depreciation of value is not based on the use of the land in its natural state but on what the land would be worth if it could be filled and used for the location of a dwelling. While loss of value is to be considered in determining whether a restriction is a constructive taking, value based upon changing the character of the land at the expense of harm to public rights is not an essential factor or controlling.

We are not unmindful of the warning in Pennsylvania Coal Co. v. Mahon (1922), 260 U.S. 393, 416, 43 S.Ct. 158, 160, 67 L.Ed. 322:

> ". . . We are in danger of forgetting that a strong public desire to improve the public condition is not enough to warrant achieving the desire by a shorter cut than the constitutional way of paying for the change."

This observation refers to the improvement of the public condition, the securing of a benefit not presently enjoyed and to which the public is not entitled. The shore-land zoning ordinance preserves nature, the environment, and natural resources as they were created and to which the people have a present right. The ordinance does not create or improve the public condition but only preserves nature from the despoilage and harm resulting from the unrestricted activities of humans.

. . .

We think that when a constitutional issue is now presented to the trial courts of this state, it is the better practice for those courts to recognize its importance, have the issue thoroughly briefed, and fully presented. The issue should be decided as any other important issue with due consideration. The practice of assuming constitutionality, until the contrary is decided by an appellate court, is no longer necessary or workable. Of course, a presumption of constitutionality exists until declared otherwise by a competent court, which we think the trial courts of Wisconsin are, because a regularly enacted statute is presumed to be constitutional and the party attacking the statute must meet the burden of proof of showing unconstitutionality beyond a reasonable doubt.

. . . the shoreland zoning ordinance of respondent Marinette County is constitutional, . . . the Justs' property constitutes wetlands and . . . the prohibition in the ordinance against the filling of wetlands is constitutional.

Questions, Materials, and Suggestions for Further Study

Just v. Marinette County

Since *Just* was decided, both the states and the federal government have sought to protect coastal areas and wetlands. The two primary federal statutes that attempt to protect such areas are the Section 404 Permit program of the Clean Water Act and the Coastal Zone Management Act. Both the federal legislation and the state laws have been continually challenged by developers. In recent years, the Supreme Court has faced these questions in a number of cases involving coastal and wetland areas and has been less sympathetic to regulations that result in serious impacts upon property rights than was the *Just* court, finding an unconstitutional taking where there is no specific nexus, or connection, between the conditions of the regulation and the goals of the regulation. Equally significant, both federal and state courts have permitted developers to bring "inverse condemnation" issues requesting compensation rather than setting the regulation aside.

Meanwhile, a detailed follow-up study of the Wisconsin wetlands program has concluded that the administrative agency, rather than follow the consequences of the *Just* decision to the letter, has tried instead to balance the need for regulation against the costs of regulations to the landowners. This conclusion reflects the experience of the authors, which is that the fundamental force of the taking challenge is to intimidate local regulators, preventing them from adopting stringent regulations.

The *Just v. Marinette County* case raises fundamental questions about the nature of private property and its protection in the modern state. Government regulation continually affects the value of property, creating windfalls (large increases in property value) and wipeouts (large declines in value). See Donald G. Hagman and Dean J. Misczynski, *Windfalls for Wipeouts: Land Value Capture and Compensation* (Washington, D.C.: American Planning Association, 1978). To what extent should the value of private property be shielded against the effects of windfalls and wipeouts that result from efforts to protect the environment?

As we attempted to point out in the introduction to this case, the preliminary question—the disarmingly simple "What is property?"—has no easy answer. It is a question with which legal philosophers have struggled for thousands of years. See Lawrence C. Becker, *Property Rights: Philosophic Foundations* (Boston: Routledge & Kegan Paul, 1977); Stephen Munzer, *A Theory of Property* (Cambridge: Cambridge University Press, 1990). Philosophers have offered different theories of property, ranging from the claim that property ownership is the natural right of the individual, existing before laws were passed, to the position that it is merely a creation of the state or community designed to serve certain practical purposes (such as producing stability for the expectations that back investment). Historians such as Jennifer Nedelsky in *Private Property and the Limits of American Constitutionalism* (Chicago: University of Chicago Press, 1990) have contributed great insight into the role of property in American history. For a modern defense of the traditional private property concept, see Gottfried Dietze's book, *In Defense of Property* (Baltimore: Johns Hopkins University Press, 1971). For a utilitarian approach, see Harold Demsetz's "Toward a Theory of Property Rights," *American Economic Review Papers and Proceedings of the American Economic Association* 57 (1967):347. One of the most creative modern studies of property views it as a vehicle of "personhood." See Margaret Jane Radin, *Reinterpreting Property* (Chicago: University of Chicago Press, 1994).

What are the proper limits of state control of private property? This complex issue has been brilliantly explored by Bruce A. Ackerman in *Private Property and the Constitution* (New Haven: Yale University Press, 1978), by Richard Epstein in *Takings: Private Property and the Power of Eminent Domain* (Cambridge, Mass.: Harvard University Press, 1985), and by Garrett Hardin and John Baden, eds., *Managing the Commons* (San Francisco: Freeman, 1977). In considering property and environmental controls, we must remember that in addition to private property, there is also common property—both the commons and state-owned property. This point is especially important for environmentalists since many polluting events take place on common property such as coastland and in airsheds. For a discussion of common property, see Mancur Olson Jr., *The Logic of Collective Action: Public Goods and the Theory of Groups* (Cambridge, Mass.: Harvard University Press, 1971), and of the impact of environmental pressures on it, see Garrett Hardin, "The Tragedy of the Commons," *Science* 162 (1968): 1243.

One basic question that environmentalists must ask themselves is whether the concept of private property is consistent with the ecological notion of the interconnectedness of ecosystems. One recent eloquent effort to explore this problem is Eric Freyfogle's *Justice and the Earth: Images for Our Planetary Survival* (New York: The Free Press, 1995). Perhaps the idea of territoriality—the presumed need of some individual species for delimited space in which to work and live—can provide the missing link between property and ecology. For a discussion of territoriality, see Robert Ardrey's *The Territorial Imperative: A Personal Inquiry into the Animal Origins of Property and Nations* (New York: Atheneum, 1966).

It may be decided that, despite environmental harms, property should be minimally regulated and disputes over environmental harms should be resolved by voluntary agreement between the parties affected. Ronald H. Coase in his article, "The Problem of Social Cost," *Journal of Law and Economics* 3 (1960):1–19, strongly implied such a position, as might those who believe in the importance of the free market. See Friedrich A. Hayek, *The Constitution of Liberty* (Chicago: University of Chicago Press, 1960).

But the existing common law of nuisance implies that people cannot use their property to harm others, that environmental harms may be nuisances, and hence the use of private property resulting in harm to others can—and should—be controlled. Control over the way in which people use their property may not be implemented through regulation but by establishing new property rights in natural resources—in the common air and water and wildlife. See William A. Fischel's *The Economics of Zoning Laws: A Property Rights Approach to American Land-Use Controls* (Baltimore: Johns Hopkins University Press, 1985); Daniel Bromley, *Environment and Economy Property Rights and Public Policy* (Oxford: Blackwell Press, 1991). At the other extreme, can that control be extended by further government action, such as government expropriation? It may be proposed that private property be abolished and control centralized in the state. See Andre Gorz's *Ecology as Politics,* translated by Patsy Vigderman and Jonathan Cloud (Boston: South End Press, 1980), or Allan Schnaiberg's *The Environment: From Surplus to Scarcity* (New York: Oxford University Press, 1980). Some authors have argued that concentrated ownership is the evil and that decentralized capital ownership is the remedy. See Louis O. Kelso and Mortimer J. Adler's *The Capitalist Manifesto* (New York: Random House, 1958). Decentralization is also favored by environmentalists such as Amory B. Lovins in *Soft Energy Paths: Toward a Durable Peace* (New York: Harper & Row, 1979). It remains to be proven, however, that decentralization of property ownership and energy production necessarily prevents pollution. The regulation of private property may be only one approach to controlling environmental pollution.

2

Property Rights

Nuisance—When Uses of Land Conflict

Case Study:
Boomer v. Atlantic
Cement Company

In the introduction to the *Just* case, we discussed the notion of property, trying to point out just how central it is to our jurisprudence. Although in *Just,* our focus was on private property, there are other sorts of property as well; underlying the environmental regime as a whole is not only our idea of private property but also of public and common property. To some extent, *Just* dealt with the transfer of private property rights from one form (their rights to develop their property) into another (the public's right to prevent them from doing so). Public property—parks and so forth—we think we understand well enough: It is property that is owned by all the members of the society, who either purchased or set it aside, and it can be used by all members with certain common-sense use restrictions. Common property, such as the use of the air, is something that we are free to use in conjunction with others. Normally, we don't think much about common property, but occasionally one member of society (such as a factory) overuses this common property (using the air as a place to dispose of soot, for example), thereby depriving others of us of our use (we now get to use their dirty air to breathe rather than our previously clean air).

As we saw in *Just,* the ownership of private property is legally protected by numerous statutes and by the Fifth and Fourteenth Amendments to the United States Constitution. In *Just,* the landowners sought to protect their property rights by asking the court to agree with them that the regulations governing their land were too

37

strict, that part of the value of their land had been taken from them by the wetlands statute.

Statutory and constitutional protections are not the only legal safeguards our laws have developed for private property. One feature of the English common-law system adopted by the colonies, which continues to the present day, is an elaborate system of private legal actions called torts. A tort is a wrong or injury done to an individual or society that does not arise out of a contract and that can be redressed by a civil, rather than criminal, legal action. Someone involved in an automobile accident might claim that the other driver had been negligent and bring a tort action against him or her. A judge or jury would then try to determine whether a harm has indeed occurred and, if so, whether the defendant is responsible for it, and whether the victim of the tort is entitled to damages (monetary payments to compensate for harm done), to an injunction (a court order to stop doing whatever it is that is doing harm), or to both.

Damages are a money penalty assessed against the person who committed the tort. Damages are paid to the victim as a form of compensation designed to make the victim "whole" again (an underlying assumption of the tort system that many would argue is simply wrong, even wrongheaded, is that money damages provide adequate recompense for harms). If we assume that monetary damages can indeed make one whole again, the tort mechanism works well enough for those harms done in the past, like the automobile accident caused by negligence. If the harm occurred at one distinct moment in the past, its cost, even its future costs in terms of additional effects, can be readily computed. But some harms are continuing: They go on into the future, repeating each day, hour, or minute. For this type of harm, the damages are not so readily quantified. An injunction is the court's remedy for this type of harm. When the court issues an injunction it orders the offending party to cease whatever it is doing that is causing the harm. Injunctions may be either temporary or permanent: Temporary injunctions normally are used to halt the offending action until the court has the opportunity to hear both sides of the dispute; a permanent injunction is just that—the court orders the party simply to stop doing whatever it is doing.

The common law recognized a number of tort actions, many termed "invasions" of one kind or another. The tort of battery, for example, is for an invasion of bodily integrity—someone who intentionally touches you without your permission has committed a battery and you are entitled to damages for that invasion. In much the same way, the tort of defamation protects an individual's good name. As to property, the common law recognized two tort actions protecting the rights of an owner or possessor of land. The first, one of the oldest of all torts, is the action for trespass. "Trespass" has been defined as the "doing of an unlawful act or of a lawful act in an unlawful manner to the injury of another's person or property." The typical trespass to land is caused when someone actually invades the possessor's premises. The offender might step onto the land, throw something over the fence, or even cause smoke particles to descend onto the property.

Trespass is an invasion of the right of possession, a right that comes with ownership. But possession is not the only right we have that comes with the ownership of real property. Included in the bundle of rights that go with landownership are those of occupation, use, and sale. When our neighbor does something that affects those rights—making them less valuable to us or to prospective purchasers—the value of our property has been reduced. This reduction of value can be brought about both directly and indirectly by the use to which our neighbors put their land. For example, they might start a fish processing plant or foundry next door and the smells or smoke might make our property less valuable. Protecting against this sort of thing, ensuring the property interests of property holders not otherwise protected by statute, is the tort of private nuisance, the "unreasonable, unwarranted, or unlawful use by a person of his property which annoys or disturbs another in the possession of his, rendering its ordinary use or occupation physically uncomfortable." There is also the category of public nuisances. These are unreasonable interferences with the rights of the general public. A number of environmental nuisances (such as offensive odors) were originally prohibited as public nuisances.

The key word in the definition of nuisance is "unreasonable." Almost any use we make of our land will affect our neighbors' use of property. But to qualify as a nuisance, some interference is not enough; the plaintiff in a nuisance case must show that the neighbor's use unreasonably interfered with his or her rights of possession. The determination of whether the interference is unreasonable is resolved by the fact finder—the jury or occasionally the judge. In arriving at its decision, the fact finder weighs the nature of the property, the nature and extent of the inconvenience, the nature of the neighborhood, and the relative veracity of the parties.

With this background, let's turn to *Boomer*. A large cement plant (one of the courts claimed that it was one of the largest in the world when built) opened operations in upper New York State. The plant cost over $45 million to build and employed over 300 nearby residents. Owners of neighboring property, including Mr. and Mrs. Boomer, brought suit against the company, claiming that the dust and vibrations caused by the plant operations created a nuisance. As is appropriate for ongoing harms under the tort of nuisance, they requested an injunction—a court order requiring the plant to stop emitting dust and causing vibrations. The crucial problem in *Boomer* is simply that with the existing technology a cement plant cannot operate without producing dust and vibrations: The only way for the company to comply with an injunction would be to close the plant down.

The lowest court that heard the case agreed with the Boomers that the plant created a nuisance: "Although the evidence in this case established that Atlantic took every available and possible precaution to protect the plaintiffs from dust, ... I find that the plaintiffs have sustained the burden of proof that Atlantic ... created a nuisance insofar as the lands of the plaintiffs are concerned" (*Boomer v. Atlantic Cement Co.*, 287 N.Y.S.2d 112, 113–114 [1976]).

But the Boomers did not win their case because the remedy they were seeking was an injunction rather than money damages. A court issues injunctions only sparingly because it orders an absolute stop to whatever activity is being complained of. In *Boomer*, that means that *no* pollution would be allowed to be emitted by the cement plant. None. And the only way that could come about would be for the court to order the plant to close down. Theoretically, the court has this power. Practically, politically, it refused to take this step.

Although an injunction would have provided an ideal solution for the Boomers, it would have had social consequences (shutting down the plant and tossing hundreds out of work) that the court was unwilling to take on. This is the central issue in *Boomer*, an issue that arises time and again in environmental law: the dilemma confronting a judge who must construct a remedy for harms proceeding into the future, especially when the harmful consequences of that remedy to the society at large seem to outweigh the present harm done to the individual plaintiff by the nuisance.

The rule in a nuisance case is clear: Once the plaintiff has demonstrated that a continuing nuisance, an ongoing, unreasonable interference, is taking place and will continue, an injunction is called for. *Whalen v. Union Paper Bag*, cited in *Boomer*, is the established common law precedent for nuisance. Under the circumstances just mentioned, an injunction should be issued by the court. The Boomers asked the trial court to issue such an injunction, but the court refused, instead allowing the plant to continue operations. The court constructed a remedy under which each plaintiff would receive permanent damages for losses sustained from September 1, 1962 (when Atlantic began operations), to June 1, 1967 (when the trial began). In addition to that amount ($185,000), the cement company was to make monthly payments equal to the fair market value of what the plaintiffs would probably get if they rented their property ($535 per month) as continuing compensation. In other words, the court allowed the company to buy its way out of an injunction.

Although the parties appealed the decision, the appeals court held that the trial court had properly considered the issues:

> Despite its conclusion that the defendant in the operation of its plant had, in fact, created a nuisance with respect to plaintiffs' properties, the trial court refused to issue an injunction. In reaching its decision on the propriety of granting the injunction relief sought, the court carefully considered, weighed and evaluated the respective equities, relative hardship and interests of the parties to this dispute and the public at large. Reexamining the record we note the zoning of the area, the large number of persons employed by the defendant, its extensive business operations and substantial investment in plant and equipment, its use of the most modern and efficient devices to prevent offensive emissions and discharges, and its payment of substantial sums of real property and school taxes. After giving due consideration to all of these relevant factors, the trial court struck a balance in defendant's favor and we find no reason to disturb that determination. *Boomer v. Atlantic Cement Co.*, 294 N.Y.S.2d 452, 453 (1968).

The case was appealed once again, this time to the highest New York State court, the New York Court of Appeals, and its decision is reprinted here. Few cases present the equitable issues of environmental law more sharply. You might try reading the decision wearing two different hats: that of the Boomers and their co-plaintiffs, who owned land in rural upstate New York only to have one of the world's largest cement plants move in next door and destroy their property, then that of the cement company, which provides jobs, pays taxes, and invests in the area only to be threatened by a handful of unappreciative local people who refuse to accept a payment that two courts have already deemed adequate.

Oscar H. BOOMER, et al.,
Appellants
v.
ATLANTIC CEMENT COMPANY, Inc.,
Respondent

Court of Appeals of New York
March 4, 1970
[26 N.Y.2d 221; 309 N.Y.S. 2d 312]

BERGAN, Judge.

Defendant operates a large cement plant near Albany. These are actions for injunction and damages by neighboring land owners alleging injury to property from dirt, smoke and vibration emanating from the plant. A nuisance has been found after trial, temporary damages have been allowed; but an injunction has been denied.

The public concern with air pollution arising from many sources in industry and in transportation is currently accorded ever wider recognition accompanied by a growing sense of responsibility in State and Federal Governments to control it. Cement plants are obvious sources of air pollution in the neighborhoods where they operate.

But there is now before the court private litigation in which individual property owners have sought specific relief from a single plant operation. The threshold question raised by the division of view on this appeal is whether the court should resolve the litigation between the parties now before it as equitably as seems possible; or whether, seeking promotion of the general public welfare, it should channel private litigation into broad public objectives.

A court performs its essential function when it decides the rights of parties before it. Its decision of private controversies may sometimes greatly affect public issues. Large questions of law are often resolved by the manner in which private litigation is decided. But this is normally an incident to the court's main function to settle controversy. It is a rare exercise of judicial power to use a decision in private litigation as a purposeful mechanism to achieve direct public objectives greatly beyond the rights and interests before the court.

Effective control of air pollution is a problem presently far from solution even with the full public and financial powers of government. In large measure adequate technical procedures are yet to be developed and some that appear possible may be economically impracticable.

It seems apparent that the amelioration of air pollution will depend on technical research in great depth; on a carefully balanced consideration of the economic impact of close regulation; and of the actual effect on public health. It is likely to require massive public expenditure and to demand more than any local community can accomplish and to depend on regional and interstate controls.

A court should not try to do this on its own as a by-product of private litigation and it seems manifest that the judicial establishment is neither equipped in the limited nature of any judgment it can pronounce nor prepared to lay down and implement an effective policy for the elimination of air pollution. This is an area beyond the circumference of one private lawsuit. It is a direct responsibility for government and should not thus be undertaken as an incident to solving a dispute between property owners and a single cement plant—one of many—in the Hudson River Valley.

The cement making operations of defendant have been found by the court at Special Term to have damaged the nearby properties of plaintiffs in these two actions. That court, as it has been noted, accordingly found defendant maintained a nuisance and this has been affirmed at the Appellate Division. The total damage to plaintiffs' properties is, however, relatively small in comparison with the value of defendant's operations and with the consequences of the injunction which plaintiffs seek.

The ground for the denial of injunction, notwithstanding the finding both that there is a nuisance and that plaintiffs have been damaged substantially, is the large disparity in economic consequences of the nuisance and of the injunction. This theory cannot, however, be sustained without overruling a doctrine which has been consistently reaffirmed in several leading cases in this court and which has never been disavowed here, namely that where a nuisance has been found and where there has been any substantial damage shown by the party complaining an injunction will be granted.

The rule in New York has been that such a nuisance will be enjoined although marked disparity be shown in economic consequence between the effect of the injunction and the effect of the nuisance.

The problem of disparity in economic consequence was sharply in focus in Whalen v. Union Bag & Paper Co., 208 N.Y. 1, 101 N.E. 805. A pulp mill entailing an investment of more than a million dollars polluted a stream in which plaintiff, who owned a farm, was "a lower riparian owner." The economic loss to plaintiff from this pollution was small. This court, reversing the Appellate Division, reinstated the injunction granted by the Special Term against the argument of the mill owner that in view of "the slight advantage to plaintiff and the great loss that will be inflicted on defendant" an injunction should not be granted. . . . "Such a balancing of injuries cannot be justified by the circumstances of this case," Judge Werner noted. . . . He continued: "Although the damage to the plaintiff may be slight as compared with the defendant's expense of abating the condition, that is not a good reason for refusing an injunction."

. . .

Although the court at Special Term and the Appellate Division held that injunction [preventing Atlantic from maintaining its nuisance] should be denied, it was found that plaintiffs had been damaged in various specific amounts up to the time of the trial and damages to the respective plaintiffs were awarded for those amounts. The effect of this was, injunction having been denied, plaintiffs could maintain successive actions at law for damages thereafter as further damage was incurred.

. . .

This result at Special Term and at the Appellate Division is a departure from a rule that has become settled; but to follow the rule literally in these cases would be to close down the plant at once. This court is fully agreed to avoid that immediately drastic remedy; the difference in view is how best to avoid it.

One alternative is to grant the injunction but postpone its effect to a specified future date to give opportunity for technical advances to permit defendant to eliminate the nuisance; another is to grant the injunction conditioned on the payment of permanent damages to plaintiffs which would compensate them for the total economic loss to their property present and future caused by defendant's operations. For reasons which will be developed the court chooses the latter alternative.

If the injunction were to be granted unless within a short period—e.g., 18 months—the nuisance be abated by improved methods, there would be no assurance that any significant technical improvement would occur.

. . . [T]echniques to eliminate dust and other annoying by-products of cement making are unlikely to be developed by any research the defendant can undertake within any short period, but will depend on the total resources of the cement industry nationwide and throughout the world. The problem is universal wherever cement is made.

For obvious reasons the rate of the research is beyond control of defendant. If at the end of 18 months the whole industry has not found a technical solution a court would be hard put to close down this one cement plant if due regard be given to equitable principles.

On the other hand, to grant the injunction unless defendant pays plaintiffs such permanent damages as may be fixed by the court seems to do justice between the contending parties. All of the attributions of economic loss to the properties on which plaintiffs' complaints are based will have been redressed.

The nuisance complained of by these plaintiffs may have other public or private consequences, but these particular parties are the only ones who have sought remedies and the judgment proposed will fully redress them. The limitation of relief granted is a limitation only within the four corners of these actions and does not foreclose public health or other public agencies from seeking proper relief in a proper court.

It seems reasonable to think that the risk of being required to pay permanent damages to injured property owners by cement plant owners would itself be a reasonable effective spur to research for improved techniques to minimize nuisance.

...

Thus it seems fair to both sides to grant permanent damages to plaintiffs which will terminate this private litigation. The theory of damage is the "servitude on land" of plaintiffs imposed by defendant's nuisance.

[Here Judge Bergan explains that the legal doctrine of a "servitude on land" will prevent the plaintiffs from bringing another action based on the same facts, thus resulting in permanent damages.]

Although the Trial Term has found permanent damages as a possible basis of settlement of the litigation, on remission the court should be entirely free to reexamine this subject. It may again find the permanent damage already found, or make new findings.

The orders should be reversed, without costs, and the cases remitted to Supreme Court, Albany County to grant an injunction which shall be vacated upon payment by defendant of such amounts of permanent damage to the respective plaintiffs as shall for this purpose be determined by the court.

JASEN, Judge (dissenting).

I agree with the majority that a reversal is required here, but I do not subscribe to the newly enunciated doctrine of assessment of permanent damages, in lieu of an injunction, where substantial property rights have been impaired by the creation of a nuisance.

It has long been the rule in this State, as the majority acknowledges, that a nuisance which results in substantial continuing damage to neighbors must be enjoined. ... To now change the rule to permit the cement company to continue polluting the air indefinitely upon the payment of permanent damages is, in my opinion, compounding the magnitude of a very serious problem in our State and Nation today.

In recognition of this problem, the Legislature of this State has enacted the Air Pollution Control Act . . . declaring that it is the State policy to require the use of all available and reasonable methods to prevent and control air pollution.

The harmful nature and widespread occurrence of air pollution have been extensively documented. Congressional hearings have revealed that air pollution causes substantial property damage, as well as being a contributing factor to a rising incidence of lung cancer, emphysema, bronchitis and asthma.

...

I see grave dangers in overruling our long-established rule of granting an injunction where a nuisance results in substantial continuing damage. In permitting the injunction to become inoperative upon the payment of permanent damages, the majority is, in effect, licensing a continuing wrong. It is the same as saying to the cement company, you may continue to do harm to your neighbors so long as you pay a fee for it. Furthermore, once such permanent damages are assessed and paid, the incentive to alleviate the wrong would be eliminated, thereby continuing air pollution of an area without abatement.

This kind of inverse condemnation [allowing a private party to "take" private property for a public purpose. Here the Cement Company is allowed to take the Boomer's property because it supposedly provides a public benefit.] . . . may not be invoked by a private person or corporation for private gain or advantage. Inverse condemnation should only be permitted when the public is primarily served in the taking or impairment of property. . . . The promotion of the interests of the polluting cement company has, in my opinion, no public use or benefit.

Nor is it constitutionally permissible to impose servitude on land, without consent of the owner, by payment of permanent damages where the continuing impairment of the land is for a private . . . This is made clear by the State Constitution . . . which provides that "[p]rivate property shall not be taken for public use without just compensation" (emphasis added). It is, of course, significant that the section makes no mention of taking for a private use.

In sum, then, by constitutional mandate as well as by judicial pronouncement, the permanent impairment of private property for private purposes is not authorized in the absence of clearly demonstrated public benefit and use.

I would enjoin the defendant cement company from continuing the discharge of dust particles upon its neighbors' properties unless, within 18 months, the cement company abated this nuisance.

...

I am aware that the trial court found that the most modern dust control devices available have been installed in defendant's plant, but, I submit, this does not mean that better and more effective dust control devices could not be developed within the time allowed to abate the pollution.

Moreover, I believe it is incumbent upon the defendant to develop such devices, since the cement company, at the time the plant commenced production (1962), was well aware of the plaintiffs' presence in the area, as well as the probable consequences of its contemplated operation. Yet, it still chose to build and operate the plant at this site.

In a day when there is a growing concern for clean air, highly developed industry should not expect acquiescence by the courts, but should, instead, plan its operations to eliminate contamination of our air and damage to its neighbors.

[Three judges concurred with Judge Bergan's majority decision.]

Questions, Materials, and
Suggestions for Further Study

Boomer v. Atlantic Cement Company

In the *Boomer* case, the court avoids addressing the question of how nuisance law—the private litigation over air pollution—is to be related to regulatory statutes governing air pollution, choosing instead to face the case as if it were simply a conflict between two private parties. This is the classic portrait of justice. Aristotle in his *Nicomachean Ethics* called this settling of conflicts between two parties corrective justice and argued that its purpose was to make the person wronged whole again. As we mentioned in the introduction to the case, this approach works well enough if harms are restricted to specific individuals; however, aren't more people affected in the *Boomer* case? When environmental harms are at issue would corrective justice call for negotiating a settlement and paying off the landowner or would it also require rehabilitating the environment to reduce downstream effects on neighbors who were not parties to the original suit? Of course, property damage is not all: The common law system exists to remedy harms to health as well as property, and one of the fastest growing areas in tort law today is the field of "toxic torts"—actions brought by neighbors or consumers for damages done to their or their families' health.

This question becomes more complicated if the damages caused by the plant were small but the costs of controlling the pollution were high. Would it make sense to pay the neighbors to accept the pollution? This was Ronald H. Coase's argument in a well-known article, "The Problem of Social Cost," *Journal of Law and Economics* 3 (1960) 1–19. The so-called Coase Theorem argues that the parties to environmental conflicts may be able to arrive at a settlement on their own, taking into account the cost of pollution, production costs, avoidance costs, and "transaction costs," or the costs of arriving at an agreement. Robert Ellickson in his *Order Without Law: How Neighbors Settle Disputes* (Cambridge, Mass.: Harvard University Press, 1991) describes how the Coase Theorem works in reality.

Treating environmental cases as private squabbles leads to the view that alternative methods of resolution—negotiation or mediation—could perhaps solve these disputes. See Lawrence Bacow and Michael Wheeler, *Environmental Dispute Resolution* (New York: Plenum, 1984). We pointed out in the introduction to the *Boomer* case that tort or private litigation is designed to compensate those who have been harmed. But tort law has other goals as well, one of which is the deterrence of similar future acts. An excellent study of the various functions of tort law can be found in Guido Calabresi's *The Costs of Accidents* (New Haven: Yale University Press, 1970). Does the decision in *Boomer* deter future pollution? Or will future plant engineers and accountants simply budget a few extra dollars to buy out the neighbors?

Underlying the *Boomer* case is a struggle over two philosophies of property. See Peter Wenz, *Environmental Justice* (Albany: State University of New York, 1988). One philosophy views property as an absolute right that operates to protect the liberty of its owner (Tibor R. Machan, ed., *The Libertarian Alternative* [Chicago: Nelson Hall,

1974]). Hence, an injunction should be given. Another theory of property sees it as a creation of society to facilitate the workings of the market (Adam Smith, *The Wealth of Nations* [London: Methuen and Co., Ltd., 1930]). Under this theory, damages might be appropriate.

Should the court have treated this case as nothing more than a conflict between private parties in the first place? If other plants might be affected and other neighbors as well as employees, perhaps the conflict should have been treated as a matter for public regulation. The federal Clean Air Act, which regulates emissions into the air, has been passed since the *Boomer* case was decided. Regulatory statutes seek to control environmental pollution by establishing certain levels or standards that would ensure a certain degree of healthfulness and then enforce those standards by assessing fines for violations. These regulatory statutes seek to benefit the entire population, not merely the parties of court cases. In fact, since *Boomer* was decided, most environmental law is carried out under statutes that do not compensate those claiming to be the victims of pollution. A real question is whether those individuals should receive compensation under environmental statutes (which would presumably provide a lesser level of compensation to a broader number of people) or whether the existing common-law regime of remedies should be strengthened to provide meaningful compensation to individuals.

The common law may also operate to check the failure of public officials acting under environmental statutes. In the 1981 case of *Wilsonville v. SCA Services*, the court upheld a public nuisance action by neighbors of a chemical waste site that had received approval under the Illinois environmental statute. But the remedy there illustrates the drawback of the injunction as clearly as *Boomer* does the weakness of paying money damages. In *Wilsonville*, the neighbors were awarded what amounted to an injunction when the court ordered the offending landfill to be dug up and transported away. Whereas this no doubt made its former set of neighbors happy, what of its new neighbors? How might you feel if you found that an entire landfill, already found to be a hazardous nuisance elsewhere, was being transported to your neighborhood and plopped down where there once was an open field. For a further analysis of the role of common law under a modern legal scheme, see Calabresi, *Common Law in an Age of Statutes* (Cambridge, Mass.: Harvard University Press, 1982).

Should damages be given to the neighbors if a statute is violated? Should we have both a private law for compensating harms to neighbors and a public regulatory system? A public regulatory system must seek to maximize public protection and should administer what Aristotle called distributive justice—the distribution of the costs of control and, depending upon the amount of control, the benefits of control. Distributive justice is discussed by Nicholas Rescher, in *Distributive Justice: A Constructive Critique of the Utilitarian Theory of Distribution* (Lanham, Md.: University Press of America, 1982). What standard should be used to determine who secures the benefits and who bears the cost of pollution control? One empirical effort to measure the distribution of costs and benefits of air pollution control is presented in Eugene P. Seskin and Lester B. Lave's *Air Pollution and Human Health*, with the assistance of Michael J. Chappie (Baltimore: Johns Hopkins University Press, 1977).

3

Personal Rights

The Constitutional Right to a Decent Environment

Case Study:
Tanner v. Armco
Steel Corporation

We all assume that we have various rights—rights of ownership; the right to speak our minds; the right to vote regardless of our skin color; even simply the right of privacy, the right to be left alone by the government. For some of these rights we can point to a clear origin. We have the right to speak our minds freely because we are given that right by the First Amendment to the U.S. Constitution. The right to vote regardless of our skin color is somewhat more complicated since the right to vote in federal elections is found in Article 1, whereas the right to be free from the discriminatory application of state laws (including voting requirements) is found in the Fourteenth Amendment and in the Civil Rights Act. The right of privacy is not mentioned in the Constitution at all. Justice William O. Douglas, however, found (and the rest of the Supreme Court agreed) that the right to privacy exists as an inescapable consequence (in the penumbra) of many of the sections of the Constitution and Bill of Rights, such as the freedom from unreasonable search and seizure. In the *Tanner* case, the plaintiff appealed to the right of privacy, attempting to extend the constitutional right that had been "found" by the Supreme Court in *Griswold v. Connecticut* to cover the existence of a pollutant in the lungs.

Where our rights come from and whether they exist independent of specific constitutions or laws are questions that have perplexed philosophers and legal theorists since thousands of years before our Constitution was even written; we are not likely to resolve them here. But under our system we know that our legal rights can be traced to our federal and state constitutions and to our statutes. Constitutions set forth the structure of the government, enumerate the duties of the various branches of government, establish qualifications for voting and holding office, and announce the broad goals, aspirations, and rights of and for citizens. Perhaps the best example of this presentation is the original Bill of Rights, the first ten amendments to the U.S. Constitution. The provisions of the Bill of Rights fall into two rough categories: those things the federal government cannot do by law (pass a statute establishing a religion, for example) and those things it must do (provide due process of law before taking away life, liberty, or property). The distinction between these categories is more than academic: For the first category the government need do nothing, but for the second it must pass statutes to ensure that the provision is carried out.

Suppose that Congress passed and the states ratified a new amendment to the Constitution: "The right of the people to a clean, healthful environment shall not be abridged." (Such an amendment has in fact been proposed by constitutional scholars and environmentalists.) What precisely would our new amendment mean and who would enforce it? A right, to have any meaning, must have an authoritative body—under our system usually a court—that can review actions that someone claims are inconsistent with the right. A person claiming a violation of that right must be able to bring legal action when he or she thinks that it has been abridged, the court must take injury of the right into account, and relief should be directed to that right. Once we decide that the new amendment creates a right that should or must be enforced, how should we set standards for it? If your next door neighbor ran a junkyard, would the constitutional amendment for a decent environment provide you with the justification for bringing a private suit? If so, the amendment would seem like merely a federalization of traditional nuisance law. If not, if the amendment were interpreted to require federal enforcement, could you merely go to the local federal attorney and request an action in the name of the United States?

Determining the proper role of the courts in defining our rights is an important consideration. In our legal scheme, courts do not typically issue advisory opinions. Federal courts define and enforce rights only when there is a case or controversy before them as required by the Constitution; most state courts also decide only specific cases and controversies. In *Tanner v. Armco Steel Corporation*, a private plaintiff was trying to halt private activity by claiming that his rights under the U.S. Constitution were being infringed upon. For strategic reasons (which we will not go into here), Mr. Tanner's attorney brought suit against Armco Steel in federal rather than Texas State court. To do this he was forced to show that he had a federal claim, one based on either the Constitution or on federal statutes, rather than a state claim.

Mr. Tanner's constitutional claim ran into problems right from the start because the Constitution does not give individual citizens a right of action against other citizens. What the Constitution does do, in the Fifth and Fourteenth Amendments, among others, is delineate what sorts of actions the government cannot take. As Judge James L. Noel points out in *Tanner*, some concrete governmental participation in the deprivation must be shown in order to invoke the Bill of Rights. One might ask, however, just how candid Judge Noel is being. A corporation has no real-world existence; it is what lawyers call a "legal fiction," existing solely because the state has either issued its charter or allowed it to register and operate within the state. Don't issuance of a charter and permission to register and operate constitute government actions that allow the corporation to continue to operate?

An even more complex problem, perhaps the one we are more sympathetic with, is the meaning of "deprivation." The Constitution, especially in the Bill of Rights, gives us rights against the government; one of those rights most certainly is *not* the right to be free from pulmonary diseases. Yet if we expand that category of disease into the only slightly larger category of health, couldn't Mr. Tanner's case begin to make sense? Couldn't the mention of life in the Fifth Amendment include health? In the famous constitutional case of *Griswold v. Connecticut,* the Supreme Court said that a state could not constitutionally outlaw the use of contraceptives by married couples and based its decision on a "right to privacy older than the Bill of Rights." Couldn't we also say that there is a right to health equally older than the Bill of Rights? And couldn't we further say that this right is implied from the Constitution? Or could we argue that the damage to health is an invasion of privacy? Such questions arise in the *Tanner* case and will undoubtedly arise in future disputes.

Constitutional scholar Laurence Tribe has argued that a value should be given constitutional protection if (1) there is widespread consensus about its worth; (2) courts can properly manage its protection; and (3) it does not receive adequate protection from other sources within the existing political system (Laurence Tribe, *American Constitutional Law* [Mineola, N.Y.: Foundation Press, 1978]). You might consider whether Mr. Tanner's right to a decent environment meets these three criteria and whether other environmental problems, if defined in terms of rights, might also meet these criteria.

George N. TANNER, Individually and wife, Stephanie Tanner et al., Plaintiffs
v.
ARMCO STEEL CORPORATION et al., Defendants

U.S. District Court, Southern District, Texas
March 8, 1972
[340 F. Supp. 532]

NOEL, District Judge.

Plaintiffs, residents of Harris County, Texas, bring this action to recover for injuries allegedly sustained as a result of the exposure of their persons and their residence to air pollutants emitted by defendants' petroleum refineries and plants located along the Houston Ship Channel. It is asserted that plaintiff George W. Tanner, as a proximate result of these emissions, has suffered pulmonary damage with consequent medical expenses and loss of income to himself and his family. By way of remedy, it appears from the rather prolix complaint that plaintiffs pray "to recover their damages from the Defendants, jointly and severally, for their personal injuries, past and future medical expenses, pain and suffering, loss of services, mental anguish, loss of support, damages to the homestead and lands of the Tanners, general damages, punitive damages and all other damages allowed by law, in the combined amount of FIVE MILLION DOLLARS."

. . .

In their jurisdictional statement, citing a potpourri of federal constitutional and statutory provisions, plaintiffs purport to construct a claim upon the following foundations: (1) the Constitution of the United States "in its entirety"; (2) the Due Process Clause of the Fifth Amendment; (3) the Ninth Amendment; (4) the Fourteenth Amendment in conjunction with the Civil Rights Act of 1871, 42 U.S.C. § 1983, and its jurisdictional counterpart, 28 U.S.C. § 1343; (5) the National Environmental Policy Act of 1969, 42 U.S.C. §§ 4321 et seq.; (6) and, finally, the general federal question jurisdictional statute, 28 U.S.C. § 1331 (a). All of the foregoing shall now be considered seriatim.

I. The allusion in the complaint to the Federal Constitution "in its entirety" is not a plain statement of the ground upon which the Court's jurisdiction depends, and is therefore insufficient pleading. . . .

II. Plaintiffs next assert that their claim arises under the Due Process Clause of the Fifth Amendment to the Federal Constitution, and is therefore cognizable in this Court. The contention is without merit. It is well settled that the Fifth Amendment operates only as a restraint upon the National Government and upon the States through the Fourteenth Amendment, but is not directed against the actions of private individuals such as defendants. . . . It is not alleged in the instant complaint that the Federal Government is involved in the activity complained of in their responsive brief, plaintiffs do assert that the Federal Government has advanced funds to the State of Texas and City of Houston for the purpose of antipollution efforts. The relevance of this is not immediately apparent; however, taken as true, it clearly does not amount to federal complicity or participation in the alleged transgressions of the defendant private corporations, and it just as clearly will not support a Fifth Amendment claim.

III. Plaintiffs next seek solace in the Ninth Amendment, and concede on brief that this is a pioneering enterprise:

> This case is believed to be unique in that counsel for the Tanners is not aware of any other cases that have sought damages for personal injuries caused by the air pollution in the United States District Courts based upon the premise that the right to a healthy and clean environment is at the very foundation of this nation and guaranteed by the laws and Constitution of the United States. Plaintiffs maintain that their right not to

be personally injured by the actions of the Defendants and their right to non-inter-
ference with their privacy and the air that they breathe are protected by the Ninth
Amendment. Responsive Brief of Plaintiffs, at p. 1.

Since its promulgation, the Ninth Amendment has lain largely quiescent, its
most ambitious sortie being in the form of a concurrence in Griswold v.
Connecticut, 381 U.S. 479, 486 (1965).... The parties have cited and the Court
has found no reported case in which the Ninth Amendment has been construed
to embrace the rights here asserted. Such a construction would be ahistorical and
would represent essentially a policy decision. In effect, plaintiffs invite this Court
to enact a law. Since our system reserves to the legislative branch the task of legis-
lating, this Court must decline the invitation. The Ninth Amendment, through its
"penumbra" or otherwise, embodies no legally assertable right to a healthful environment. Environmental Defense Fund, Inc. v. Corps of Engineers, 325 F.Supp.
728, 739 (E.D.Ark. 1971).

IV. Plaintiffs also contend that this action is entertainable by reason of the
Fourteenth Amendment in conjunction with the Civil Rights Act of 1871, 42
U.S.C. § 1983, and its jurisdictional counterpart, 28 U.S.C. § 1343. The Supreme
Court of the United States, in Adickes v. S.H. Kress & Co., 398 U.S. 144, 90 S.Ct.
1598, 26 L.Ed.2d 142 (1970), has recently defined plaintiffs' task:

> The terms of § 1983 make plain two elements that are necessary for recovery. First,
> the plaintiff must prove that the defendant has deprived him of a right secured by the
> "Constitution and laws" of the United States. Second, the plaintiff must show that the
> defendant deprived him of this constitutional right "under color of any statute, ordi-
> nance, regulation, custom, or usage, of any State or Territory." This second element
> requires that the plaintiff show that the defendant acted "under color of law."

> ...

> 398 U.S. at 150, ...

Therefore, it is clear that a sufficiently stated claim under section 1983 must
embrace two elements properly alleged: (1) a constitutional deprivation, and (2)
state action. On brief, all parties have devoted considerable attention to state action, the second requisite.

This Court is persuaded that plaintiffs have not alleged the quantum of state or
municipal regulatory involvement necessary to clothe defendants with the mantle
of the State for the purposes of Section 1983.... However, it is unnecessary to
dwell upon the point at length. For, assuming arguendo that state action were present, the fact remains that the first requisite of a Section 1983 suit—constitutional
deprivation—has not been satisfied.

Taking as true all factual allegations in the complaint, plaintiffs have failed to
allege a violation by defendants of any judicially cognizable federal constitutional

right which would entitle them to the relief sought. Once again, the parties have cited and the Court has found no reported case which persuasively suggests that the Fourteenth Amendment is susceptible to the interpretation urged. Although there has been something of a boom recently in what Judge Seals of this Court has described as "grandiose claims of the right of the general populace to enjoy a decent environment," . . . such claims "have been more successful in theory than in operation." . . . In view of the dearth of supportive authority, this Court must decline "to embrace the exhilarating opportunity of anticipating a doctrine which may be in the womb of time, but whose birth is distant." Spector Motor Service v. Walsh, 139 F.2d 809, 823 (2nd Cir. 1943)(L. Hand J., dissenting).. . .

First, there is not a scintilla of persuasive content in the words, origin, or historical setting of the Fourteenth Amendment to support the assertion that environmental rights were to be accorded its protection. To perceive such content in the Amendment would be to turn somersaults with history. For, as the Congressional sponsor of a proposed federal environmental amendment recently observed:

> We are frank to say that such a provision to the Constitution would have been meaningless to those attending the Constitutional Convention in Philadelphia almost 200 years ago. Indeed, this amendment would have been altogether unpersuasive twenty years ago, although the handwriting was then visible on the wall, if one cared to look for it. Remarks of Representative Richard L. Ottinger of New York, Cong. Rec. 17116 (1968). . . .

Second, it is apparent that nowhere in the Fourteenth Amendment—or its "incorporated" amendments—can be found the decisional standards to guide a court in determining whether the plaintiffs' hypothetical environmental rights have been infringed, and, if so, what remedies are to be fashioned. Such a task would be difficult enough with the guidance of a statute, but to undertake it in the complete absence of statutory standards would be simply to ignore the limitations of judicial decisionmaking.

Third, from an institutional viewpoint, the judicial process, through constitutional litigation, is peculiarly ill-suited to solving problems of environmental control. Because such problems frequently call for the delicate balancing of competing social interests, as well as the application of specialized expertise, it would appear that their resolution is best consigned initially to the legislative and administrative processes. Furthermore, the inevitable trade-off between economic and ecological values presents a subject matter which is inherently political, and which is far too serious to relegate to the ad hoc process of "government by lawsuit" in the midst of a statutory vacuum.

Finally, to the extent that an environmental controversy such as this is presently justiciable, it is within the province of the law of torts, to wit: nuisance. . . . There would seem little good reason in law or policy to conjure with the Fourteenth

Amendment and Section 1983 for the purpose of producing the wholesale transformation of state tort suits into federal cases. In any event, if such a result is deemed desirable in order to cope with pollution on a nationwide scale, then it should be accomplished by Congress through legislation, and not by jurisdictional alchemy. Therefore, this Court must follow Guthrie v. Alabama By-Products Co., supra, where the Court, in dismissing a similar pollution suit, observed that several bills have been introduced to challenge conduct alleged to result in environmental pollution. From this, Chief Judge Lynne of the Northern District of Alabama quite reasonably concluded that:

> Though this circumstance may be only faintly persuasive, it does indicate that the sponsors of these bills believe that the right to maintain such suits in federal court is not provided by existing legislation. This Court is firmly of the opinion that if plaintiffs are to be allowed to bring private damage suits for injuries traditionally local in nature and already covered by local statutory and common law, additional federal legislation is imperative. Such authority cannot be found in the existing law. 328 F. Supp. at 1149.

For the foregoing reasons, this Court holds that no legally enforceable right to a healthful environment, giving rise to an action for damages, is guaranteed by the Fourteenth Amendment or any other provision of the Federal Constitution. As the United States Supreme Court recently observed in rejecting a similarly imaginative constitutional claim, "the Constitution does not provide judicial remedies for every social and economic ill." Lindsey v. Normet, 405 U.S. 56 (1972). . . . It follows, of course, that a claim under Section 1983 has not been stated and subject matter jurisdiction under 28 U.S.C. § 1343 has not been invoked.

V. Next, plaintiffs urge this Court to find an implied civil damage remedy in certain provisions of the National Environmental Policy Act of 1969, 42 U.S.C. § 4321 et seq. In this, the Court is again apparently invited to break new ground, for no case has been cited in which such a remedy was inferred. The absence of such authority is understandable. By its terms, the statute is directed only to the agencies and instrumentalities of the Federal Government, with a primary purpose being full disclosure of the environmental consequences of federal governmental activities. It follows that plaintiffs may derive from the statute no private cause of action against these private defendants. For the sake of thoroughness, however, each section of the Act cited by plaintiffs shall be separately considered.

(a) As to 42 U.S.C. § 4321, this is merely a preamble to the Act, in which Congress declares its purpose to encourage harmony between man and his environment, to promote efforts for the prevention of environmental damage, to enrich man's understanding of his environment, and to establish a Council on Environmental Quality. In so doing, Congress said nothing of rights or remedies. As it embodies no prescriptive command and creates no duties or liabilities, this section of the statute clearly cannot be made to embrace a private cause of action. . . .

(b) In their jurisdictional statement, plaintiffs also cite 42 U.S.C. §§ 4331(a) and (b) as supportive of this action. There is contrary authority on the point, and we need look no further than Environmental Defense Fund, Inc. v. Corps of Engineers, supra, in which the Court held that these sections of the statute create no substantive private rights. . . .

(c) Plaintiffs' reliance upon 42 U.S.C. § 4331(c) is similarly misplaced. This section provides only that "(t)he Congress recognizes that each person should enjoy a healthful environment and that each person has a responsibility to contribute to the preservation and enhancement of the environment." Like the language of Section 4321, these words are almost precatory in nature. Had the Congress intended to create a positive and enforceable legal right or duty, it would have said so, and would not have limited itself to words of entreaty. In the absence of any clear statement, this Court must assume that no such intention existed. Although such a reading stands by itself as the only plausible construction, it is interesting to note that it is supported by the legislative history of the provision in question. Originally, the Senate version, Senate Bill 1075, provided that "[t]he Congress recognizes that each person has a fundamental and inalienable right to a healthful environment. . . ." [emphasis added.] However, these strong words did not survive the conference committee, where they were deleted lest they be interpreted to create legal consequences which the Congress did not intend. In the words of the Conference Report:

> Section 101(c) of the conference substitute states that "Congress recognizes that each person should enjoy a healthful environment and that each person has a responsibility to contribute to the preservation and enhancement of the environment." The language of the conference substitute reflects a compromise by the conferees with respect to a provision in the Senate bill (but which was not in the House amendment) which stated that Congress recognizes that "each person has a fundamental and inalienable right to a healthful environment. . . ." The compromise language was adopted because of doubt on the part of the House conferees with respect to the legal scope of the original Senate provision. See Conference Report No. 91–765, 1969 U.S. Code Cong. & Admin. News, pp. 2767, 2768.

This "doubt" was resolved by stripping the Senate bill of the language which might arguably have been construed as creating a legally enforceable right to a "healthful environment." As the Congress took assiduous care to foreclose the possibility of such an interpretation, this Court is obviously powerless to adopt it. From this it follows that no claim upon which relief can be granted has been stated under 42 U.S.C. § 4331(c).

. . .

Accordingly, for the foregoing reasons, this action must be dismissed because of plaintiffs' failure to state a claim upon which relief can be granted. Rule 12(b)(6), Fed.R.Civ.P.

Judgement shall enter for the defendants.

Questions, Materials, and Suggestions for Further Study

Tanner v. Armco Steel Corporation

Judge Noel clearly does not think much of Mr. Tanner's assertion that Armco Steel's operations have deprived him of his health, that his health is a constitutional right or one granted indirectly by other statutes, and that the company therefore owes him damages. It might be appropriate to study Judge Noel's opinion as an exercise in judicial rhetoric. To conduct this study requires a careful review of the relationship between legal reasoning and rhetoric. For one such study, see Chaim Perelman, *The Idea of Justice and the Problem of Argument* (London: Routledge & Kegan Paul, 1963), translated by John Petrie.

In what ways is this case similar to *Boomer?* Note that in *Boomer* the plaintiff brought a nuisance action. The judge seems to think that the action in *Tanner* should be a nuisance action. Should it? In *Tanner,* the plaintiff claims rights under a federal statute and the federal Constitution. Based on what you have read so far, could you distinguish between common law, statutory, and constitutional rights? Constitutional rights protect the rights holder against government action. Statutes establish both private rights and rights against governments. Common-law rules protect individuals against private action. Does this segregation between public and private rights, enshrined in Sir William Blackstone's *Commentaries on the Laws of England* and our Constitution, make any sense in the 1990s? The relationship between the common-law rights and emerging constitutional rights is discussed in Roscoe Pound's *The Spirit of the Common Law* (Boston: Marshall Jones, 1925).

As the court says, the Ninth Amendment of the U.S. Constitution—which states, "the enumeration in the Constitution of certain rights shall not be construed to deny or disparage others retained by the people"—is not used very much these days and, until Mr. Tanner's claim, had never been used to advance such a claim as his. But should that be a reason for so abruptly dismissing the claim? Who should be forced to justify his case—Tanner, to show that health is protected by the law, or the state, to show that it is not?

The court emphasizes Representative Ottinger's remarks that the founding fathers would not have understood an environmental rights amendment. But suppose that they were given the health information now available: Many of them were eighteenth-century projectors, experimenters who might have grasped the problems immediately. And, to take another tack, isn't their understanding beside the point if the Constitution is a flexible rather than a rigid document? Doesn't the Ninth Amendment permit the court to be flexible?

If the court is being flexible, shouldn't it recognize a right to health? Or would this new right be a moral or human right, not enforceable by the courts? Not surprisingly, there has been a great deal of discussion in philosophical and ethical studies about moral and human rights. See, for example, Alan Gewirth, *Human Rights* (Chicago:

University of Chicago Press, 1982). Among those considering the issue, there does appear to be general agreement that health is a moral or human right because it is a basic good. See John Finnis, *Natural Law and Natural Rights* (Oxford: Clarendon Law Series, 1980). If that is so, if health is a basic good and a moral right, does it necessarily follow that laws should protect it? When and under what circumstances should laws be established to protect these "basic goods"? Even if established by law, need a right be enforced by a court?

Blackstone, in his eighteenth-century commentary on English law, maintained that the individual right to health should be protected by the common law. If this is so, why not by the Constitution as well? Or, would formulating such a right (or attempting to enforce one in the absence of any formulation) create even broader and more intractable problems than it resolves?

The *Tanner* case raises the issue of the existence and content of a constitutional right to a decent environment. This issue moves us into the world of the Constitution—what it is and what it means. A magnificent treatise on the subject is Laurence H. Tribe's *American Constitutional Law* (Mineola, N.Y.: Foundation Press, 1978). Charles H. McIlwain's short and readable *Constitutionalism: Ancient and Modern* (Ithaca: Cornell University Press, 1958) gives a broad historical view, and Rexford G. Tugwell's *The Compromising of the Constitution* (South Bend, Ind.: University of Notre Dame Press, 1976) gives a more modern, realistic, and less legalistic view of the constitutional structure of the United States. Although this text looks only to the environmental rights invoked by the Tanners and the right of property protected under the Fifth and Fourteenth Amendments to the United States Constitution, many different rights have been cited in various environmental conflicts. For a full account of these, see Richard O. Brooks, "A Constitutional Right to a Healthful Environment," 16 *Vermont Law Review* 1063 (1992).

When a plaintiff refers to an environmental right being based on the "constitution in its entirety," one meaning of the phrase is that a viable constitution requires, in turn, a viable ecosystem. This argument is spelled out in detail in William Ophuls, et al., *Ecology and the Politics of Scarcity Revisited*, (San Francisco: W. H. Freeman, 1977). One curious aspect of a right to a decent environment is that it may be a right of the majority against a polluting minority rather than the more common situation in which the Constitution guarantees a right to a minority. This notion is discussed in Malcolm F. Baldwin and James K. Page, eds., *Law and the Environment* (New York: Walker, 1970).

What kind of value is being protected in a right to a decent environment? Is it, for example, the right to a healthful environment? (See Norman Dorsen, David Haber, and Thomas Irwin Emerson, *Political and Civil Rights in the United States* [Boston: Little, Brown and Co., 1976].) Or is it the right to untouched nature, as discussed in William O. Douglas's *Wilderness Bill of Rights* (Boston: Little, Brown and Co.,1965)? Is there any such thing as "untouched Nature" in the first place? See Bill McKibben, *The End of Nature* (New York: Random House, 1989). Or are we protecting the rights of the natural objects themselves? (See, for example, Tom Regan's *The Case for Animal Rights* [Berkeley: University of California Press, 1983].)

Would a constitutional right to a decent environment protect future generations? Under the Constitution, does our government owe them a clean environment or the highest level of prosperity achievable regardless of environmental cost? Did previous generations worry about what they should leave to us? Should a constitutional right be used to protect future generations? Who should invoke it? As might be expected, vigorous argument has erupted over the nature of our obligations—if any—to future generations. For a discussion of these obligations see R. I. Sikora and Brian Barry, eds., *Obligations to Future Generations* (Philadelphia: Temple University Press, 1978), Ernest Partridge, ed., *Responsibilities to Future Generations* (Buffalo, N.Y.: Prometheus Books, 1980) and Edith Weiss *In Fairness to Future Generations: International Law, Common Patrimony, and International Equity*. (U.N. University, 1989).

For the most part, in the Bill of Rights the Constitution offers negative protection for individuals from government action. But should the government place affirmative duties upon individuals to protect the environment? And should the government itself have affirmative obligations to protect the environment? This is part of the more general question of the duties of citizens and the state that Mortimer J. Adler discussed in *The Common Sense of Politics* (New York: Holt, Rinehart & Winston, 1971). Peter Wenz, in *Environmental Justice* (Albany: State University of New York Press, 1988) argued for a positive right to environmental protection. What would be the cost of implementing such a right? What form(s) would those rights take and who would pay them? Rexford Tugwell, in *The Compromising of the Constitution*, proposed a constitutional clause making it obligatory for both individuals and government to protect the environment. In the legal literature the issue of our duties to others is most often discussed in cases where we might be expected to assist injured or threatened strangers. James M. Ratcliffe, *The Good Samaritan and the Law* (Garden City, N.Y.: Doubleday, 1966). Once one begins to articulate a duty of citizens to protect the environment, what are the limits of that duty? Are U.S. citizens responsible for the environmental degradation of Africa? See James S. Fishkin, *The Limits of Obligation* (New Haven: Yale University Press, 1982).

Part 2

Environmental Statutes

As we suggested in Part 1, the gradual trend in our jurisprudence has been away from the one-on-one pattern of conflict resolution typical of the common law toward a statutory approach to remedying environmental wrongs. The decision arrived at in *Boomer,* and the difficulty the judges had dealing with that decision, suggest that statutes provide very real advantages over the common law, particularly when they are enforced by a state or central government that is in a position to apply them evenhandedly whether those claiming to have been harmed are close by or far away. Statutes are also very easy to write (if more difficult to embody in regulations or to enforce) and, frequently, provide as well a very nearly ideal way to sooth an inflamed political base or pressure group. For the legislator, attractively written statutes plus publicity equals legislative success, more votes in the next election and the likelihood of continuing to do good for his or her constituents.

Environmental statutes are nothing new; the Rivers and Harbors Act of 1899 is still cited in most interstate pollution briefs. But over the past twenty-five years, the growth of environmental statutes in both number and scope has been little short of astonishing. Perhaps the most significant of the new environmental statutes in its implications was also one of the first. In The National Environmental Policy Act of 1969 (NEPA), the federal government required that every "significant" federal action be accompanied by an environmental impact statement assessing the effects of the action on the environment, both pros and cons.

Since the passage of NEPA, older statutes have been strengthened (The Federal Water Pollution Control Act, or Clean Water Act, and The Clean Air Act) and newer ones added to the lists: The Endangered Species Act of 1973; The Solid Waste Disposal Act (itself containing The Resource Conservation and Recovery Act); The Toxic Substances Control Act; The Coastal Zone Management Act; and The Comprehensive Environmental Response, Compensation, and Liability Act. Some might also include statutes governing the "built environment" such as the Historic Preservation Act. Just how broad this movement has been is only vaguely reflected in the titles of the statutes since each statute requires a set of federal regulations and an enforcement mechanism to make it work. Moreover, most of these federal statutes, in turn, provide both the justification and models for equivalent state legislation. Every state now has an environmental agency with a bureaucracy and legislative agenda all its own.

Throughout *Green Justice* we will be dealing in more detail with most of these statutes and the agencies that administer them, but in Part 2 we will be focusing primarily upon the National Environmental Policy Act and The Wilderness Act (*Lyng*), the Clean Air Act (*Ethyl Corp.*), and the Endangered Species Act (*Palila*). In *Lyng,* we will look more closely at just what the phrase "governmental action" actually means. As we'll see, the definition is not as clear as it might at first seem. In *Ethyl Corp.* we raise the much broader question of just how well statutes and the agencies that administer them deal with the problem of future, unquantifiable, or hypothetical risk. *Palila* raises the question of just how we define "take" and "harm"; what is and is not allowable if one is to limit the harm to a species.

4

Statutes

*The National Environmental Policy Act
and The Wilderness Act*

Case Study:
Sierra Club v. Lyng

At the heart of any statute is something beyond the scope of either the legislature that passed it or the executive who signed it into law with a well-photographed flourish: its enforcement. And the enforcement of a statute, in turn, is closely governed by how the statute is interpreted by a court. The growth in the number of environmental statutes during the twenty-five years since 1970 has led to the need to interpret these statutes as they apply to specific situations. Gaps in statutory coverage, use of vague terms, conflicting provisions, and unanticipated circumstances following a statute's adoption are only a few of the reasons that courts and administrative agencies must interpret and reinterpret statutes long after they have been passed.

The court before which an alleged violation comes for the first time can construe even the most closely worded and tightly drawn statute so loosely that it is rendered almost frivolous, an empty husk safely ignored by an already underfunded and overburdened agency. Conversely, a broad, general directive—precisely the sort of abstract principle that an agency could avoid or pay lip service to—can be turned by an activist court into a stringent mandate with far-reaching consequences. The initial reception of the National Environmental Policy Act (NEPA) fell into the second camp. Writing in *Calvert Cliffs' Coordinating Committee v. United States Atomic Energy Commission,* Judge Skelly Wright of the Washington, D.C., Circuit Court of Appeals determined that the analysis of its actions, which NEPA required of each agency, was not to be merely a pro forma review in which the eventual agency action was assumed to be the outcome, but to be a real, meaningful analysis. The history of environmental law in the United States has not been the same since Judge Wright's decision.

NEPA was divided into three sections: a statement of policy and goals; a section establishing the Council on Environmental Quality; and a section concerning miscellaneous provisions governing research and development. The first section, "Policy and Goals" was, to all intents and purposes, hortatory, containing a broad general statement of governmental policy with which almost no one could disagree: The resources of the United States should be used "in a manner calculated to foster and preserve the general welfare, to create and maintain conditions under which man and nature can exist in productive harmony, and fulfill the social, economic, and other requirements of present and future generations of Americans."

To carry all this out, NEPA contained a section requiring all federal agencies to carry out studies of any proposed "major federal action" to determine whether the project would, in the main, be beneficial, whether its long-term benefits would outweigh its long-term costs. This evaluative document, an environmental impact statement (EIS), must use "a systematic, interdisciplinary approach" to evaluate the effect that "legislation and other Federal actions" would have on the environment.

What was to happen to these EISs? What form was the statement to take, who was to draw it up, who was to review it, and to what end, were all questions left unaddressed in Subchapter I of the statute? Subchapter II at least partially answered these questions by creating the Council on Environmental Quality (CEQ), thought to be equivalent to the Council of Economic Advisors. The CEQ was to direct research, inform the president, and evaluate governmental actions in light of Subchapter I. As part of that advisory function it was to read over the EISs.

But then what? Establishing the Council and having it read over the impact statements and advising the president is one thing. It is quite another to authorize the Council to reject projects on the basis of the statements. This simply wasn't addressed. If an agency action looked as if it would result in more harm than good, could (should) the proposed action be rejected? What if an agency turned a blind eye to a handful of detriments in its impact statement, instead sprinkling benefits about liberally in order to justify a project? And how does one go about quantifying all these benefits and costs? Must it be done in dollars? If so, just how does one assign a dollar value to intangible harms or benefits? How could an agency valuate a sunset, a wilderness (which, by definition, cannot be used), a canyon, or an increased susceptibility to disease? How could even the most conscientious study include such anomalies as an increased dust or particulate level that may enhance certain environmental amenities (the color of a sunset) while at the same time, diminishing others?

Whatever else the court in *Calvert Cliffs* may have done, it attempted to establish once and for all that the environmental impact statement was not to be merely pro forma, not lip service by an advocacy agency, no mere sop to environmentalists that was stapled to a sheaf of papers being shuffled through an agency. As Judge Wright put it in dismissing the Atomic Energy Commission's position that an EIS had merely to "accompany" the agency decision through the administrative process and not be seriously considered:

> We believe that the Commission's crabbed interpretation of NEPA makes a mockery of the Act. What possible purpose could there be in the Section 102(2)(C) requirement (that a "detailed statement" accompany proposals through agency review processes) if "accompany" means no more than physical proximity—mandating no more than the physical act of passing certain folders and papers, unopened, to reviewing officials along with other folders and papers? What possible purpose could there be in requiring the "detailed statement" to be before hearing boards, if the boards are free to ignore entirely the contents of the statement? NEPA was meant to do more than regulate the flow of papers in the federal bureaucracy. The word "accompany" in Section 102(2)(C) must not be read so narrowly as to make the Act ludicrous. . . .

The Supreme Court thought Judge Wright was misinformed. Despite Judge Wright's bold language, the Supreme Court would later interpret the NEPA requirements as procedural, taking away what he had so eloquently given: Although an agency was required to "consider" the EIS in its deliberations, the Supreme Court held, once that consideration had been accomplished (and a record made to show that the deliberations had taken place), the agency could do pretty much what it wanted.

This is not to say that the EIS process has been without effect. The EISs, produced at great expense by the agencies involved, have proven to be a mine of information for those affected by the governmental projects, which information those people use when and if they decide to oppose the project. Typically, neighbors, for example, could not begin to afford the scientific studies necessary to oppose the extension of an airport runway, but the EIS compiles and amasses all of the most relevant information in one place, saving the opponents countless thousands of dollars in research.

The extent to which a court can demand that an agency follow statutory requirements is made clear in *Sierra Club v. Lyng*, a case primarily having to do with The Wilderness Act. Under the Wilderness Act, certain areas of the United States are designated "wilderness," areas in which the activities of all humans, even those of the Forest Service, which is charged with "administering" them, are severely circumscribed. Within a designated wilderness, no vehicles or engines are allowed—even the Forest Service trail crews must use hand tools rather than chain saws.

Of course, the very existence of a trail crew in a wilderness brings the inherent contradictions to the fore. If an area were truly a wilderness there would be no trail crew, just as a true wilderness would have no need for an administrator in the first place. Trails would be created simply by repeated use—whether animal or human—and not by the planning efforts of an individual or group of Forest Service employees.

The fact is that a modern wilderness is an artificial creation that both relies on and affects the neighboring "non-wilderness" areas. The land has been carved out and set aside on the basis of its being a certain size, having no roads, and having little or no commercial value. But it does affect the neighboring area and uses. The current debate over bison and the reintroduction of wolves into Yellowstone National Park is only the most obvious example. Ranchers complain that bison ranging out of the park carry brucellosis, which can be transmitted to their herds, and that reintroducing wolves will result in herd predation.

It is in this gray area that *Sierra Club v. Lyng* takes place: What is the obligation of the Forest Service to fulfill its mandate to administer the wilderness in its charge when that administration directly affects neighboring commercial interests?

SIERRA CLUB and the Wilderness Society, Plaintiffs
v.
Richard E. LYNG, et. al., Defendants

United States District Court, District of Columbia
Jan. 14, 1987
[662 F. Supp. 40]

GESELL, District Judge.

By a complaint filed July 12, 1986, Sierra Club and the Wilderness Society have challenged the legality of a program initiated by the United States Forest Service under direction of the Secretary of Agriculture to control infestations of the Southern Pine Beetle in federally designated Wilderness Areas located in Arkansas, Louisiana and Mississippi. They claimed that the program was being conducted without first developing an environmental impact statement ("EIS"), in violation of the National Environmental Policy Act ("NEPA"), 42 U.S.C. §§ 4321–4847 (1982); that it violates the Endangered Species Act, 16 U.S.C. §§ 1531–1543 (1982), by harming the redcockaded woodpecker, an endangered species which inhabits these areas; and that the extensive tree-cutting and chemical spraying campaign involved is prohibited under Section 2 of the Wilderness Act, 16 U.S.C. §§ 1131–1136 (1982). After preliminarily enjoining the program in the three areas involved (subject only to a limited exception allowing some cutting for the benefit of the woodpeckers) pending development of an EIS, see *Sierra Club v. Block,* 614 F. Supp. 488 (D.D.C.1985), the Court now, for the second time, considers plaintiffs' long-deferred motion for summary judgment on its basic Wilderness Act claims, prompt development of an EIS having been repeatedly delayed. There has been full argument, and accompanying briefs, affidavits and documents have been considered.

Section 4(d)(1) of the Wilderness Act, 16 U.S.C. §1133(d)(1), authorizes the Secretary of Agriculture to control insects within Wilderness Areas in the following terms: "such measures may be taken [by the Secretary] as may be necessary in the control of fire, insects, and diseases, subject to such conditions as the Secretary deems desirable." Plaintiffs' primary contention is that the Secretary is not authorized to undertake an insect control program in a designated Wilderness Area unless the Secretary can demonstrate that the program is necessary in the sense that it is effective, and that the program for the Southern Pine Beetle infestations which are under attack here must be restrained since the program is ineffective. They argue that the Wilderness Areas were being destroyed by extensive and continuing spot cutting of infestations pursuant to the Secretary's program without any appreciable success in curbing the pest and that wilderness values Congress sought to preserve as a matter of affirmative national policy were, as a consequence, being permanently injured. The complex life cycle of the Southern Pine Beetle, an indigenous, well-known pest, has been elaborately studied and plaintiffs offered considerable data indicating the program's dubious effectiveness.

The Secretary presents both a legal and factual opposition. First, he asserts that the Court has no authority to consider the motion since Section 4(d)(1) leaves all management decisions affecting Wilderness Areas to his nonreviewable discretion. It is further suggested that since a different program may emerge with the eventual publication of the EIS the Court is being asked to issue an advisory opinion. Factually, the Secretary contends the program is effective in the sense that although continued cutting of spot infestations would be required, the program has somewhat slowed the appearance of new infestations as more and more mature pine trees are cut down and destroyed.

The Wilderness Act, as the Secretary urges, clearly places broad discretion in the Secretary to manage designated Wilderness Areas. Each area differs. There are no standards indicated for control of fire, insects or disease. Technical information and research must in the end guide the Secretary in the sensitive task of keeping nature's precarious balance within each area stable. Resolution of these decisions through litigation is surely counter indicated except upon the most explicit showing of arbitrary irresponsibility.

However, a further circumstance overhangs this particular dispute which must be considered. The Southern Pine Beetle program is not limited to Wilderness Areas and indeed the purpose and effect of the program is solely to protect commercial timber interests and private property, including, of course, national forests in which more draconian steps can be taken to eliminate the beetle. The extensive cutting in the Wilderness Areas that was being carried out under the program until preliminarily enjoined was conducted solely to aid outside adjacent property interests, not to further wilderness interests or to further national wilderness policy.

Both plaintiffs and the Secretary agree that Congress also intended by Section 4(d)(1) to authorize the Secretary to take actions within Wilderness Areas where necessary to control fire, insects, or disease from spreading beyond the areas and harming adjacent or neighboring private or commercial interests. The legislative history sustains this view. Plaintiffs' case therefore poses the declared national policy to preserve pristine wilderness ecology and values into sharp juxtaposition with the program's effectiveness, or lack of effectiveness, in controlling the harm being caused by pine beetles on adjacent property. Management of wilderness areas as such is not involved and the program could not be approved as a wilderness-management program.

Unfortunately, the material submitted on the motion provides no clear answers to the dilemma suggested. Pine beetles have a considerable range of flight and studies leave in doubt the extent to which they may migrate to or from adjacent pine land. There is no way the Court can determine from the material submitted to what extent beetle migration out of these particular Wilderness Areas into commercial timber properties may be adequately controlled under the program. Nor is it clear whether adjacent properties can be equally well controlled against beetle infestation by measures taken outside of the Wilderness Areas that would be wholly inappropriate within the Wilderness Areas.

Thus this case does not involve the management of Wilderness Areas as such. Rather, it presents a different question, one that is not wholly addressed by the Act itself. That question is whether the Secretary has been given the same Section 4(d)(1) broad management discretion previously noted when he takes actions within the Wilderness Areas for the benefit of outside commercial and other private interests. This question must be answered in the negative because in a situation like this the Secretary is not managing the wilderness but acting contrary to wilderness policy for the benefit of outsiders.

A fair reading of the Wilderness Act places a burden on the Secretary affirmatively to justify his actions under these circumstances. Where such actions are shown to contravene wilderness values guaranteed by the Wilderness Act, as they do here, then the Secretary must, when challenged, justify them by demonstrating they are necessary to effectively control the threatened outside harm that prompts the action being taken. Here the Secretary has not addressed this affirmative burden.

Plaintiffs have amply demonstrated that the Southern Pine Beetle program as carried out in these three Wilderness Areas was wholly antithetical to the wilderness policy established by Congress.

The destruction of many acres of pine trees by chain sawing, and chemical spraying accompanied by noise and personnel in a continuing process unlimited in scope, is hardly consonant with preservation and protection of these areas in their natural state. These are delicate, sensitive places where the often mysterious and unpredictable process of nature were to be preserved for the study and enjoyment of mankind. Congress directed that man must tread lightly in these areas, in awe and with respect. Ruthless intrusion in disregard for these values was condemned as a matter of national policy. While many facts remain unclear, the record before the Court suggests that within Wilderness Areas, as mature pines are destroyed by the beetle there will be less and less possibility of outbreaks infecting neighboring areas. Only a clear necessity for upsetting the equilibrium of the ecology could justify this highly injurious, semi-experimental venture of limited effectiveness.

The Secretary has failed to demonstrate that the Southern Pine Beetle program as carried out in the three Wilderness Areas is necessary to control the presence of that pest in neighboring pine forests or that it has in any way been more than marginally effective in doing so. There is little evidence relating to the effect of the program on the beetle's tendency, if any, to move out of the Wilderness Areas. Conversely, the Court has not received any material indicating whether adjacent pine land, which has been already infected by the beetle, could be managed with less effective controls in the absence of the accompanying Wilderness authority. Nor is the Secretary's weighing of alternatives apparent. The record strongly suggests that the beetle cannot be irradicated and the solution of the problem is longterm, dependent for its ultimate efficacy upon further research and scientific study.

While the Secretary's program covers the South, this particular case only concerns a limited aspect. Serious problems exist in other southern regions and indeed the United States District Court for the Eastern District of Texas has before it a challenge to the Southern Pine Beetle program as it affects five Wilderness Areas in Texas, See *Sierra Club v. Lyng,* No. L-85-69-CA (E.D.Tex.). That Court has also been awaiting the EIS. The problems in different regions in all probability vary and what may be a necessity in one Wilderness Area, or effective there, may not be so in another. The very generality of the Secretary's approach suggests inadequate sensitivity to his wilderness duties.

Because this Court's analysis raises issues not fully addressed in the papers and because it suggests a need to particularize any approach to the Southern Pine Beetle program in terms of each Wilderness Area, area by area, the Court has concluded that final resolution of the motion can most appropriately await the EIS. The Court directs the parties to file further papers in support of or opposition to the motion within 30 days of the publication of the final EIS with emphasis upon the Secretary's burdens as set out herein in the light of whatever Southern Pine Beetle program emerges in the EIS. In the meantime, the preliminary injunction remains in effect and final action on the motion will be held in abeyance. An appropriate Order is filed herewith.

For convenience, we have reproduced here the relevant passages from The Environmental Policy Act of 1969:

. . .

Section 4332

The Congress authorizes and directs that, to the fullest extent possible: (1) the policies, regulations, and pubic laws of the United States shall be interpreted and administered in accordance with the policies set forth in this chapter, and (2) all agencies of the Federal Government shall —

(C) include in every recommendation or report on proposals for legislation and other major Federal actions significantly affecting the quality of the human environment, a detailed statement by the responsible official on —

  (i)   the environmental impact of the proposed action;

  (ii) any adverse environmental effects which cannot be avoided should the proposal be implemented;

  (iii) alternatives to the proposed action;

  (iv) the relationship between local short-term uses of man's environment and the maintenance and enhancement of long-term productivity; and

  (v)   any irreversible and irretrievable commitments of resources which would be involved in the proposed action should it be implemented. . . .

Questions, Materials, and Suggestions for Further Study

Sierra Club v. Lyng

The Wilderness Act seeks to preserve lands that appear to be unaffected by humans and offer opportunities for solitude and "primitive" recreation. These lands may also contain significant geological, ecological, scenic, scientific, educational, and historical values. The notion of protecting these lands cuts across the pragmatic grain of American character. Roderick Nash in his classic, *Wilderness and the American Mind,* 3d. edition (New Haven and London: Yale University Press, 1982), traces the changing attitudes of Americans toward wilderness. A more general history is Max Oelschlaeger's *The Idea of Wilderness: From Prehistory to the Age of Ecology* (New Haven and London: Yale University Press, 1991).

Each of the purposes behind the protection of wilderness: preservation, human solitude, primitive recreation, and respect for the intrinsic value of nature itself, has generated a huge amount of writing. The ideal of preservation is explored in John Passmore's *Man's Responsibility for Nature: Ecological Problems and Western Traditions* (New York: Charles Scribner & Sons, 1974). Of course, classics such as Thoreau's *Walden* have discussed human solitude in nature, but the theme has also been explored philosophically by Philip Koch's *Solitude: A Philosophical Encounter* (Chicago: Open Court Publishing, 1994). "Primitive recreation," such as hiking, bird-watching, fishing, and hunting, has its own extensive literature. Joseph Sax, in his *Mountains Without Handrails* (Ann Arbor: University of Michigan Press, 1980) articulates a theory of primitive recreation within the context of national parklands.

Most attention to the issue of wilderness has been focused upon the intrinsic value of nature itself. The proliferation of environmental ethicists has created a cottage industry cranking out justifications of the intrinsic value of untouched nature. Bill McKibben, in his *The End of Nature* (New York: Random House, 1989), argues that, in fact, there is no such thing as untouched nature. Various theories have been offered as to how and why nature can have intrinsic value. One approach, set forth by Paul Taylor, in his *Respect for Nature* (Princeton: Princeton University Press, 1986), is to claim to find value in nature, independent of humans. Others, such as Aldo Leopold in *A Sand County Almanac* (New York: Oxford University Press, 1949), find value in a community that includes both humans and nature. This latter approach, poetically set forth by Leopold, is philosophically supported by the writings of J. Baird Callicott in *In Defense of Nature* (New York: State University of New York Press, 1989). The recognition of the intrinsic value of nature has been championed by "deep ecologists" who seek to set forth an entire worldview of science and nature; see Bill Devall and George Sessions, *Deep Ecology* (Salt Lake City: Peregrine Smith Books, 1985).

Both the Wilderness Act and the National Environmental Policy Act can find their justification in the science of ecology. This science, which sees nature as an evolving, interdependent tissue of biotic and abiotic elements and energy, offers a unique perspective on the natural world. See Eugene Odum, *Ecological and Endangered Life-Support Systems* (Sunderland, Mass.: Smaller Assoc., 1993). Some theorists believe that one can draw from ecology a unique ethic and political philosophy (Laura Westra, *An Environmental Proposal for Ethics: The Principle of Integrity* [Lanham, Md.: Rowman & Littlefield, 1994]; John Dryzek, *Rational Ecology* [Oxford: Basil Blackwell, 1987]). Others are more skeptical (K. S. Shrader-Frechette and E. D. McCoy, *Method in Ecology: Strategies for Conservation* (Cambridge: Cambridge University Press, 1993).

Perhaps the best way to evaluate the contribution of ecology is to explore how it works out in the laws that embody its approach. One such study was conducted by one author of NEPA, ecologist Lynton Caldwell, in *Science and the National Environmental Policy Act: Redirecting Policy Through Procedural Reform* (University: University of Alabama Press, 1982). The holistic approach required by ecology leads to an emphasis on ecological planning. Laws such as the Coastal Zone Management Act and the National Forest Management Act are two of the many laws that authorize planning. For an excellent account of planning in national forests, see Charles Wilkinson and H. Michael Anderson, *Land and Resource Planning in the National Forests* (Washington, D.C.: Island Press, 1987).

5

Statutes

Future Risk and Administrative Agencies

Case Study: *Ethyl Corporation v. United States Environmental Protection Agency*

Few things we do are free from risk: Driving invites the chance of injury; failure to wear seatbelts increases that risk; drinking alcohol prior to driving increases it yet more. Environmental risks are merely another class of risk—the chance that harm will befall us as we go through life. Frequently, avoiding one harmful or unpalatable result merely increases the chance that other, potentially even more harmful, results will come about. We may increase both our yield of tomatoes and our chance of disease when we use certain pesticides in the garden. We stuff the walls and ceilings of our houses with insulation to conserve heat, but that same insulation traps fumes inside and we breathe the fumes continually, increasing our risk of respiratory ailments. But most respiratory ailments are not severe, and we continue to insulate our homes because we decide, consciously or not, that the monetary savings is worth the extra coughing and wheezing. An alternative would be to purchase an air purifier; but that in turn requires electricity, and the increased electrical demand means that more fuel will be burned by our utility, which will, in its turn, pollute the air outside our houses all the more. Again, we perform a little mental equation: The increased pollution outside is minuscule compared to the dramatic improvement inside. We feel that the increased risk of contracting a respiratory ailment outside is well worth the improved air quality inside.

There is nothing particularly wrong with bouncing from one risk to another: We must somehow accommodate ourselves to life's imperfections without thinking

73

about them. Occasionally, however, our decisions directly affect the quality of our own life and of the lives of others. At that point the consequences of these decisions cannot in good conscience be ignored. Insulating my own house at my own and my family's risk is one thing, but saving money by installing an airtight woodstove is something else again. Such stoves send up the chimney a witch's brew of potential carcinogens that are then inhaled by my neighbors' families. Now the risks are no longer clear cut enough for one individual acting for private financial benefit to weigh properly. How do I weigh my personal savings against someone else's increased risk of health damage? For that matter, since we both live in the same neighborhood, how do I weigh my increased risk against my stove-owning neighbor's savings? The real question is whether any one individual should be forced unwillingly or unknowingly to accept a higher risk of disease so that another can save money.

If the woodstove example seems trivial (though it shouldn't), imagine that you are a manufacturer and that rather than a woodstove, we are discussing the costs and effects of chemical waste disposal. These are precisely the sorts of questions with which environmental law deals every day. If society demands more electricity, the util- ity company has the legal obligation to make it available at the lowest possible cost, consistent with the sound management of the investors' money. The environmental problem with this otherwise clear-cut description of interrelated obligations is that there is no provision for what economists call downstream costs—for the environ- mental costs that the utility's operation puts on the environment, the water, and the air. These costs will be paid in one form or another. The cost of allowing air pollution to continue even within supposedly safe limits will be paid in the form of shortness of breath and of a statistically greater risk of pulmonary disease to society at large. We could choose to pay this cost in dollars by financing the installation of pollution- control equipment through the utility rate structure. Either way, the society will pay; the only question is what form that payment will take. Ratepayers currently do not seem willing to pay enough for their electricity to allow local utilities to install the most effective pollution-control equipment in their power generation plants. They register this decision through the public utilities commissions of their various states, politically sensitive bodies that control the amount that utilities can charge for elec- tricity. By default, we force downwind residents to pay in health or other environ- mental degradation for our reduced electric bills.

As we saw in the house insulation example, risks taken with knowledge seem somehow more acceptable to us. But our recently increased knowledge of how the environment actually works suggests that the probability of harm from our various activities may be greater than we had previously imagined. We are now in the posi- tion of having once decided consciously or unconsciously that certain behavior was worth the risks involved only to discover that the actual risks may have been far greater (or less) than we had suspected. The ultimate effects of acid precipitation, haz- ardous wastes, or thermal pollution are currently unknown and are probably un- knowable because of the almost infinite number of variables involved in tracing their consequences. If we knew the results for certain we could at least make rational decisions about what would or would not be an appropriate risk. But as it is we do not know for certain whether any harm will occur, we do not know what form that harm might take if it does occur, we do not know the magnitude of that potential harm, and we certainly don't know whether it is prudent to take steps now to lessen the potential for harm.

Furthermore, in the previous examples, it is we, individually, who have made the little equations governing just how much risk we will expose ourselves to. In the last decade of the twentieth century, however, that decisionmaking power has been taken away from us; we do not make the decisions—for better or ill it is a government agency, operating out of sight of virtually all of us, that makes decisions each day that directly affect the amount of risk we will face. Our only recourse is to affect these agencies through the political process, a recourse that many feel is too remote.

The issues raised in the *Ethyl* case by Judge Skelly Wright go to the heart of the functioning of administrative agencies under our modern statutory/administrative system. In *Ethyl*, an administrative agency (EPA), has made a determination that airborne lead poses a threat to human health. It has made that decision based upon a number of studies, many of which are referred to in the decision, but it is still a *risk-based* determination. To the EPA, no more than to the rest of us, certain knowledge of future events is not given.

Because the issues of risk assessment and risk evaluation are so difficult, the federal and state governments have taken several different approaches to dealing with them. The National Research Council has sought to offer scientific advice regarding risk assessment. Several laws, including parts of the Clean Air Act, have recently been amended to delete references to risk, attempting instead to regulate on the basis of available technology.

Administrative Agencies

To understand the position and functioning of administrative agencies such as the Environmental Protection Agency, we must first return to the Constitution. The bulk of the U.S. Constitution is devoted to establishing the relationships between the three branches of the U.S. government: the legislative (dealt with in Article I), the executive (Article II), and the Judiciary (Article III). The Constitution carefully delineates the spheres of power and responsibility proper to each branch as well as the functions of each in relation to those of the others. Despite the masterful job of drafting, however, many areas were either inadequately considered at the convention, deliberately left vague, or simply not foreseen. Although sometimes frustrating, vagueness and imprecision can give rise to creativity, particularly when change is needed. Just how completely the Constitution can accommodate change may be seen in the growth of administrative agencies, those faceless bureaucrats who have such enormous influence on our everyday lives and, in the opinion of many, amount to a fourth branch of government, a nonconstitutional one at that.

Administrative agencies may well act as a fourth branch of government. In the mid-twentieth-century United States, administrative agencies have enormous influence on our lives: They regulate the food we eat, the clothes we wear, the cars we drive. A governmental agency set the standards for the hospitals we were born in and will do the same for the caskets we will be buried in. Thousands of people are employed by the federal bureaucracy. The Department of Health and Human Services oversees a budget that is larger than the entire budgets of all but a handful of other countries. The Interior Department's Bureau of Land Management is the largest single landholder in the United States. The Department of Agriculture oversees a budget of billions of dollars and a workforce of thousands of men and women administering programs as diverse as crop management, agricultural research, university extension services, national forests, and wilderness areas.

All agencies are created by statute. The so-called New Deal Agencies were established by broadly, even vaguely, worded statutes, in effect delegating to the agencies the responsibility of solving a general problem identified in the statute. Since 1970, agencies have been governed by much more precisely focused and worded statutes that seek to force agencies to accomplish specific tasks. Many of these new statutes also have elaborate provisions for juridical review and provisions enabling citizens to bring suit against an administrator who acts arbitrarily or capriciously.

Administrative agencies share two related characteristics: longevity and expertise. Administrative agencies remain in place and power independent of the political party in power at any given moment. This continuity, today ensured by the civil service system, guarantees that policies and projects undertaken by one administration will not automatically be jettisoned merely because a new administration moves in. Related to this longevity is the expertise that characterizes these agencies; because they deal with technical issues they tend to employ specialists in those fields, and they gradually become reservoirs of technical expertise not otherwise available. Expertise in this context is typically of two types: scientific knowledge and information and administrative experience in dealing with the issue.

This expertise is particularly relevant to regulatory agencies—agencies that exist to regulate, to take away certain freedoms of operation from those over whom they have control. The extent of this regulation may be as seemingly insignificant as requiring a breakfast cereal company to list percentages of minimum daily vitamin and mineral requirements on their box (daily requirements themselves established by another agency) or as significant as collecting taxes, closing down stores and plants, even shutting down entire industries. To regulate efficiently and equitably an agency needs technical expertise.

Agencies also need expertise because the legislation that affects our lives has become so complex. Before passing legislation Congress needs experts it can rely on to assess problems and evaluate proposed solutions. Those experts typically come from inside the governmental agencies that will eventually enforce the new statute. When legislation is finally passed, Congress passes a seemingly specific statute even if the legislation can only be implemented by further much more precise rule making that will be carried out by the same agency.

Agencies adopt regulations that serve the purpose not only of preventing injuries that in turn prevent the high cost of after-the-fact pollution suits but also of economically handling groups of polluters under a common plan and accompanying regulation, hence reducing the costs of case-by-case resolution of conflicts. A common plan is also needed to compare present costs/benefits with predicted future costs/benefits. Such coordination is exemplified in the variety of statutory planning requirements of environmental law, including the state air quality implementation plans, river quality management plans, plans for nuclear wastes, and industrial siting plans.

Administrative agencies devote most of their energies toward the rule making required to implement legislation and toward the enforcement of those plans. Most environmental statutes have a deadline by which the agency is expected to promulgate a set of rules and standards that will bring about the statute's goal (for example, clean the air). The agency typically begins by asking for comments from those who are regulated—the smokestack owners or automobile manufacturers—as well as from those promoting the regulations. The agency will then draw up a set of proposed regulations and invite various interested parties—the "regulated community" of industry and interested citizens' groups as well as individuals—to comment on the proposals. After making the changes that it deems necessary the agency will promulgate final regulations that have the force of law; as with any law, the parties governed by the regulations are entitled to challenge them in court as either too strict or too lenient.

Just as the constitutional branches of government keep each other under control by a system of checks and balances, agencies are regulated by the other branches through legislative oversight and the judicial review of agency decisions. The most dramatic form of control is played out as each new president selects cabinet heads who appear before the Senate for confirmation. Although lower-level employees are protected from the political winds, the department heads do change; they set new policies within the agencies and are subject to political pressure from the executive and legislative branches.

Because agencies are created by statute and do not have constitutional status, their powers can be modified. Entire agencies can be created or abolished by statute. As a creation of the legislature, not the constitution, an agency can do no more than it is enabled to do by the legislature that created it. If it attempts to exceed its mandate, it is acting ultra vires (that is, beyond its authority), and its regulations will be struck down by the courts. Attempts to bring agencies under control typically arise either from those whose activities are regulated, who claim that the agency is acting ultra vires and regulating too much, or from those whom the agency is intended to help, who claim that the agency is not doing enough, not fulfilling its congressional mandate.

Final agency decisions, like congressional legislation, can be appealed to the courts, and this is the background of the *Ethyl* case. When agency decisions are appealed, the pivotal questions concern the "scope of review"—the extent to which the court will let agency decisions stand and the extent to which courts will substitute their own decisions for the agency's.

Because one main reason for establishing agencies is to provide a reservoir of technical expertise for the government, what sort of standard should courts use to review the work of an agency challenged in court? What sort of deference should a court give to agency decisions? Should it reverse a decision that came about as a result of months, or even years, of research by experts merely because it does not think it is right? One judge's opinion, surely, cannot outweigh the accumulated expertise of an entire department of government. Then again, why not? As we pointed out in the Introduction, although the information going into a decision may be technical, the choice of whether or not to implement that decision is based on political, moral, and legal motives. Why shouldn't the judiciary take an active part in the process when the implementation of the statute will affect the rights of all citizens?

Under the Administrative Procedures Act or the substantive statute, an agency must propose rules and regulations consistent with the mandate in the particular statute (in the *Ethyl* case, the Clean Air Act), hold hearings on those proposed rules, and either adopt or revise them based upon the hearings. If anyone objects that the proposed rules are excessive, wrong, or for some other reason defective, that individual may petition the Washington, D.C., Circuit Court of Appeals, to have the regulations revised or thrown out. The court may do this only if it determines that the agency (in the *Ethyl* case, EPA) has been "arbitrary, capricious, or [committed an] abuse of discretion." Essentially, the court is acting as a reviewing panel to ensure that in carrying out its mandate the agency has acted rationally, not trampling on the rights of those regulated.

The specific issue in *Ethyl* is whether the EPA has been arbitrary or capricious in making a determination that the lead additive level in gasoline should be reduced not because it poses an *actual* harm, but because it poses the *risk* of harm; in effect, where the statute called for control of those substances that "will" endanger the public health, the agency looked at the evidence and regulated those that "probably" will. Obviously, the manufacturers of the additives want the court to decide that in making this decision the agency has misused the studies it has examined and that it has, thus, been arbitrary and capricious. But Judge Wright keeps coming back to his conclusion that the decision made by the agency was a perfectly rational one under the circumstances.

Throughout his decision, Judge Wright refers to the earlier Eighth Circuit Court of Appeals decision in *Reserve Mining v. United States Environmental Protection Agency*. *Reserve Mining* was also a risk-based case, one in which the Reserve Mining Company argued that the known economic benefits of its activities (the provision of iron ore for the steel industry and the consequent employment in both mining and manufacture) should be permitted despite the arguably harmful, unknown effects of asbestos fibers that inevitably accompanied the taconite tailings that were dumped into Lake Superior.

In *Reserve Mining*, although the harm was statistically predictable, determining who would incur it was not. This is a common dilemma in environmental cases, a variation of which is at issue in *Ethyl*. We can state that a given course of action will result in a statistically certain increase of one cancer per 100,000 individuals over a five-year period. We cannot, however, predict who, if anyone, will contract that one case. In *Reserve Mining*, the court accepted as a fact that the risk of contracting a taconite-related disease had been increased. But what do these figures mean in human terms? No potential cancer can be attributed directly to the source, so reimbursing a potential victim becomes impossible; and each person who contracts the disease cannot be reimbursed for a percentage of the disease attributable to the source. At the same time, almost no one would say that those responsible for the harmful source should not pay some compensation. We are confronted with a difficult conceptual problem: How do we weigh this abstract, anonymous harm with specific horrific, personal consequences, none of which are directly traceable, against the positive gains from continuing the operation (employment, tax revenues, increased standard of living for thousands more than are harmed) and the costs of preventing a merely possible risk.

The same sorts of arguments arise in *Ethyl*. Just what is the certainty that anyone will suffer from the additive? If there is no certainty, if the risk is of a mere possibility, is the severity of that merely possible risk relevant? Is an agency the proper decisionmaker and the court the proper reviewer? One might also remember that courts, no less than agencies, are creatures of politics: The bench as well as an agency may reflect the philosophy of the political party that appointed it. Those of you who read *Ethyl* and come away secure in the belief that the case illustrates the "proper" workings of the agency and court systems should remember that agencies and judges with beliefs diametrically opposed to those on display here may be only an election away. Under those circumstances, with a court upholding the "reasonableness" of an agency actually increasing the allowable lead additives, would you feel so secure with the procedures now in place?

ETHYL CORPORATION, *et al.*,
Petitioners
v.
ENVIRONMENTAL PROTECTION AGENCY, *et al.*,
Respondents

United States Court of Appeals,
District of Columbia Circuit
March 19, 1976
[541 F.2d 1]

J. SKELLY WRIGHT, Circuit Judge.

Man's ability to alter his environment has developed far more rapidly than his ability to foresee with certainty the effects of his alterations. It is only recently that we have begun to appreciate the danger posed by unregulated modification of the world around us, and have created watchdog agencies whose task it is to warn us, and protect us, when technological "advances" present dangers unappreciated or unrevealed by their supporters. Such agencies, unequipped with crystal balls and unable to read the future, are nonetheless charged with evaluating the effects of unprecedented environmental modifications, often made on a massive scale. Necessarily, they must deal with predictions and uncertainty, with developing evidence, with conflicting evidence, and, sometimes, with little or no evidence at all. Today we address the scope of the power delegated one such watchdog, the Environmental Protection Agency (EPA). We must determine the certainty required by the Clean Air Act before EPA may act to protect the health of our populace from the lead particulate emissions of automobiles.

Section 211(c)(1)(A) of the Clean Air Act authorizes the Administrator of EPA to regulate gasoline additives whose emission products "will endanger the public health or welfare * * *." 42 U.S.C. § 1857f-6c(c)(1)(A). Acting pursuant to that power, the Administrator, after notice and comment, determined that the automotive emissions caused by leaded gasoline present "a significant risk of harm" to the public health. Accordingly, he promulgated regulations that reduce, in stepwise fashion, the lead content of leaded gasoline. We must decide whether the Administrator properly interpreted the meaning of Section 211(c)(1)(A) and the scope of his power thereunder, and, if so, whether the evidence adduced at the rule-making proceeding supports his final determination. Finding in favor of the Administrator on both grounds, and on all other grounds raised by petitioners, we affirm his determination.

I. The Facts, the Statute, the Proceedings, and the Regulations

Hard on the introduction of the first gasoline-powered automobiles came the discovery that lead "antiknock" compounds, when added to gasoline, dramatically increase the fuel's octane rating. Increased octane allows for higher compression engines, which operate with greater efficiency. Since 1923 antiknocks have been regularly added to gasoline, and a large industry has developed to supply those compounds. Today, approximately 90 percent of motor gasoline manufactured in the United States contains lead additives, even though most 1975 and 1976 model automobiles are equipped with catalytic converters, which require lead-free gasoline. From the beginning, however, scientists have questioned whether the addition of lead to gasoline, and its consequent diffusion into the atmosphere from the automobile emission, poses a danger to the public health. As use of automobiles, and emission of lead particulates, has accelerated in the last quarter century, this concern has mounted. The reasons for concern are obvious (and essentially undisputed by petitioners): (1) lead in high concentrations in the body is toxic; (2) lead can be absorbed into the body from the ambient air; and (3) lead particulate emissions from gasoline engines account for approximately 90 percent of the lead in our air. Despite these apparent reasons for concern, hard proof of any danger caused by lead automotive emissions has been hard to come by. Part of the reason for this lies in the multiple sources of human exposure to lead.

Lead is an ubiquitous element. It is found in the land, in the sea, in plants, in animals, and, ultimately, in humans. Traces of lead ranging from 10 to 40 micrograms per 100 grams of blood (10–40 mcg/100g) are found in everyone, including those living in environments with almost no atmospheric lead. National Academy of Sciences Committee on Biologic Effects of Atmospheric Pollutants, Airborne Lead in Perspective 118 (1972) (hereinafter NAS Report). Despite its universal presence, however, lead serves no known purpose in the human body, and at higher concentrations is toxic, causing anemia, severe intestinal cramps, paralysis of nerves, fatigue, and even death. Clinical symptoms of lead poisoning appear at blood lead levels of 80–100 mcg or higher, and symptomatic lead poisoning may appear at levels of 50–60 mcg, particularly in the presence of anemia. EPA's Position on the Health Implications of Airborne Lead (hereinafter Third Health Document) at III–1, Joint Appendix (hereinafter JA) 54–55.

[Judge Wright discusses dietary lead sources and the tendency of children to ingest lead paint in older—pre-1948—housing units.]

The last remaining major source of lead exposure for humans is the ambient air. This source is easily the most controllable [of the three sources], since approximately 90 percent of lead in the air comes from automobile emissions, and can be simply eliminated by removing lead from gasoline. While the extent to which such lead actually enters the body is vigorously contested by petitioners and lies at the heart of this appeal, all parties agree that, to some extent at least, airborne lead can be absorbed through the lungs as a person breathes lead-contaminated air and that it can be eaten by children with pica after larger lead particles fall to the ground and mix with dust. Once the lead is in the body, however, its source becomes irrelevant; all lead in the bloodstream, from whatever source, is essentially fungible. Thus so long as there are multiple sources of lead exposure it is virtually impossible to isolate one source and determine its particular effect on the body. The effect of any one source is meaningful only in cumulative terms.

The multiple sources of human exposure to lead explain in part why it has been difficult to pinpoint automobile lead emissions as a danger to public health. Obviously, any danger is caused only by the additive effect of lead emissions on the other, largely uncontrollable, sources of lead. For years the lead antiknock industry has refused to accept the developing evidence that lead emissions contribute significantly to the total human lead body burden. In the Clean Air Act Amendments of 1970, Pub.L. 91–604, December 31, 1970, 84 Stat. 1698–1700, however, Congress finally set up a legal mechanism by which that evidence could be weighed in a more objective tribunal. It gave the newly-created EPA authority to control or prohibit the sale or manufacture of any fuel additive whose emission products "will endanger the public health or welfare * * *." 42 U.S.C. § 1857f-6c(c)(1)(A) (1970). It is beyond question that the fuel additive Congress had in mind was lead.

Given this mandate, EPA published on January 31, 1971 advance notice of proposed rule-making. The Administrator announced he was considering possible controls on lead additives in gasolines, both because of their possible danger to health and because of their incompatibility with the newly-developed catalytic converter emission control system. 36 Fed.Reg. 1486 (1971). Proposed regulations were issued a year later, February 23, 1972, supported by a document Health Hazards of Lead (hereinafter First Health Document), prepared by the EPA scientific staff. Comments were invited for a 90-day period, later reopened for an additional 30 days. 37 Fed.Reg. 11786–11787 (1972). At the same time public hearings were held in Washington, D. C., Dallas, and Los Angeles.

[The court recounts the lengthy history of rule making and legal challenges.]

The regulations are challenged by petitioners on a variety of grounds, all of which will be addressed below. Their primary claims, and the ones on which the division majority based its reversal, are that the Administrator misinterpreted the statutory standard of "will endanger" and that his application of that standard is without support in the evidence and arbitrary and capricious.

II. The Statutory Requirements

Under Section 211(c)(1)(A) the Administrator may, on the basis of all the information available to him, promulgate regulations that control or prohibit the manufacture, introduction into commerce, offering for sale, or sale of any fuel or fuel additive for use in a motor vehicle or motor vehicle engine (A) if any emission products of such fuel or fuel additive will endanger the public health or welfare * * *. 42 U.S.C. § 1857f-6c(c)(1)(A). The Administrator cannot act under Section 211(c)(1)(A), however, until after "consideration of all relevant medical and scientific evidence available to him, including consideration of other technologically or economically feasible means of achieving emission standards under (Section 202)." Section 211(c)(2)(A), 42 U.S.C. § 1857f-6c(c)(2)(A). Section 202 of the Act, 42 U.S.C. § 1857f-1, allows the Administrator to set standards for emission of pollutants from automobiles (as opposed to standards for the composition of the gasoline that produces the emissions), and is thus the preferred although not the mandatory alternative under the statutory scheme, presumably because it minimizes Agency interference with manufacturer prerogatives.

The Administrator is also required, before prohibiting a fuel or fuel additive under Section 211(c)(1)(A), to find, and publish the finding, that in his judgment any fuel or fuel additive likely to replace the prohibited one will not "endanger the public health or welfare to the same or greater degree * * *." Section 211(c)(2)(C), 42 U.S.C. § 1857f-6c(c)(2)(C). It is significant that this is the only conclusion the Administrator is expressly required to "find" before regulating a fuel or fuel additive for health reasons.

A. The Threshold Determination

In making his threshold determination that lead particulate emissions from motor vehicles "will endanger the public health or welfare," the Administrator provided his interpretation of the statutory language by couching his conclusion in these words: such emissions "present a significant risk of harm to the health of urban populations, particularly to the health of city children." 38 Fed.Reg. 33734. By way of further interpretation, he added that it was his view that the statutory language * * * does not require a determination that automobile emissions alone create the endangerment on which controls may be based. Rather, the Administrator believes that in providing this authority, the Congress was aware that the public's exposure to harmful substances results from a number of sources which may have varying degrees of susceptibility to control. Id. It is petitioners' first claim of error that the Administrator has erroneously interpreted Section 211(c)(1)(A) by not sufficiently appreciating the rigor demanded by Congress in establishing the "will endanger" standard. Therefore, petitioners argue, the Administrator's action is "short of statutory right," in violation of Section 10(e)(2)(C) of the Administrative Procedure Act (APA), 5 U.S.C. § 706(2)(C) (1970).

Petitioners argue that the "will endanger" standard requires a high quantum of factual proof, proof of actual harm rather than of a "significant risk of harm." See supplemental brief of petitioner Ethyl Corporation (hereinafter Ethyl Supp.Br.) at 20. Since, according to petitioners, regulation under Section 211(c)(1)(A) must be premised upon factual proof of actual harm, the Administrator has, in their view, no power to assess risks or make policy judgments in deciding to regulate lead additives. Moreover, petitioners argue, regulation must be based on the danger presented by lead additives "in and of themselves," so it is improper to consider, as the Administrator did, the cumulative impact of lead additives on all other sources of human exposure to lead. We have considered these arguments with care and find them to be without merit. It is our view that the Administrator's interpretation of the standard is the correct one.

1. The Precautionary Nature of "Will Endanger." Simply as a matter of plain meaning, we have difficulty crediting petitioners' reading of the "will endanger" standard. The meaning of "endanger" is not disputed. Case law and dictionary definition agree that endanger means something less than actual harm. When one is endangered, harm is threatened; no actual injury need ever occur. Thus, for example, a town may be "endangered" by a threatening plague or hurricane and yet emerge from the danger completely unscathed. A statute allowing for regulation in the face of danger is, necessarily, a precautionary statute. Regulatory action may be taken before the threatened harm occurs; indeed, the very existence of such precautionary legislation would seem to demand that regulatory action precede, and, optimally, prevent, the perceived threat. As should be apparent, the "will endanger" language of Section 211(c)(1)(A) makes it such a precautionary statute.

The Administrator read it as such, interpreting "will endanger" to mean "presents a significant risk of harm." 38 Fed.Reg. 33734. We agree with the Administrator's interpretation. This conclusion is reached not only by reference to the plain meaning of the statute, but by juxtaposition of Section 211(c)(1)(A) with other sections of the Clean Air Act and by analysis of pertinent precedent.

. . .

While petitioners have little more to offer to prove that the "will endanger" standard demands proof of actual harm and is not precautionary in nature, we may turn, in support of our interpretation, to the relevant case law. While cases interpreting the meaning of "endanger" are few in number, at least one recent case is directly on point and fully in accord with our view.

In *Reserve Mining Co. v. EPA,* 514 F.2d 492 (8th Cir. 1975) (en banc), the Eighth Circuit addressed, among other issues, the meaning of the phrase "endangering the health or welfare of persons" under Section 112 of the Federal Water Pollution Control Act of 1970 (FWPCA), 33 U.S.C. § 1160. FWPCA and the Clean Air Act together constitute the bulk of this nation's substantive environmental protection legislation. As such, and because of their contemporaneous enactment, interpretations of provisions of one Act have frequently been applied to comparable provisions of the other. See, e.g., *Natural Resources Defense Council, Inc. v. Train,* 166 U.S.App.D.C. 312, 321–322, 510 F.2d 692, 701–702 (1975). Thus Reserve Mining's interpretation of "endangering" is relevant to the meaning of the term "endanger" in the Clean Air Act. Indeed, it is particularly relevant because in construing the language before it the Eighth Circuit borrowed extensively from the interpretation of the "will endanger" language of Section 211 expressed in the dissent from the division opinion in this case, the same interpretation we adopt here. See *Reserve Mining Co. v. EPA,* supra, 514 F.2d at 528–529. After analysis of the plain meaning of the FWPCA provision, comparison with other sections of that Act, and reference to our division's dissent, the Eighth Circuit's unanimous conclusion fully supports our view of the "will endanger" standard:

In the context of this environmental legislation, we believe that Congress used the term "endangering" in a precautionary or preventive sense, and, therefore, evidence of potential harm as well as actual harm comes within the purview of that term. Id. at 528.

In sum, based on the plain meaning of the statute, the juxtaposition of Section 211 with Sections 108 and 202, and the Reserve Mining precedent, we conclude that the "will endanger" standard is precautionary in nature and does not require proof of actual harm before regulation is appropriate.

Perhaps because it realized that the above interpretation was the only possible reading of the statutory language, petitioner Ethyl addresses this interpretation and argues that even if actual harm is not required for action under Section 211(c)(1)(A), the occurrence of the threatened harm must be "probable" before regulation is justified. Ethyl Supp.Br. 12. While the dictionary admittedly settles on "probable" as its measure of danger, we believe a more sophisticated case-by-case analysis is appropriate. Danger, the Administrator recognized, is not set by a fixed probability of harm, but rather is composed of reciprocal elements of risk and harm, or probability and severity. Cf. *Carolina Environmental Study Group v.*

United States, 166 U.S.App.D.C. 416, 419, 510 F.2d 796, 799 (1975); *Reserve Mining Co. v. EPA,* supra, 514 F.2d at 519–520. That is to say, the public health may properly be found endangered both by a lesser risk of a greater harm and by a greater risk of a lesser harm. Danger depends upon the relation between the risk and harm presented by each case, and cannot legitimately be pegged to "probable" harm, regardless of whether that harm be great or small. As the Eighth Circuit found in *Reserve Mining,* these concepts "necessarily must apply in a determination of whether any relief should be given in cases of this kind in which proof with certainty is impossible." 514 F.2d at 520.

In *Reserve Mining* the issue was whether asbestiform wastes flushed into Lake Superior by the Reserve Mining Company endangered health. The polluted lake waters formed the drinking supply of several surrounding communities, while a medical theory, bolstered only by inconclusive evidence, suggested that ingestion of the wastes caused cancer. See pages———of—U.S.App.D.C., pages 45–46 of 541 F.2d infra. Applying the "endangering the health or welfare of persons" standard of the FWPCA, the court found the wastes to be a danger cognizable under the Act. The court did not find that the danger was probable; rather it found the wastes to be "potentially harmful," 514 F.2d at 528, and potential harm to be embraced by the "endangering" standard, id. See page—of—U.S.App.D.C., page 17 of 541 F.2d supra. The court concluded:

The record shows that Reserve is discharging a substance into Lake Superior waters which under an acceptable but unproved medical theory may be considered as carcinogenic. As previously discussed, this discharge gives rise to a reasonable medical concern over the public health. We sustain the district court's determination that Reserve's discharge into Lake Superior constitutes pollution of waters "endangering the health or welfare of persons" within the terms of §§1160(c)(5) and (g)(1) of the Federal Water Pollution Control Act and is subject to abatement. 514 F.2d at 529 (footnote omitted; emphasis added). The court thus allowed regulation of the effluent on only a "reasonable" or "potential" showing of danger, hardly the "probable" finding urged by Ethyl as the proper reading of the "endanger" language in Section 211. The reason this relatively slight showing of probability of risk justified regulation is clear: the harm to be avoided, cancer, was particularly great. However, because the risk was somewhat remote, the court did not order the immediate cessation of asbestiform dumping, but rather ordered such cessation within "a reasonable time." Id. at 538.

Reserve Mining convincingly demonstrates that the magnitude of risk sufficient to justify regulation is inversely proportional to the harm to be avoided. Cf. *Carolina Environmental Study Group v. United States,* supra. It would be a bizarre exercise in balancing horrors to determine whether cancer or lead poisoning is a greater harm to be avoided, but fortunately such balancing is unnecessary in this case. Undoubtedly, the harm caused by lead poisoning is severe; nonetheless, the Administrator does not rely on a "potential" risk or a "reasonable medical concern" to justify the regulations before us. Instead, he finds a "significant" risk of harm to health. While this finding may be less than the "probable" standard urged by Ethyl, it is considerably more certain than the risk that justified regulation in Reserve Mining of a comparably "fright-laden" harm. Cf. *Environmental Defense Fund, Inc. v. EPA,* 150 U.S.App.D.C. 348, 358, 465 F.2d 528, 538 (1972). Moreover, like the Reserve Mining court, in the face of this still less than certain risk the Administrator did not order the cessation of use of lead additives, but rather directed a phased step-down to a plateau level. Thus we conclude that however far the parameters of risk and harm inherent in the "will endanger" standard might reach in an appropriate case, they certainly present a "danger" that can be regulated when the harm to be avoided is widespread lead poisoning and the risk of that occurrence is "significant."

. . .

Questions involving the environment are particularly prone to uncertainty. Technological man has altered his world in ways never before experienced or anticipated. The health effects of such alterations are often unknown, sometimes unknowable. While a concerned Congress has passed legislation providing for protection of the public health against gross environmental modifications, the regulators entrusted with the enforcement of such laws have not thereby been endowed with a prescience that removes all doubt from their decisionmaking. Rather, speculation, conflicts in evidence, and theoretical extrapolation typify their every action. How else can they act, given a mandate to protect the public health but only a slight or nonexistent data base upon which to draw? Never before have massive quantities of asbestiform tailings been spewed into the water we drink. Never before have our industrial workers been occupationally exposed to vinyl chloride or to asbestos dust. Never before has the food we eat been permeated with DDT or the pesticides aldrin and dieldrin. And never before have hundreds of thousands of tons of lead emissions been disgorged annually into the air we breathe. Sometimes, of course, relatively certain proof of danger or harm from such modifications can be readily found. But, more commonly, "reasonable medical concerns" and theory long precede certainty. Yet the statutes and common sense demand regulatory action to prevent harm, even if the regulator is less than certain that harm is otherwise inevitable.

Undoubtedly, certainty is the scientific ideal to the extent that even science can be certain of its truth. But certainty in the complexities of environmental medicine may be achievable only after the fact, when scientists have the opportunity for leisurely and isolated scrutiny of an entire mechanism. Awaiting certainty will often allow for only reactive, not preventive, regulation. Petitioners suggest that anything less than certainty, that any speculation, is irresponsible. But when statutes seek to avoid environmental catastrophe, can preventive, albeit uncertain, decisions legitimately be so labeled?

The problems faced by EPA in deciding whether lead automotive emissions pose a threat to the public health highlight the limitations of awaiting certainty. First, lead concentrations are, even to date, essentially low-level, so that the feared adverse effects would not materialize until after a lifetime of exposure. Contrary to petitioners' suggestion, however, we have not yet suffered a lifetime of exposure to lead emissions. At best, emissions at present levels have been with us for no more than 15–20 years. Second, lead exposure from the ambient air is pervasive, so that valid control groups cannot be found against which the effects of lead on our population can be measured. Third, the sources of human exposure to lead are multiple, so that it is difficult to isolate the effect of automobile emissions. Lastly, significant exposure to lead is toxic, so that considerations of decency and morality limit the flexibility of experiments on humans that would otherwise accelerate lead exposure from years to months, and measure those results. Cf. *Environmental Defense Fund, Inc. v. EPA* (Shell), 167 U.S.App.D.C. 71, 78, 510 F.2d 1292, 1299 (1975).

The scientific techniques for attempting to overcome these limitations are several: toxicology can study the distribution and effect of lead in animals; epidemiological techniques can analyze the effects of lead emissions on entire populations; clinical studies can reproduce in laboratories atmospheric conditions and measure under controlled circumstances the effects on humans. All of these studies are of limited usefulness, however. Dr. J. H. Knelson, Director of EPA's Human Studies Laboratory, has described, in the context of setting ambient air standards, the limitations of these various investigative tools: Each of these investigative approaches classic toxicology, epidemiology, and clinical research has its advantages and disadvantages. The toxicologist can control the dose and use invasive or destructive techniques in measuring response in the animal, but is always faced with the problem of extrapolating results to humans. Epidemiology is most relevant because it studies phenomena actually occurring in humans under "natural" conditions, but can only draw inference from observed correlations rather than prove cause and effect relationships. Clinical research can provide the most accurate dose-response relationships in the species of interest. Precisely because the study subjects are humans, however, many experimental design problems are encountered in assuring their safety. Although the dose of an atmospheric pollutant can be carefully controlled and measured in the clinical laboratory, qualitative comparability to the multiplex variable of atmospheric pollution cannot always be assured. The best scientific criteria for establishing air quality standards result from interactions between these disciplines. Clinical studies must be preceded by exhaustive toxicological assessment in other species; observations from population studies should play an important role in the experimental design of clinical research. Biomedical data from all these sources, taken in their entirety, should be used for the prudent definition of air pollution control needs. JA 582–583. The best biomedical evidence will be derived from relating all three research approaches. This EPA did. That petitioners, and their scientists, find a basis to disagree is hardly surprising, since the results are still uncertain, and will be for some time. But if the statute accords the regulator flexibility to assess risks and make essentially legislative policy judgments, as we believe it does, preventive regulation based on conflicting and inconclusive evidence may be sustained. Recent cases have recognized this flexibility in similar situations.

. . .

All of this is not to say that Congress left the Administrator free to set policy on his own terms. To the contrary, the policy guidelines are largely set, both in the statutory term "will endanger" and in the relationship of that term to other sections of the Clean Air Act. These prescriptions direct the Administrator's actions. Operating within the prescribed guidelines, he must consider all the information available to him. Some of the information will be factual, but much of it will be more speculative scientific estimates and "guesstimates" of probable harm, hypotheses based on still-developing data, etc. Ultimately he must act, in part on "factual issues," but largely "on choices of policy, on an assessment of risks, (and) on predictions dealing with matters on the frontiers of scientific knowledge * * *." *Amoco Oil Co. v. EPA,* supra, 163 U.S.App.D.C. at 181, 501 F.2d at 741. A standard of danger, fear of uncertain or unknown harm, contemplates no more.

3. Propriety of the Cumulative Impact Approach. In addition to demanding that the Administrator act solely on facts, petitioner Ethyl insists that those facts convince him that the emission product of the additive to be regulated "in and of itself," i. e., considered in isolation, endangers health. The Administrator contends that the impact of lead emissions is properly considered together with all other human exposure to lead. See page—of—U.S.App.D.C., page 12 of 541 F.2d supra. We agree.

. . .

. . . The Administrator found endangerment, but recognized that the national lead exposure problem is caused, not by air pollution alone, but by an aggregate of sources, including food, water, leaded paint, and dust. He believed that regulation was justified because the aggregate was dangerous, and because leaded gasoline was a significant source that was particularly suited to ready reduction. 38 Fed.Reg. 33734. To the question whether the Administrator was correct in his belief, comparison with the "contribute to" language of Section 202 provides no guidance.

. . .

. . . Congress understood that the body lead burden is caused by multiple sources. It understood that determining the effect of lead automobile emissions, by themselves, on human health is of no more practical value than finding the incremental effect on health of the fifteenth sleeping pill swallowed by a would-be suicide. It did not mean for "endanger" to be measured only in incremental terms. This the Administrator also understood. He determined that absorption of lead automobile emissions, when added to all other human exposure to lead, raises the body lead burden to a level that will endanger health. He realized that lead automobile emissions were, far and away, the most readily reduced significant source of environmental lead. And he determined that the statute authorized him to reduce those emissions on such a finding. We find no error in the Administrator's use of the cumulative impact approach.

4. Summary of the "Will Endanger" Determination. In sum, we must reject petitioners' cramped and unrealistic interpretation of Section 211(c)(1)(A). Their reading would render the statute largely useless as a basis for health-related regulation of lead emissions. Petitioners' arguments are rebuffed by the plain meaning of the statute and the Administrator's interpretation of it, by the legislative history and the implications that can be drawn from other sections of the same statute, by the relevant precedents, and by the established maxim that health-related legislation is liberally construed to achieve its purpose.

We believe the Administrator may regulate lead additives under Section 211(c)(1)(A) when he determines, based on his assessment of the risks as developed by consideration of all the information available to him, and as guided by the policy judgment inherent in the statute, that lead automobile emissions significantly increase the total human exposure to lead so as to cause a significant risk of harm to the public health. Before so regulating, he must consider the possibility of regulation under Section 202. This interpretation of Section 211 does not allow for baseless or purposeless regulation, but does grant the Administrator the flexibility needed to confront realistically the public health problem presented by massive diffusion of lead emissions from automobiles.

B. Comparison with Substitute Additives

Even when the Administrator has determined that a fuel or fuel additive causes emissions which endanger the public health, he is not yet free to prohibit the substance under Section 211. He must first find, and publish his finding, that in his judgment such prohibition will not cause the use of any other fuel or fuel additive which will produce emissions which will endanger the public health or welfare to the same or greater degree than the use of the fuel or fuel additive proposed to be prohibited. Section 211(c)(2)(C), 42 U.S.C. § 1857f-6c(c)(2)(C).

Preliminarily it must be noted that the section requires a finding only before the Administrator "prohibits" a fuel or fuel additive under Section 211. Since the proposed regulations only "control" lead additives, the findings requirement, on its face, does not apply to the EPA action. If the requirement is read to apply, however, it plainly demands no more than the findings requirement of Section 211(c)(2)(B), as construed in Amoco, see pages———of—U.S.App.D.C., page 23 of 541 F.2d supra. This conclusion is compelled by the identical genesis of the two provisions, plus the fact that the Section 211(c)(2)(C) finding is judgmental by its own terms. Thus where the judgment turns "on factual issues" we will "demand sufficient attention to these in the statement to allow the fundamental rationality * * * to be ascertained." *Amoco Oil Co. v. EPA,* supra, 163 U.S.App.D.C. at 180–181, 501 F.2d at 740–741. By contrast, where the judgment is necessarily more speculative, we will "demand adequate reasons and explanations, but not 'findings' of the sort familiar from the world of adjudication." Id., 163 U.S.App.D.C. at 181, 501 F.2d at 741.

After making the "will endanger" determination and the "substitute additives" finding, EPA has complied with the statutory mandate and is free to regulate the fuel or fuel additive under Section 211.

. . .

C. Summary of the Evidence

From a vast mass of evidence the Administrator has concluded that the emission products of lead additives will endanger the public health. He has handled an extraordinarily complicated problem with great care and candor. The evidence did not necessarily always point in one direction and frequently, until EPA authorized research, there was no evidence at all. The Administrator reached his conclusion only after hearings spread over several months, consideration of thousands of pages of documents, publication of three health documents, three formal comment periods, and receipt of hundreds of comments. Each study was considered independently; its worth was assessed only after it was measured against any critical comments. From the totality of the evidence the Administrator concluded that regulation under Section 211(c)(1)(A) was warranted.

In tracking his path through the evidence we, in our appellate role, have also considered separately each study and the objections petitioners make thereto. In no case have we found the Administrator's use of the evidence to be arbitrary or capricious. Having rejected the individual objections, we also reject the overall claim of error. We find the Administrator's analysis of the evidence and assessment of the risks to be well within the flexibility allowed by the "will endanger" standard. Accordingly, we affirm his determination that lead emissions "present a significant risk of harm to the health of urban populations, particularly to the health of city children." 38 Fed.Reg. 33734.

. . .

V. Conclusion

The complex scientific questions presented by this rule-making proceeding were "resolved in the crucible of debate through the clash of informed but opposing scientific and technological viewpoints." *International Harvester Co. v. Ruckelshaus,* 155 U.S.App.D.C. 411, 448, 478 F.2d 615, 652 (1973) (concurring opinion of Chief Judge Bazelon). On January 31, 1971 the EPA began the debate by publishing advance notice of proposed rule-making concerning possible controls on lead additives in gasolines because of their possible danger to health. On February 23, 1972 it published the proposed regulations supported by a document, Health Hazards of Lead (First Health Document), prepared by the EPA scientific staff. It invited comment from the lead industry, the scientific community, and the concerned public. The EPA held public hearings in Washington, D.C.,

Dallas, and Los Angeles to give people across the country an opportunity to join the debate.

On January 10, 1973 the EPA reproposed the regulations in slightly changed form, supported by a Second Health Document which reflected the scientific comments on the first and brought the scientific information on the subject up to date. Scientific studies, pro and con, which had become available since the proposed regulations were first published were included. Again the EPA invited the parties, the scientific community, and the concerned public to comment. Finally, on November 28, 1973, almost three years after the debate was joined, the EPA promulgated its regulations accompanied by a 10,000-word opinion, thoroughly and comprehensively analyzing the various scientific studies and giving its reasons why it resolved the scientific debate it had provoked in favor of protecting the public from the danger of lead emissions. A Third Health Document, extensively detailing and reviewing the current state of scientific knowledge of the health effects of airborne lead, also accompanied the regulations and the reasons for their issuance.

Because of the importance of the issues raised, we have accorded this case the most careful and exhaustive consideration. We find that in this rule-making proceeding the EPA has complied with all the statutory procedural requirements and that its reasons as stated in its opinion provide a rational basis for its action. Since we reject all of petitioners' claims of error the Agency may enforce its low-lead regulations.

AFIRMED.

Questions, Material, and Suggestions for Further Study

Ethyl v. U.S. EPA

Because actual harm had not been evident at the time the case was decided, *Ethyl* illustrates a problem unique to environmental law but all too common within it: The central question the case poses is, what risks—as opposed to actual harms—should our society seek, through its legal system, to control or prevent? That question, in turn, leads us inevitably to examine the nature of risk itself.

"Risk" can be defined as the chance of harm; and as Mary Douglas and Aaron Wildavsky have shown in their provocative book, *Risk and Culture: An Essay on the Selection of Technological and Environmental Dangers* (Berkeley: University of California Press, 1983), our society faces risks in such areas as foreign affairs, crime, pollution, and economics. Which risks are selected and highlighted by a society depends upon its culture. In the authors' words, "risk is a collective societal construct." We must remember that our society has rewarded risk taking in the past. Some economists, such as Frank H. Knight in his classic *Risk Uncertainty and Profit* (Chicago:

University of Chicago Press, 1921, reprinted in 1971), have argued that such risk taking leads to economic progress. We have a rich tradition of praising the risks taken
by the heroes in literature. See Paul Zweig, *The Adventurer: The Fate of Adventure in
the Western World* (Princeton: Princeton University Press, 1981). Many of the activities
that contribute to our environmental problems (economic activity, technological
growth, population growth) may be seen as the result of the desire of people to take
risks. Microbiologist Rene Dubos, in *Man Adapting* (New Haven: Yale University
Press, 1965), argued that we will always be out of balance with our environment because of human initiative and risk taking. Perhaps environmental law requires an ethic
of risk taking—a reflection on when and under what circumstances the taking of risk
is ethically acceptable. One recent discussion of the ethics of risk taking is given in
Mary Gibson, ed., *To Breathe Freely: Risk, Consent, and Air* (Totowa, N.J.: Rowman &
Allanheld, 1985).

If risk is the probability of harm, inherent in the idea of risk is the notion that we
do not fully know whether any specific harm will definitely result, and we may not
know what its magnitude will be. An ecosystem view of the environment that shows
nature in all its complexity also reveals how much we may not know about the environment because of that complexity. A scheme or system of environmental laws that
seeks to control threats to complex ecosystems faces especially serious problems
precisely because of that lack of knowledge. Thus, in a sense, even the implementation of environmental laws, designed to reduce risk, can actually increase other risks.

How to make decisions in the face of relative ignorance has been the prime concern of the complex new fields of risk analysis, decision theory, and the economics of
information. A few well-known works in these complex fields include K. S. Shrader-
Frechette, *Risk Analysis and Scientific Method: Methodological and Ethical Problems
with Evaluating Societal Hazards* (Boston: Reidel, 1985); Baruch Fischoff et al.,
Acceptable Risk (New York: Cambridge University Press, 1981); David Braybrooke and
Charles E. Lindblom, *Strategy of Decision* (New York: Free Press, 1970); and Malcolm
Galatin and Robert D. Leiter, eds., *Economics of Information* (Hingham, Mass.: Kluwer
Academic Publishers Group, 1981). But despite these complicated techniques for handling uncertainty, we all know common-sense ways of coping with risk: hedging our
bets, insuring against loss, putting our eggs in more than one basket. Some of these
common-sense techniques can be used in devising ways of controlling projects that
pose threats to the environment.

6

Statutes

Extinction and Governmental Action

Case Study:
Palila v. Hawaii

A pitfall of using legal cases as precedent to analyze subsequent conflicts is a tendency to categorize cases and categories of cases glibly, not wisely. Lawyers speak of such and such case as if it had only one possible application when in reality, any case may serve as precedent for any number of issues. It is all too easy to speak of *Just v. Marinette* as a "Taking Case," of *Boomer* as a "Nuisance Case," or *Tanner* as a "Con[stitutional] Law Case." Obviously life isn't that simple and if, as your authors believe, case law is no more or less than the conflicts of life writ large, dealing with cases isn't going to be that simple either.

Perhaps no other case in this book illustrates this point quite as clearly as *Palila*. Although in the end it may not make much difference, your two authors view this case in different ways: To one of us it's an "Endangered Species Case," and to the other it's an "Administrative Law Case." We ask that before reading the case, you think about these two ways of interpreting what is here and then, after reading, make up your own minds about just what *Palila* is all about and how it is best approached. Might these two approaches yield different results? *Should* they?

Both authors agree that the case has at its roots the application of the Endangered Species Act (one would be hard pressed to deny that) and that the Endangered Species Act was an attempt by Congress to "protect" certain species of wildlife, animals, and plants from extinction. One of the authors pretty much accepts that human beings have an obligation to existing species as well as to future generations of human beings, to attempt to protect existing species from the negative effects of human existence and behavior, thereby "preserving" them. The other author is not so sure, tending to view species extinction more as a natural part of existence and seeing man as no more or less disruptive of life on Earth than any other species, the success of any one of which may inevitably lead to the extinction of others. He views the current impetus for the protection of species as essentially aesthetic rather than moral: We *like* bears and wolves so we protect them; we don't particularly care for the smallpox bacillus (just another species, after all) or the Norway rat, so we'd be content to wipe them off the face of the earth.

To begin our analysis where we so often do in *Green Justice*, we need to ask what does it *mean* to say that we will "preserve" a species? And, as a consequence, just who are *we* to decide such a thing in the first place? The concept that entire species will from time to time and for various reasons (or for no evident reason at all) simply disappear from the face of the earth—vanish, become extinct—did not exist until the mid-eighteenth to mid-nineteenth century. One consequence of the extraordinary ferment in biological studies from about 1760 to 1860—the product of such intellectual prodigies as Jean-Baptiste Lamarck, Carolus Linnaeus, Erasmus Darwin, and Charles Darwin—was acceptance of the notion that species, not merely individuals, could appear on the earth, thrive, and quietly sink back into oblivion. Earlier, in the Elizabethan period, the more common assumption was that the Creation was just that, something created by a Creator who knew just what He was doing and included in it precisely the correct number of plants and animals, all of which existed in some specific, definable relationship one to another. The world was a plenum, a space to which nothing could be added or subtracted.

The modern, very different view of the universe has replaced the plenum and its satisfying solidity with a blooming, buzzing, busy world in which species must compete for the factors necessary for their continued existence. We know now, for example, that in the extremely brief period since 1600, over 700 species have become extinct. Of these, something like 290 were mammals, 200 were birds, and 210 were reptiles and amphibians. Is there any reason to look at species extinction as anything other than the inevitable working-out of evolution? Older, more established species give way to newer ones that have more efficiently adapted to the changing environment; it is the way of the world. There are no guarantees in this life: no guarantee that a given species will become extinct over a certain time span, no guarantee that it will not. In the absence of a more efficiently adapted and competing species, the horseshoe crab has scurried about for 500 million years and may well outlive all of us. By one estimate, only 1 percent of all the species that have ever existed are alive at present, leading to the astonishing deduction that 99 percent have become extinct. To believe that extinction can't happen to human beings and the other species that happen to inhabit the earth at the same time we do is hubris on a cosmological scale.

Species arise from an indistinct past, flourish for years, decades, or millennia, and disappear. The cycle appears to be inevitable. To succeed for the brief time it is here a species has a handful of requirements: There must be a certain number of individuals, each of which requires a minimum amount of territory for support. The most obvious and dramatic instances of species extinction occur when all individuals of a given species are killed outright. The great auk and the dodo (both of which became extinct in the nineteenth century) were killed off because their lack of fear made them easy prey for hungry sailors, and they provide probably the best contemporary examples of this mechanism of extinction. The flightless rails that inhabited many Pacific islands at the time of Captain Cook's voyages in the eighteenth century were driven to extinction by the introduction of alien animals.

The more insidious attack upon a species' reproductive ability is a less dramatic but equally destructive action of habitat deprivation. Each individual of a species requires a certain amount of space containing a certain amount of food and other features that enable it to live and reproduce. This space, the individual's habitat, is crucial to its survival; the survival of the species, in turn, depends upon the survival and reproduction of an adequate number of individuals. Just how these two factors interrelate can be seen in the history of the American passenger pigeon, a dove that existed by the billions in the United States until it disappeared from the wild in 1904, and completely by 1914. Passenger pigeons were hunted, probably overhunted, but their doom was sealed by axes rather than guns: When their native forests were cut down the species could not reproduce, and those that died could not be replaced.

There are other more timely examples as well. The grizzly bear, once common throughout large portions of North America, has been hunted and deprived of its habitat until the species is on the verge of extinction in the contiguous United States. Its range in the lower forty-eight states has been reduced to a smattering in pockets of isolated wilderness and park areas of Idaho, Wyoming, Montana, and, possibly, Washington. Ironically, there is currently a debate over whether the bear population has increased too much in those areas. The debate, which includes consideration of such factors as increased human pressure, the possible growth of the bear population beyond the yield of its food supplies, and the relationship between an individual bear's range and the number of square miles of habitat needed to support it, promises to continue for some time. A similar dispute pits ranchers around Yellowstone National Park against the National Park Service and a number of wildlife groups attempting to reintroduce wolves into the Yellowstone and central Idaho ecosystems.

In disputes over preserving species, no one seems to know for sure what is being done, why it is being done, whether it is worth doing, or whether we should keep doing whatever it is that we are doing just to keep doing something. Do we wish to preserve the species? If so, perhaps we should simply round up as many individuals as possible, place them in zoos, and ensure through proper breeding records that there is no more (and no less) interbreeding than would occur in the wild. Is our wish actually to preserve the habitat at least as much as it is to preserve the species? If so, we must decide at the start that the "wild habitat" will remain "wild"—that we will not intervene even though in making that decision we may be sealing the doom of the species we want to preserve, taking the chance, for example, that a wild population within the habitat will outgrow its resources and suffer a catastrophic crash, during which all but a few individuals will die, perhaps not even leaving enough survivors to continue the species.

Resolving the dilemmas we face with those species defined by federal legislation as "endangered" raises other problems as well. We have so far been remarkably successful in breeding captive populations of whooping cranes, peregrine falcons, black-footed ferrets and several species of African antelope. But to what end? This sort of specialized attention is not cheap, and in periods when many members of our own society are having trouble making ends meet, we need good arguments to justify spending our precious resources on animals.

Proponents for protecting endangered species argue that recent population growth, development, and pollution may "speed up" the process of extinction. The wholesale elimination of species may be an indicator of more dangerous changes in the ecosystems, changes that may be dangerous to the survival of our own species. But this argument is essentially anthropocentric: The species are indicators *for* human beings and our existence is assumed to be more cosmically significant. They are our miners' canaries. Some defenders of threatened wildlife argue that all species have an intrinsic value, perhaps a "right to exist" at least equal to ours. Some even argue that human beings can rise above the blind processes of evolution and offer a version of an "environmental welfare state" for nonhumans.

Can we justify such expenses another way? A way that ignores economics and a cost/benefit analysis? According to medieval theological theory, humans, the noblest animals, those made in God's own likeness, were put on Earth as stewards, not as exploiters. Many people today find it hard to accept the possibility that our needs, significant or frivolous, might lead to the elimination of an entire species. Perhaps we really do have a duty to attempt to preserve species other than our own. But if so, that duty can't come from the Nature we have come to understand since Darwin. It must come from outside the ecosystem.

If we cannot justify our duty by the medieval notion that we were placed here to be stewards, perhaps we can take our lead from modern scientific fact. One very clear biological reason to preserve individuals is to maintain as many characteristics as possible in the gene pool. This is an excellent argument against over-hybridization within an individual species (the idea being that a monoculture with no diversity is particularly apt to crash). Many people, however, would find it hard to accept the argument that preserving whooping cranes, black-footed ferrets, grizzly bears, louse-worts, and a random handful of bugs would benefit the world as a whole, particularly humans. With so many serious problems—poverty, famine, war, and disease—we cannot irresponsibly spend our resources on a few fashionable causes; we must set priorities in establishing social, political, and economic goals.

One of the most far-reaching of all environmental statutes, if for no other reason than its capability of bedeviling developers, is the Endangered Species Act of 1973, 16 U.S.C. §1531 *et seq.* In the first section the objectives of the act were clearly set forth: "The purposes of this Act are to provide a means whereby the ecosystems upon which endangered species and threatened species depend may be conserved; and to provide a program for the conservation of such endangered species and threatened species" (16 U.S.C. §1531(b)). To achieve these goals the Secretary of the Interior was required to maintain a list of endangered and threatened species and to ensure that those species would be protected:

> The Secretary shall review other programs administered by him and utilize such programs in furtherance of the purposes of this chapter. All other Federal departments and agencies shall, in consultation with and with the assistance of the Secretary, utilize their authorities in furtherance of the purposes of this chapter . . . and by taking such action necessary to insure that actions authorized, funded, or carried out by them do not jeopardize the continued existence of such endangered species and threatened species or result in the destruction or modification of habitat of such species which is determined by the Secretary, after consultation as appropriate with the affected states, to be critical. (16 U.S.C. 1536, 1976)

One of the first applications of the new law was its use in the Tellico Dam dispute [*TVA v. Hill*, 437 U.S. 153 (1978)] in which The Supreme Court held, in effect, that the law meant what it said: If a species were endangered, it was protected. In that case, the Supreme Court held that because the building of the Tellico Dam would disrupt the habitat of the snail darter (a fish of about three or four inches in length), the Dam (which its supporters saw as providing a badly needed economic boost to an economically depressed area) could not be built.

One of the more intriguing things about the *TVA v. Hill* case, and about many environmental disputes, is that the statute became used by the parties not so much for its own sake as for its value as an offensive weapon in a lawsuit, one with which to bludgeon developers of a project that is actually being opposed for any number of reasons: economic, aesthetic, political, or cultural, few, if any, of which have a thing to do with endangered species.

Which brings us back to *Palila*. You might ask yourself what is going on here. What is the basis of the judge's decision? (See case excerpts that follow.) Clearly he has decided that the sheep have got to go. But on what grounds did he decide this? Do you think he believes this argument? Suppose, for a moment that the judge did not believe the palila were in any danger whatever—could he have decided the case the same way? Why did he decide the way he did? Was it on the grounds that the sheep were depriving the palila of its habitat? What if each and every palila were roasted for Thanksgiving? Would we be any the poorer for it?

As an aide in understanding just what it means to interpret statutes, we reproduce here three extremely small portions of The Endangered Species Act. The decision in the *Palila* case rests largely upon these sections:

Section 1531(b). Purposes.
The purposes of this chapter are to provide a means whereby the ecosystems upon which endangered species and threatened species depend may be conserved, to provide a program for the conservation of such endangered species and threatened species, and. . . .

Section 1532.   Definitions.
(5) the term "critical habitat" for a threatened or endangered species means—
  (i)   the specific area within the geographical areas occupied by the species, . . . on
        which are found those physical or biological features (I) essential to the con-
        servation of the species and (II) which may require special management con-
        siderations of protection and;
  (ii) specific areas outside the geographical area occupied by the species . . . [that
        are] essential for the conservation of the species. . . .
  (19) The term "take" means to harass, harm, pursue, hunt, shoot, wound, kill, trap,
        capture, or collect, or to attempt to engage in any such conduct. . . .

Section 1538.   Prohibited Acts.
(a) Generally
  (1) . . . it is unlawful for any person subject to the jurisdiction of the United States
       to—
        . . .
  (B) take any such species within the United States or the territorial sea of the
       United States; . . .

**PALILA (Loxioides bailleui, formerly Psittirostra bailleui),
an endangered species;
et al.,
Plaintiffs-Appellees
v.
HAWAII DEPARTMENT OF LAND
AND NATURAL RESOURCES;
et al.,
Defendants-Appellants**

**United States Court of Appeals,
Ninth Circuit
Decided July 22, 1988
[852 F.2d 1106]**

O'SCANNLAIN, Circuit Judge.

This is the fourth round of judicial activity involving a six-inch long finch-billed
bird called palila, found only on the slopes of Mauna Kea on the Island of Hawaii.

As an endangered species under the Endangered Species Act ("Act"), 16 U.S.C.
§§ 1531–43 (1982), the bird (Loxioides bailleui), a member of the Hawaiian hon-
eycreeper family, also has legal status and wings its way into federal court as a
plaintiff in its own right. The Palila (which has earned the right to be capitalized
since it is a party to this proceeding) is represented by attorneys for the Sierra

Club, Audubon Society, and other environmental parties who obtained an order directing the Hawaii Department of Land and Natural Resources ("Department") to remove mouflon sheep from its critical habitat. Sports hunters, represented by the Hawaii Rifle Association, among others, had intervened to dispute the contention that the Palila was "harmed" by the presence of mouflon sheep. Hence, these appeals. But, first, some history.

Facts and Proceedings

In 1978 the Sierra Club and others brought an action under the Act on behalf of the Palila, claiming that the Department's practice of maintaining feral goats and sheep (animals that originally were domesticated but were allowed to run wild) in the Palila's critical habitat constituted an unlawful "taking" under the Act. The district court agreed and ordered the Department to remove the animals because it found that the goats and sheep destroyed the mamane-naio woodlands upon which the Palila depend. *Palila v. Hawaii Dept. of Land & Natural Resources* ("*Palila I*"), 471 F.Supp.985 (D.Haw.1979). This court affirmed. *Palila v. Hawaii Dept. Land & Natural Resources* ("*Palila II*"), 639 F.2d 495 (9th Cir.1981).

In 1984 the Sierra Club reopened the 1978 proceeding by moving to amend its original complaint to add mouflon sheep as destructive animals to be removed from the Palila's habitat. The mouflon sheep had been introduced by the Department between 1962 and 1966 for the enjoyment of sport hunters. Apparently, they had not been the target of the original complaint because research into their effect upon the Palila's habitat had not been completed. The mouflon sheep, like the feral sheep and goats before them, feed on the mamane trees.

In November 1986 the district court ruled in favor of the *Sierra Club. Palila v. Hawaii Dept. of Land & Natural Resources* ("*Palila III*"), 649 F. Supp.1070 (D.Haw.1986). It found that presence of mouflon sheep "harmed" the Palila within the meaning of 50 C.F.R. § 17.3's definition of "harm" in two ways: (1) the eating habits of the sheep destroyed the mamane woodland and thus caused habitat degradation that could result in extinction; (2) were the mouflon to continue eating the mamane, the woodland would not regenerate and the Palila population would not recover to a point where it could be removed from the Endangered Species list.

The Department and intervenors filed timely appeals. We granted the United States amicus curiae status to represent the view of the Secretary that Judge King's order should be affirmed, but for reasons different than those stated in his opinion.

Discussion
I

The Department argues that the district court construed the definition of "harm" in 50 C.F.R. § 17.3 too broadly. The scope of the definition of harm is important because it in part sets the limit on what acts or omissions violate the Act's prohibition against "taking" an endangered species.

In making this argument, the Department suggests dichotomy between "actual" and "potential" harm. The Department believes that actual harm only includes those acts which result in the immediate destruction of the Palila's food sources; all other acts are "potential" harm no matter how clear the causal link and beyond the reach of the Act. Thus, the Department challenges the district court's finding that habitat destruction which could drive the Palila to extinction constitutes "harm."

We inquire whether the district court's interpretation is consistent with the Secretary's construction of the statute since he is charged with enforcing the Act, and entitled to deference if his regulation is reasonable and not in conflict with the intent of Congress. See *United States v. Riverside Bayview Homes, Inc.,* 474 U.S. 121, 131, 106 S.Ct. 455, 461, 88 L.Ed.2d 419 (1985).

While promulgating a revised definition of harm, the Secretary noted that harm includes not only direct physical injury, but also injury caused by impairment of essential behavior patterns via habitat modification that can have significant and permanent effects on a listed species. 46 Fed.Reg. 54748, 54750 (1981) (codified at 50 C.F.R. § 17.3). Moreover, in that same promulgation notice, the Secretary let stand the district court's construction of harm in *Palila I.* Id. at 54749–50. In *Palila I,* the district court construed harm to include habitat destruction that could result in the extinction of the Palila—exactly the same type of injury at issue here. See generally *Palila I,* 471 F. Supp. at 985. We conclude that the district court's inclusion within the definition of "harm" of habitat destruction that could drive the Palila to extinction falls within the Secretary's interpretation.

The Secretary's inclusion of habitat destruction that could result in extinction follows the plain language of the statute because it serves the overall purpose of the Act, which is "to provide a means whereby the ecosystems upon which endangered species and threatened species depend may be conserved. . . ." 16 U.S.C. § 1531(b). The definition serves the overall purpose of the Act since it conserves the Palila's threatened ecosystem (the mamane-naio woodland).

The Secretary's construction of harm is also consistent with the policy of Congress evidenced by the legislative history. For example, in the Senate Report on the Act: "'Take' is defined in . . . the broadest possible manner to include every conceivable way in which a person can 'take' or attempt to 'take' any fish or wildlife." S.Rep. No. 307, 93d Cong., 1st Sess. (1973), reprinted in 1973 U.S. Code Cong. & Admin. News 2989, 2995. The House Report said that the "harassment" form of taking would "allow, for example, the Secretary to regulate or prohibit the activities of birdwatchers where the effect of those activities might disturb the birds and make it difficult for them to hatch or raise their young." H.R.Rep. No. 412, 93d Cong., 1st Sess. (1973), 1973 U.S.Code Cong. & Admin.News 2989, reprinted in 4 House Miscellaneous Reports on Public Bills, 93d Cong., 1st Sess. 11 (1973). If the "harassment" form of taking includes activities so remote from actual injury to the bird as birdwatching, then the "harm" form of taking should include more direct activities, such as the mouflon sheep preventing any mamane from growing to maturity.

II

The Department contends that the district court erred when it found an unlawful "taking" within the meaning of Section 9 of the Act. (Section 9—codified as 16 U.S.C. § 1538—lists the conduct prohibited by the Act). The Department argues that no taking exists because the evidence shows that (1) a huntable number of sheep (a flock large enough to sustain sports hunting) could co-exist with the Palila; and (2) the Palila are doing poorly because of the recently removed feral sheep and goats, not the mouflon sheep. Our review is for clear error. Oregon Envtl. Council v. Kunzman, 817 F.2d 484, 493 (9th Cir.1987).

A. Co-existence

The Department's witnesses conceded that a large number of mouflon sheep in one area could significantly damage the mamane-naio woodlands and thereby drive the Palila to extinction. However, these witnesses maintained that a huntable number of mouflon sheep could co-exist with the Palila. In support of its co-existence thesis, the Department makes four arguments. First, since the removal of the feral sheep and goats, the mamane-naio woodland has regenerated. This regeneration will support both the mouflon sheep and the Palila. Second, the Department has begun a number of regeneration projects (replanting, fertilizing, etc.). Third, the mouflon sheep would not cause significant degradation if the Department controlled their density. Fourth, the population of the Palila has increased since January 1985.

The Sierra Club's witnesses controverted the Department's thesis of co-existence. First, although regeneration (new mamane seedlings and sprouts) has occurred in many areas, it takes twenty-five years for the mamane seedlings and sprouts to become mature trees capable of providing food and shelter for the Palila. However, for the first ten to fifteen years of this growth period, the mouflon sheep can kill the mamane trees and no significant regeneration would occur, at least not sufficient to sustain the Palila unless the trees survive to twenty-five years of age. Second, the Sierra Club's witnesses showed that the Department's additional programs as an alternative to removal of the mouflon sheep would not work. Third, they disagreed with the premise that the mouflon sheep population could co-exist with the Palila if the Department controlled their density. Fourth, the Sierra Club witnesses stated that the Palila's population, despite short-term fluctuations, has been static over the long term.

The Sierra Club witnesses put forth their own thesis: Because the grazing and browsing habits of the mouflon sheep destroy the mamane woodland upon which the Palila depend entirely for their existence, the sheep must be removed. This thesis received the support of one of the state's witnesses. This witness conceded that he believes that the mouflon sheep must be removed to ensure the survival of the Palila.

The Sierra Club's witnesses are not contradicted by the documentary evidence (i.e., studies of the Palila, mouflon sheep, etc.), and the Sierra Club witnesses advanced a coherent and plausible thesis. On the issue of coexistence, then, the district court's decision to accept the Sierra Club's witnesses' testimony as more credible cannot be clearly erroneous.

B. Feral Sheep and Goats Versus Mouflon Sheep

The Department's witnesses asserted that there had been significant regeneration wherever the feral animals had been removed. The Sierra Club's witnesses agreed, but they went on to argue that where mouflon sheep have appeared, no significant regeneration has occurred.

On the question of which animals—the feral sheep and goats or the mouflon—damage the mamane, the district court again gave more credibility to the Sierra Club's witnesses; this preference cannot be clearly erroneous where the Sierra Club's witnesses were not contradicted by documentary evidence. Indeed, the testimony given by the Sierra Club witnesses—noticeable regeneration has occurred only where the feral animals have been removed and no mouflon sheep have appeared—is both plausible and consistent.

We affirm the district court's finding that the Department's permitting mouflon sheep in the area constitutes a "taking" of the Palila's habitat. The district court made its findings based on the testimony of the Sierra Club witnesses, which was not contradicted by extrinsic evidence. Therefore, the district court's findings should not be held clearly erroneous. See *Anderson v. City of Bessemer City, N.C.,* 470 U.S. 564, 575, 105 S.Ct. 1504, 1512, 84 L.Ed.2d 518 (1985)("When a trial judge's finding is based on his decision to credit the testimony of one of two or more witnesses, each of whom has told a coherent and facially plausible story that is not contradicted by extrinsic evidence, that finding, if not internally inconsistent, can virtually never be clear error").

III

Under this resolution of the appeal, we do not reach the issue of whether harm includes habitat degradation that merely retards recovery. The district court's (and the Secretary's) interpretation of harm as including habitat destruction that could result in extinction, and findings to that effect are enough to sustain an order for the removal of the mouflon sheep.

Conclusion

The district court's finding of habitat degradation that could result in extinction constitutes "harm." The district court's finding of a "taking" was not clearly erroneous. We do not reach the issue of whether the district court properly found that harm included habitat degradation that prevents recovery of an endangered species.

AFFIRMED.

Questions, Materials, and Suggestions for Further Study

Palila v. Hawaii

Since the early days of the Endangered Species Act, many species have been listed and many critical habitats have been identified. States have adopted their own endangered species acts to supplement the federal law. Steven Yaffee has written two excellent studies of the act. In 1982, Yaffee wrote *Prohibitive Policy: Implementing the Federal Endangered Species Act* (Cambridge, Mass.: MIT Press). He pointed out that unlike most environmental laws, which rely on permits, the Endangered Species Act prohibits actions on pain of criminal and civil penalties. More recently, Yaffee studied the past ten years of the law in light of the controversy over the spotted owl in *The Wisdom of the Spotted Owl* (Washington, D.C.: Island Press, 1994).

In recent years, there have been two major related shifts in how the Endangered Species Act is perceived. First, it has come to be more fully recognized that the major threat to species is habitat destruction, and hence habitat conservation is crucial. See Kathryn Kohner, *Balancing on the Brink of Extinction: The Endangered Species Act and Lessons for the Future* (Washington, D.C.: Island Press, 1991). Second, it has become increasingly evident that it is not merely the big and beautiful species that are important to the ecosystem, but the myriad of smaller species as well. As a consequence, the preservation of ecosystem biodiversity has become the principal goal of environmentalists. This shift, however, has created serious political problems, since, as an abstraction, preserving biodiversty is not as popular as protecting specific animals: bears, wolves, whooping cranes, and snowy egrets. Moreover, habitat protection, especially on private lands threatens private property claims. The biology behind this shift is set forth in Michael Soule and B. A. Wilcox, *Conservation Biology: An Evolutionary-Ecological Perspective* (Sunderland, Mass.: Sinauer Associates, 1980). The ideal of biodiversity is set forth in E. O. Wilson's *Biophilia: The Human Bond with Other Species* (Cambridge: Harvard University Press, 1984). A more popular treatment is R. E. Grumbine's *Ghost Bears: Exploring the Biodiversity Crisis* (Washington, D.C.: Island Press, 1992).

Part 3

Fundamental Causes of the Environmental Crisis

For children, laying blame is a favorite pastime. This is true of adults as well, but to save face we tell ourselves that we are laying blame for a good reason: to identify those individuals, entities, or forces that have made something go wrong and, knowing that, to set out to remedy or "fix" it. There is probably no better example than just this phenomenon than the U.S. approach to what many today perceive as our "environmental crisis." It follows as the night the day: If there is a "crisis" someone or something must have caused it. And, further, if we could identify and correct whatever it is that has gone wrong, the crisis would disappear.

Ever optimistic, we assume that if only we could adequately define our environmental problems and find out precisely why and how things happen the way they do, if only we could identify the causes, then we could fix the problems: Deft surgeons, we could reach in, carve out the causes, and all would be well—the rain pure, the fish healthy, the air fit to breathe. As rational men and women we probably accept in our heart of hearts that this return to Eden will not come about overnight, but we tell ourselves that if we could enumerate the causes of our environmental problems we could begin to line up the remedies and that from there it would be only a matter of getting on with the job of correcting things.

Where to begin? In reading the next four cases of *Green Justice,* you will find that what may have seemed merely a suggestion in Parts 1 and 2, quickly becomes apparent in Part 3: We are dealing with issues so multifaceted in terms of their social, political, economic, and even philosophical and aesthetic dimensions that pinning down the cause or causes of our current environmental crisis is precisely what we cannot do. Significant numbers of our fellow citizens would even deny that there is any crisis at all. Those who believe a crisis is imminent have no lack of candidates. One school of thought bravely proclaims that the pressures of overpopulation have produced our problems. Another cries nonsense; the earth has plenty of resources to provide for the present population and many more to boot;

the problem, they might claim, lies in the technologies we use to get at or distribute those resources. Some may find the cause of the crisis in the expansion and use of our military might, with its consequent pollution, in war, nuclear testing, and waste at military bases. Yet others may say that the real problem lies not so much in those technologies themselves as in our inability or lack of desire to control the social effects of using them; if we could only devise a bureaucracy that would ensure the proper allocation of resources and costs, all would be well (seldom being very clear about what that "proper" allocation might be or who would get to determine it). And there are moralists who insist that the root of our problem lies in individual and corporate greed that uses natural resources (including the cleanness of air and water) without paying for them in the form of pollution-control equipment, thereby increasing their own return on investment at the cost of everyone else's health. The fact is that many of our natural resources, including our air and water, are part of an unregulated commons, not subject to the rules governing private, or even public, property. The wages of greed are various forms of pollution, they maintain, and it is about time that individuals and companies begin to clean up after themselves.

One of the major problems of using the law as an instrument for achieving ecological justice is that our legal system does not handle ultimate causes very well. Law deals best with symptomatic problems, with individuals and groups seeking specific results, with mandating specific actions in the real world. Legislatures and agencies are good at picking an environmental medium (air, soil, or water), choosing a substance (cadmium, say), designating an amount (1 ppm), specifying a test (the Toxicity Characteristic Leaching Process or TCLP test), and declaring that any material that has served its useful life, is being discarded and contains 1 ppm of cadmium when tested by the TCLP test is a "hazardous" waste that must be handled in accordance with specific regulations. The ultimate reason the waste exists—population, technology, bureaucracy, greed, whatever—is ignored, as is the reason the cadmium got into the waste in the first place. But the law handles the concrete fact of its presence very effectively.

Technology is, of course, one of the more visible candidates, one that many advance as the primary candidate for the role of chief environmental culprit but, in truth, there are many possibilities. Some would choose population, others point at market economies, still others rail at the bureaucracies that sustain the modern state as causes in one form or another of the current state of affairs. To still others, the problem is essentially moral, attributable to a general ethical laxness or absence of responsibility: If those who "dirty" the environment would "clean up after themselves," all this would go away.

Perhaps one of the many reasons why the law does not address the fundamental causes of our environmental problems is that each cause (population growth, technology, consumerism, the growth of international markets, etc., etc., etc.) is in reality a collection of diffuse practices and institutions in our society. Only large-scale planning could cope with such diffuse causes and such planning is not popular in the United States. Out of the huge number of fundamental causes of environmental problems, only technology and population have received the attention of planners. Despite the Technological Assessment Act of 1972, the United States has rejected a comprehensive technology policy (Otis Graham, *Closing Time: The Industrial Policy Debate* [Cambridge, Mass.: Harvard University Press, 1992]). In the United States, we sought to adopt a population plan in the early 1970s, but the effort collapsed soon thereafter. Other nations have succeeded in adopting comprehensive population policies, with mixed results. Most scholars are also afraid to "think big" about the fundamental causes of environmental problems. No such fear intimidates Allan Schnaiberg, *The Environment from Surplus to Scarcity* (Oxford: Oxford University Press, 1980).

In Part 3 of *Green Justice,* we will look at cases involving the consequences that arise from technological change, population growth, and the growth of an international market economy and questions that arise when the values that have given rise to our consumer economy crash headlong into those that have given rise to our desire for that pesticide-free apple pie we referred to in the Introduction. In none of these cases do the issues that arise come about as starkly as one might at first glance wish. There is no *Techno-nerd v. Luddite* case, no "morning after" pill case, no foreign nationalization of American assets case, no chemical company marketing its pesticides as food additives case.

7

Fundamental Causes

Technology

Case Study:
du Pont v. Train

We begin Part 3 of *Green Justice* with an older case, *du Pont v. Train*, because it, more succinctly than most, brings out the difficulties of regulating the effects of technology in modern society. As we discussed in the introduction to Part 3 technology is one candidate for the dubious mantle of ultimate cause for the problem of pollution. When used in this sense, "technology" means those specialized industrial, mechanical, electronic, or chemical processes that go into producing the objects, gadgets, and goodies that our society has decided it needs. You may not remember it now, but you probably first heard about the extent of our current environmental crisis on a television or a radio, the making of which generated hazardous wastes (its circuit boards were etched with acids, the joints soldered); most people drive their cars to meetings to discuss clean air.

Technological advances need not be dramatic to have long-range effects. Thomas Jefferson's curved moldboard on the horse-drawn plow was a technological advance with far-ranging consequences, malign as well as benign. The more effective plow led to deeper furrows, more acreage under cultivation, and a reduced need for labor. Since being cast in steel (Jefferson's was wood) and ganged on the back of another technological wonder, the mechanical tractor, the moldboard has contributed significantly not only to the dramatic successes of modern agriculture but also to the excess yield and lost topsoil that characterize modern farming techniques.

Not that the pressures of progress left all this devastation to the lowly moldboard. Agricultural mechanization was only a few generations away when Jefferson first worked on his invention. The McCormick reaper, the combine, and the milking machine have all contributed to current agricultural woes. And agriculture was not alone in manifesting the effects—both beneficial and detrimental—of technological growth. Before World War II there were few artificial fertilizers, no DDT, and no handheld calculators. A "computer" at work on the Manhattan Project during World War II was just that: a human being with pencil, paper, and slide rule who computed as accurately as possible, probably spending as much time erasing as figuring.

Our ability to control our surroundings—evinced in the growth of technology since World War II—has been staggering. Alloys unimagined only fifteen years ago enable us today to carry hundreds of passengers through the sky at speeds over 500 miles per hour. Millions of U.S. homes have microwave ovens, cellular telephones, home computers, and satellite dishes receiving television signals bounced down from orbiting satellites.

Yet we pay a price for all this technological glitter. The production of those newer alloys generates increasingly complex hazardous waste problems; the wizardry that has blessed us with electronic marvels has cursed us with rivers of acid-etching fluids and fogs of carcinogenic vinyl chloride. By international agreement many nations will be phasing out chlorofluorocarbons because of their effects on stratospheric ozone. More down to earth, we have increased the amounts of air- and water-borne pollution to the extent that many are giving serious thought to banning the use of chlorine in manufacturing processes, a possibility inconceivable a mere five or six years ago. We have lived to rediscover that not only is there no ecological free lunch, there are precious few cheap snacks.

Since the technology that causes environmental problems bears both good and evil fruit, our focus will be on the ways in which the legal system deals with the effects of technology rather than on control of the technology itself. Thus, the focus in *du Pont* is the ways in which three groups—the legislative branch in enacting the Clean Water Act, the executive branch in enacting administrative regulations intended to implement the statute, and the court in evaluating those regulations when they were under challenge by the manufacturers—tried to use technology and technological processes embodied in the best available technology (BAT) standard to regulate, offset, perhaps even negate, the deleterious effects of yet other technologies.

E. I. du PONT de NEMOURS AND COMPANY
et al.,
v.
Russell E. TRAIN,
Administrator, Environmental Protection Agency,
et al.,

Decided Feb. 23, 1977
[430 U.S. 112]

Mr. Justice STEVENS delivered the opinion of the Court.

Inorganic chemical manufacturing plants operated by the eight petitioners in Nos. 75-978 and 75-1473 discharge various pollutants into the Nation's waters and therefore are "point sources" within the meaning of the Federal Water Pollution Control Act (Act), as added and amended by §2 of the Federal Water Pollution Control Act Amendments of 1972, 86 Stat. 816, 33 U.S.C. §1251 et seq. (1970 ed., Supp. V). The Environmental Protection Agency has promulgated industry-wide regulations imposing three sets of precise limitations on petitioners' discharges. The first two impose progressively higher levels of pollutant control on existing point sources after July 1, 1977, and after July 1, 1983, respectively. The third set imposes limits on "new sources" that may be constructed in the future.

These cases present three important questions of statutory construction: (1) whether EPA has the authority under §301 of the Act to issue industrywide regulations limiting discharges by existing plants; (2) whether the Court of Appeals, which admittedly is authorized to review the standards for new sources, also has jurisdiction under §509 to review the regulations concerning existing plants; and (3) whether the new-source standards issued under §306 must allow variances for individual plants. As a preface to our discussion of these three questions, we summarize relevant portions of the statute and then describe the procedure which EPA followed in promulgating the challenged regulations.

The Statute

The statute, enacted on October 18, 1972, authorized a series of steps to be taken to achieve the goal of eliminating all discharges of pollutants into the Nation's waters by 1985, §101(a)(1). The first steps required by the Act are described in §304, which directs the Administrator to develop and publish various kinds of technical data to provide guidance in carrying out responsibilities imposed by other sections of the Act. Thus, within 60 days, 120 days, and 180 days after the date of enactment, the Administrator was to promulgate a series of guidelines to assist the States in developing and carrying out permit programs pursuant to §402. §§304(h),(f),(g). Within 270 days, he was to develop the information to be used in formulating standards for new plants pursuant to §306. §304(c). And within one year he was to publish regulations providing guidance for effluent limitations on existing point sources. Section 304(b) goes into great detail concerning the contents of these regulations. They must identify the degree of effluent reduction attainable through use of the best practicable or best available technology for a class of plants. The guidelines must also "specify factors to be taken into account" in determining the control measures applicable to point sources within these classes. A list of factors to be considered then follows. The Administrator was also directed to develop and publish, within one year, elaborate criteria for water quality accurately reflecting the most current scientific knowledge, and also technical information on factors necessary to restore and maintain water quality. §304(a). The title of §304 describes it as the "information and guidelines" portion of the statute.

Section 301 is captioned "effluent limitations." Section 301(a) makes the discharge of any pollutant unlawful unless the discharge is in compliance with certain enumerated sections of the Act. The enumerated sections which are relevant to this case are §301 itself, §306, and §402. A brief word about each of these sections is necessary.

Section 402 authorizes the Administrator to issue permits for individual point sources, and also authorizes him to review and approve the plan of any State desiring to administer its own permit program. These permits serve "to transform generally applicable effluent limitations . . . into the obligations (including a timetable for compliance) of the individual discharger(s). . . . " *EPA v. California ex rel. State Water Resources Control Board,* 426 U.S. 200, 205, 96 S.Ct. 2022, 2025, 48 L.Ed.2d 578. Petitioner chemical companies' position in this litigation is that §402 provides the only statutory authority for the issuance of enforceable limitations on the discharge of pollutants by existing plants. It is noteworthy, however, that although this section authorizes the imposition of limitations in individual permits, the section itself does not mandate either the Administrator or the States to use permits as the method of prescribing effluent limitations.

Section 306 directs the Administrator to publish within 90 days a list of categories of sources discharging pollutants and, within one year thereafter, to publish regulations establishing national standards of performance for new sources within each category. Section 306 contains no provision for exceptions from the standards for individual plants; on the contrary, subsection (e) expressly makes it unlawful to operate a new source in violation of the applicable standard of performance after its effective date. The statute provides that the new-source standards shall reflect the greatest degree of effluent reduction achievable through application of the best available demonstrated control technology.

Section 301(b) defines the effluent limitations that shall be achieved by existing point sources in two stages. By July 1, 1977, the effluent limitations shall require the application of the best practicable control technology currently available; by July 1, 1983, the limitations shall require application of the best available technology economically achievable. The statute expressly provides that the limitations which are to become effective in 1983 are applicable to "categories and classes of point sources"; this phrase is omitted from the description of the 1977 limitations. While §301 states that these limitations "shall be achieved," it fails to state who will establish the limitations.

Section 301(c) authorizes the Administrator to grant variances from the 1983 limitations. Section 301(e) states that effluent limitations established pursuant to §301 shall be applied to all point sources.

To summarize, §301(b) requires the achievement of effluent limitations requiring use of the "best practicable" or "best available" technology. It refers to §304 for a definition of these terms. Section 304 requires the publication of "regulations, providing guidelines for effluent limitations." Finally, permits issued under §402 must require compliance with §301 effluent limitations. Nowhere are we told who sets the §301 effluent limitations, or precisely how they relate to §304 guidelines and §402 permits.

. . .

The Issues

The broad outlines of the parties' respective theories may be stated briefly. EPA contends that §301(b) authorizes it to issue regulations establishing effluent limitations for classes of plants. The permits granted under §402, in EPA's view, simply incorporate these across-the-board limitations, except for the limited variances allowed by the regulations themselves and by §301(c). The §304(b) guidelines, according to EPA, were intended to guide it in later establishing §301 effluent-limitation regulations. Because the process proved more time consuming than Congress assumed when it established this two-stage process, EPA condensed the two stages into a single regulation.

In contrast, petitioners contend that §301 is not an independent source of authority for setting effluent limitations by regulation. Instead, §301 is seen as merely a description of the effluent limitations which are set for each plant on an individual basis during the permit-issuance process. Under the industry view, the §304 guidelines serve the function of guiding the permit issuer in setting the effluent limitations.

. . .

I

We think §301 itself is the key to the problem. The statutory language concerning the 1983 limitation, in particular, leaves no doubt that these limitations are to be set by regulation. Subsection (b)(2)(A) of §301 states that by 1983 "effluent limitations for categories and classes of point sources" are to be achieved which will require "application of the best available technology economically achievable for such category or class." (Emphasis added.) These effluent limitations are to require elimination of all discharges if "such elimination is technologically and economically achievable for a category or class of point sources." (Emphasis added.) This is "language difficult to reconcile with the view that individual effluent limitations are to be set when each permit is issued." *American Meat Institute v. EPA*, 526 F.2d 442, 450 (C.A.7 1975). The statute thus focuses expressly on the characteristics of the "category or class" rather than the characteristics of individual point sources. Normally, such classwide determinations would be made by regulation, not in the course of issuing a permit to one member of the class.

Thus, we find that §301 unambiguously provides for the use of regulations to establish the 1983 effluent limitations. Different language is used in §301 with respect to the 1977 limitations. Here, the statute speaks of "effluent limitations for point sources," rather than "effluent limitations for categories and classes of point sources." Nothing elsewhere in the Act, however, suggests any radical difference in the mechanism used to impose limitations for the 1977 and 1983 deadlines. See *American Iron & Steel Institute v. EPA*, 526 F.2d 1027, 1042 n.32 (C.A.3 1975). For instance, there is no indication in either §301 or §304 that the §304 guidelines play a different role in setting 1977 limitations. Moreover, it would be highly anomalous if the 1983 regulations and the new-source standards were directly reviewable in the Court of Appeals, while the 1977 regulations based on the same administrative record were reviewable only in the District Court. The magnitude and highly technical character of the administrative record involved with these regulations makes it almost inconceivable that Congress would have required duplicate review in the first instance by different courts. We conclude that the statute authorizes the 1977 limitations as well as the 1983 limitations to be set by regulation, so long as some allowance is made for variations in individual plants, as EPA has done by including a variance clause in its 1977 limitations.

The question of the form of §301 limitations is tied to the question whether the Act requires the Administrator or the permit issuer to establish the limitations. Section 301 does not itself answer this question, for it speaks only in the passive voice of the achievement and establishment of the limitations. But other parts of the statute leave little doubt on this score. Section 304(b) states that "(f)or the purpose of adopting or revising effluent limitations . . . the Administrator shall" issue guideline regulations; while the judicial-review section, §509(b)(1), speaks of "the Administrator's action . . . in approving or promulgating any effluent limitation or other limitation under section 301 . . . ." See infra, at 979. And §101(d) requires us to resolve any ambiguity on this score in favor of the Administrator. It provides that "(e)xcept as otherwise expressly provided in this Act, the Administrator of the Environmental Protection Agency . . . shall administer this Act." (Emphasis added.) In sum, the language of the statute supports the view that §301 limitations are to be adopted by the Administrator, that they are to be based primarily on classes and categories, and that they are to take the form of regulations.

. . .

Th[e] legislative history supports our reading of §301 and makes it clear that the §304 guidelines are not merely aimed at guiding the discretion of permit issuers in setting limitations for individual plants.

What, then, is the function of the §304(b) guidelines? As we noted earlier, §304(b) requires EPA to identify the amount of effluent reduction attainable through use of the best practicable or available technology and to "specify factors to be taken into account" in determining the pollution control methods "to be applicable to point sources . . . within such categories or classes." These guidelines are to be issued "(f)or the purpose of adopting or revising effluent limitations under this Act." As we read it, §304 requires that the guidelines survey the practicable or available pollution-control technology for an industry and assess its effectiveness. The guidelines are then to describe the methodology EPA intends to use in the §301 regulations to determine the effluent limitations for particular plants. If the technical complexity of the task had not prevented EPA from issuing the guidelines within the statutory deadline, they could have provided valuable guidance to permit issuers, industry, and the public, prior to the issuance of the §301 regulations.

. . .

The petitioners' view of the Act would place an impossible burden on EPA. It would require EPA to give individual consideration to the circumstances of each of the more than 42,000 dischargers who have applied for permits, Brief for Respondents in No. 75-978, p. 30 n.22, and to issue or approve all these permits well in advance of the 1977 deadline in order to give industry time to install the necessary pollution-control equipment. We do not believe that Congress would have failed so conspicuously to provide EPA with the authority needed to achieve the statutory goals.

. . .

Consequently, we hold that EPA has the authority to issue regulations setting forth uniform effluent limitations for categories of plants.

. . .

III

The remaining issue in this case concerns new plants. Under §306, EPA is to promulgate "regulations establishing Federal standards of performance for new sources . . . ." §306(b)(1)(B). A "standard of performance" is a "standard for the control of the discharge of pollutants which reflects the greatest degree of effluent reduction which the Administrator determines to be achievable through application of the best available demonstrated control technology, . . . including, where practicable, a standard permitting no discharge of pollutants." §306(a)(1). In setting the standard, "(t)he Administrator may distinguish among classes, types, and sizes within categories of new sources . . . and shall consider the type of process employed (including whether batch or continuous)." §306(b)(2). As the House Report states, the standard must reflect the best technology for "that category of sources, and for class, types, and sizes within categories." H.R.Rep. No. 92-911, p. 111 (1972), Leg.Hist. 798.

. . . [I]t is what Congress intended for these regulations. It is clear that Congress intended these regulations to be absolute prohibitions. The use of the word "standards" implies as much. So does the description of the preferred standard as one "permitting no discharge of pollutants." (Emphasis added.) It is "unlawful for any owner or operator of any new source to operate such source in violation of any standard of performance applicable to such source." §306(e) (emphasis added). In striking contrast to §301(c), there is no statutory provision for variances, and a variance provision would be inappropriate in a standard that was intended to insure national uniformity and "maximum feasible control of new sources." S.Rep. No. 92–414, p. 58 (1971), Leg.Hist. 1476.

That portion of the judgment of the Court of Appeals in 541 F.2d 1018 requiring EPA to provide a variance procedure for new sources is reversed. In all other aspects, the judgments of the Court of Appeals are affirmed. It is so ordered.

Questions, Materials, and Suggestions for Further Study

du Pont v. Train

The best available technology standard at issue in the *du Pont* case is an example of the many efforts by environmental statutes to "force technology," that is, to require a level of pollution-control technology beyond current practice. The Clean Air Act has also sought to both force and encourage technology through various incentives. Some of the early major environmental cases, contained and discussed in the first edition of *Green Justice*, *Calvert Cliffs Coordinating Committee, Inc. v. U.S. Atomic Energy Commission*, (449 F.2d 1109, 1971) and *International Harvester Company v. William D. Ruckelshaus* (478 F.2d 615, 1973) involved conflicts over efforts to promote technology controls of nuclear energy and automobiles. In the 1990s, an effort has been made to adopt policies that would encourage "green technologies," new forms of manufacturing producing less pollution. If new technologies, in the form of new less-polluting machines or improved pollution-control devices, are friends of the environment, then other technologies can be less friendly. In one of the most famous books on the environment, *The Closing Circle*: *Nature, Man, and Technology* (New York: Knopf, 1971), Barry Commoner argued that the new chemical technology is especially harmful to the environment.

The way in which we think about technology may affect our view of the *du Pont* case. Jacques Ellul, in *The Technological Society* (New York: Random House, 1967), and Carl Mitcham in *Thinking Through Technology* (Chicago: University of Chicago Press, 1994), view technology as a fundamental way of thought that infuses a society. From their point of view, a specific technology such as nuclear energy cannot be controlled unless we change the way we think about technology in our entire society. Albert Borgmann, in *Technology and the Character of Contemporary Life: A Philosophical Inquiry* (Chicago: University of Chicago Press, 1984), documented how technology has penetrated our way of living. David Rothenberg, in *Hands End: Technology and the Limits of Nature* (Berkeley: University of California Press, 1994) has argued that our view of technology has affected the way we view nature. On a less philosophical level, Victor C. Ferkiss, in *Technological Man: The Myth and the Reality* (New York: Braziller, 1969) and *Nature, Technology, and Society: Cultural Roots of the Current Environmental Crisis* (New York: New York University Press, 1993), viewed technology as an assemblage of techniques having both good and bad effects that can be controlled on a case-by-case basis. The approach of environmental law has been similar to that of Ferkiss—seeking to control technology's bad effects through law on a case-by-case basis, without giving up its benefits. But is this the best approach to controlling technology?

The specific underlying causes of technological growth can be linked to a deep desire for power and control over nature; this desire for power is the central theme of Lewis Mumford's view of technology described in *Technics and Civilization* (New York: Harcourt Brace, 1934) and *The Pentagon of Power: The Myth of the Machine* (New York: Harcourt Brace Jovanovich, 1970). From Mumford's viewpoint, the purpose of the environmental impact statement would be to control the federal agency's power to damage nature when implementing its project. Mumford's view has been expanded by William Leiss, who, in his *Dominion of Nature* (Boston: Beacon Press, 1972), argues that man's technological approach to nature is rooted in both Christian thought and the historical origins of modern science.

Barry Commoner views harmful technology as the product of a modern reductionist science, which in turn results from a predatory economic system. Thus, the environmental impact statement, in Commoner's view, serves to balance a reductionist scientific view with the ecosystems view contained in the environmental impact statement, whereas the court helps those threatened by the project to counter the economic motives that stimulate the proposed project. Of course, Commoner would like to see a socialist restructuring of the economy, blindly ignoring the depredations wreaked upon the environment by socialist countries. See Marshall Goldman, *The Spoils of Progress* (Cambridge, Mass.: MIT Press, 1972); Boris Komorov, *The Destruction of Nature in the Soviet Union* (White Plains, N.Y.: M. E. Sharpe, 1980).

Students of technology draw different conclusions about its relative impact upon the environment. Some see the impacts of such technology as threatening the entire global ecosystem. In Ralph Nader and John Abbott's *The Menace of Atomic Energy* (New York: Norton, 1977), the authors saw the spread of the use of atomic energy leading to large-scale catastrophe. Others regarded the threat of technology as less serious and consequently not requiring drastic action. What is the level of threat posed by our technology?

The U.S. government has always, directly or indirectly, subsidized developing technologies. Provisions were made in the Constitution for the protection of patents, and the federal government early on financed research in agriculture at the University of Virginia. The Morrill Act of 1862 established the entire complex of land grant colleges and universities by providing a grant of 30,000 acres for each congressman, which would be sold and the proceeds used to found colleges emphasizing "such branches of learning as are related to agriculture and the mechanical arts ... in order to promote the liberal and practical education of the industrial classes in the several pursuits and professions in life." This act changed the face of U.S. education and society forever by funding research in science and agriculture at state universities. More recently, the shelter provided by federal subsidies may have enabled nuclear power to achieve a position of dominance that, its critics maintain, could not be sustained on economic grounds alone. As Laurence H. Tribe pointed out in *Channelling Technology Through Law* (Chicago: Bracton Press, 1973), the government is now beginning to take a role in controlling technological development. This new role is illustrated by the Technology Assessment Act of 1972, by which Congress weighs the effects of new technologies but carefully keeps its hands off technological research itself.

Several methods are available to enable the government to control technologies in addition to the regulatory approach of the National Environmental Policy Act. Congress may seek to offer incentives for control or to change property rights in new inventions. Or it may seek to build into organizations engaged in technological development new committees of control (such as scientific review committees within pharmaceutical companies). One recent discussion of the proper way for government to control science and technology is given in William Lowrance's *Modern Science and Human Values* (New York: Oxford University Press, 1985).

As the *du Pont* case exemplifies, government may seek to force more benign technology through its environmental laws. A more radical approach to the problem of technology is offered by the appropriate technology movement, which urges a smaller, more ecologically sensitive kind of technology development. See E. F. Schumacher, *Small is Beautiful: Economics as if People Mattered* (New York: Harper & Row, 1973). This approach, as applied to energy, is illustrated by Amory B. Lovins, who, in *Soft Energy Paths: Toward a Durable Peace* (New York: Harper & Row, 1979), advocates reliance upon conservation and biomass, solar, wind, and small-scale hydro energy to meet our future needs.

8

Fundamental Causes

Population

Case Study:
Guo Chun Di v. Carroll

To many environmental activists, population growth is public enemy number one. And although there are respected natural resource economists who would disagree, it certainly has some intuitive appeal to say that an ever-growing population will put an ever-growing strain on the world's resources, making them less and less available; increasing their price or their scarcity (different ways of saying much the same thing). Similar arguments in favor of limiting population growth have been proposed at least since Thomas Malthus's *An Essay on the Principle of Population: And a Summary View of the Principle of Population* in 1798 (Harmondsworth, England: Penguin, 1970); the modern locus of the argument is probably Paul Ehrlich's *The Population Bomb* (New York: Ballantine Books, 1968), which, along with The Club of Rome's (Donella and Dennis Meadows) *The Limits to Growth: A Report for the Club of Rome's Project on the Predicament of Mankind* (New York: Universe Books, 1972), was one of the more influential environmental studies in the 1970s.

Just whose population are we talking about when we discuss "overpopulation," the "population explosion," or the "population bomb"? The problem with discussing population is that very soon we realize that dealing with the abstraction is easy, but that in the concrete, we are dealing with the social behavior of individuals: We are actually discussing ethnic, political, social, and economic issues, frequently in ways we don't (and probably shouldn't) feel very comfortable about. One example of this is the way in which middle-class Americans immediately identify other nations and cultures as the "cause" of the population problems that they see as bedeviling us all. To many, it is the "overpopulation" caused by the sheer numbers, and increasing numbers, of Asian (predominantly India and China), African, and South American nations. What should a contemporary American make of the German State of Brandenburg paying a bounty for the birth of German children at the same time the central German government supports population-control efforts in the Third World? How different is this from the income tax deduction provided to Americans for each child?

Whether the sheer numbers are relevant is a nice question. Ehrlich has pointed this out and prefers to deal with a unit of population that he calls the "Indian baby," a fictitious unit that takes into account that one child born in China, India, Africa, or Central or South Asia actually creates far less impact upon the world's resources than one child born in the United States, Europe, or Japan.

This is Ehrlich's way of pointing out that mere numbers don't mean much: the *impact* of the numbers does. In a culture where there are no disposable diapers, no two or even three cars apiece, no multiple television sets, bicycles, refrigerators, telephones, rayons, nylons, or plastic fixtures, far fewer of the earth's natural resources are extracted and developed; over the course of a generation many thousands of those individuals would have far less impact upon the earth's resources than one American, European, or Japanese at today's standard of living.

The desire to curb population growth, although it may sound admirable in the abstract, also comes quickly smack up against fiercely held individual beliefs concerning family planning, birth-control, and abortion. For many in the United States, not just those labeled "conservative Christians," but also for many Jews, Muslims, and others, population control is at best questionable, at worst, despicable. Recently, some of the more vocal feminists in the United States have suggested that birth control and abortion are simply newer, more initially palatable, ways in which males assert themselves over women.

Virtually any population decision is, in large part, a political one. At the most recent United Nations Population Conference, held in Cairo, Egypt, the emphasis was not on positive birth control at all but on the education and economic betterment and reproductive health of women, since the statistics appear to demonstrate that the better educated the female populace, the lower the birth rate. This, in turn, led to a discussion of the political and economic status of women in various societies. In a number of these societies, the specter of large numbers of educated women is far more intimidating to their (generally) male-dominated political classes, than a growing population could ever be.

This entire discussion leaves aside entirely the central question of whether a reduction in population would be a good or bad thing economically. Despite the drain on the world's resources, there does appear to be a case for arguing that a growing population is necessary for continued economic growth and, thus, long-term economic stability. Many natural resource economists maintain that it is impossible to run out of resources and that a growing population is an unallayed boon to any society.

The *Guo* case, seeming at first an unusual case to use to discuss population, begins to make sense in the larger context of the political environment in which we make decisions concerning population. Essentially, is the court in *Guo* dealing with an international population-related decision, a political decision, a human rights decision, an immigration decision, or an administrative law decision? Does Mr. Guo's claim that he is escaping from political persecution because of his opposition to sterilization make any sense? And if it does, which should be given precedence—the political statement of his position that lends itself to our Bill of Rights (that he has the human right to have children) or the political statement that lends itself to his being characterized as a lawbreaker in his own country, the position that happens to be consistent with the current fashion of limiting population.

And, most importantly, assuming that we are able to come to some conclusion, just how could our position be phrased so that it could be applied consistently and across the board in future similar cases? One might ask whether the court, in resolving this case on administrative law grounds, has avoided the difficult questions.

GUO CHUN DI, Petitioner
v.
William J. CARROLL,
District Director of the United States Immigration
and
Naturalization Service, Respondent

United States District Court, E.D. Virginia
Jan. 14, 1994
[842 F. Supp. 858]

ELLIS, District Judge.

I.

This petition for a writ of habeas corpus presents the question whether aliens who have a well-founded fear that they will be arrested and involuntarily sterilized because they oppose and refuse to obey their country's coercive population control policies may be granted asylum on the ground of "persecution * * * on account of ... political opinion." 8 U.S.C. §1101(a)(42)(A) (hereafter "the Act"). Imbedded in this general question are subsidiary, predicate questions concerning the validity and effect, if any, of various administrative efforts to construe the Act. Finally, because the Court concludes that the cacophonous administrative record merits no judicial deference, the central question presented is whether the Act, properly construed, extends asylum to an alien who fled his country to avoid arrest, imprisonment and involuntary sterilization because he and his wife oppose and will not obey their country's policy of coercive population control through involuntary sterilization and abortion.

II.

1. Petitioner's History

Petitioner, Guo Chun Di, is a 28 year old citizen of the Peoples Republic of China ("PRC"), who fled his country aboard the vessel Golden Venture, which ran aground in New York harbor on June 6, 1993. When this occurred, petitioner was one of many aliens on the ship who jumped overboard and attempted to swim to shore. While still in the water, petitioner was rescued, and then detained and taken into custody by the Immigration and Naturalization Service ("INS"). The INS charged petitioner with attempting to enter the United States without valid documents in violation of federal law. Petitioner, who asserted a claim for political asylum under the Act, was transferred to a state detention facility in Winchester, Virginia, pending completion of an exclusion and deportation proceeding initiated against him by INS pursuant to 8 U.S.C. §1226. At a hearing before an immigration judge in Arlington, Virginia, petitioner testified through an interpreter and described the events that led to his decision to flee his country. Specifically, he testified that following the birth of his first child, government family planning officials ordered his wife to report to a local hospital for a sterilization operation. Strongly opposed to this involuntary sterilization, his wife fled from the village in which they lived to relatives in a distant city. At this point, government planning officials then sent petitioner a similar notice to report to a local hospital for a sterilization operation. Firmly opposed to the government-ordered involuntary sterilization, petitioner also fled his home village and joined his wife in the city. While living in the city, petitioner received word from relatives living in his home village that government officials had visited his home, confiscated his and his wife's personal property and then destroyed the portion of the house in which petitioner and his wife had lived. On receiving this information, petitioner decided to leave the PRC and come to the United States. In his own words, his reasons for doing so were as follows: Q. And can you say exactly why you wanted to leave China? A. Because I feared that China has no freedom. Because I only have one child, I want to have two more child, but they don't let me have. If . . . I afraid that if they find me, they will took me to get sterilize operation. Q. Why did you want to come to the United States instead of some other country? A. Because I heard about the U.S.A. is a freedom country. Q. What do you think would happen to you if you were sent back to China? A. They . . . first they will sent me to the jail and then they will force me to do the sterilize [sic] operation. The immigration judge found petitioner truthful and accepted petitioner's account of the facts and circumstances that led to petitioner's decision to flee government persecution in the PRC and to come to America. Even so, however, the immigration judge ruled that petitioner (i) was "not a 'refugee' as that term is defined by law," (ii) was therefore ineligible for asylum, and (iii) was subject instead to exclusion and deportation. In reaching this conclusion, the immigration judge relied on Matter of Chang, Int.Dec. 3107, 1989 WL 247513 (BIA 1989), a decision of the Board of

Immigration Appeals ("BIA") purporting to hold that government persecution in furtherance of a coercive population control policy that includes involuntary sterilization does not constitute "persecution on account of race, religion, nationality, membership in a particular social group, or political opinion." 8 U.S.C. §1101(a)(42)(A). Petitioner appealed this ruling to the BIA on the ground that certain federal regulations had invalidated Chang. The Board rejected petitioner's appeal after noting that Chang was still valid controlling administrative precedent, as the regulations petitioner cited "were not codified and have no force or effect." This petition for a writ of habeas corpus followed.

2. Regulatory History

Chang issued in May 1989. Almost a year earlier, the Department of Justice had issued policy guidelines to the INS designed to ensure that asylum could be granted to persons who could show well-founded fear of government persecution stemming from the PRC's involuntary sterilization and abortion programs. INS did not implement these guidelines and the Board in Chang expressly stated it was not bound by the guidelines.

Soon after the May 1989 Chang decision, efforts were made in Congress to overturn it. These efforts culminated in the Armstrong-DeConcini Amendment to the Emergency Chinese Immigration Relief Act of 1989, H.R. 2712, which was drafted and offered for the express purpose of overruling Chang. Sponsors of the amendment expressed frustration that the Attorney General's guidelines were not implemented by the INS. By November 1989, the Senate had unanimously passed the amendment and the House, by a substantial margin, had voted to concur in the amendment. While in agreement with the amendment, President Bush vetoed the Emergency Chinese Immigration Relief Act of 1989, citing concerns with other portions of the bill. See Memorandum of Disapproval for the Emergency Chinese Immigration Relief Act of 1989, Weekly Comp.Pres.Doc. 1853–54 (Nov. 30, 1989). The House of Representatives voted to override the veto, but the Senate failed by five votes to do so. Several Senators voting to uphold the veto noted that they did so in reliance on the President's assurances that administrative action would be taken to ensure that Chang was reversed. Faithful to his assurances and reflecting his agreement with the amendment, if not the entire bill, President Bush issued instructions to the Attorney General to take appropriate action.

Responding to this instruction, the then Attorney General, in January 1990, promulgated an interim rule amending the existing regulations governing asylum and withholding of deportation (hereinafter "January 1990 Interim Rule"). Specifically, the January 1990 Interim Rule amended then-existing C.F.R. §208.5 to provide that:

1. Aliens who have a well-founded fear that they will be required . . . to be sterilized because of their country's family planning policies may be granted asylum on the ground of persecution on account of political opinion.
2. An applicant who establishes that the applicant (or the applicant's spouse) has refused . . . to be sterilized in violation of a country's family planning

policy, and who has a well-founded fear that he or she will be required . . . to be sterilized or otherwise persecuted if the applicant were returned to such country may be granted asylum.

Approximately three months after the promulgation of the January 1990 Interim Rule, an executive order issued underscoring the substance of the January 1990 Interim Rule. The executive order stated:

The Secretary of State and the Attorney General are directed to provide for enhanced consideration under the immigration laws for individuals from any country who express a fear of persecution upon return to their country related to that country's policy of forced abortion or coerced sterilization, as implemented by the Attorney General's regulation effective January 29, 1990.

The next chapter in this regulatory saga occurred in July 1990, when the Attorney General published a final rule setting forth extensive changes in the regulations pertaining to asylum and withholding of deportation. See 55 Fed.Reg. 30674 (July 27, 1990) (hereinafter "July 1990 Rule"). The July 1990 Rule inexplicably made no mention whatever of the January 1990 Interim Rule, nor did it refer in any way to the issue of asylum for persecution on the basis of opposition to coercive family planning policies, including policies involving involuntary abortions and sterilizations. Still, this July 1990 Rule rewrote, among other things, the sections of the Code of Federal Regulations that were ostensibly amended by the January 1990 Interim Rule so that when the Code of Federal Regulations was published in January 1991, the January 1990 Interim Rule had quite simply and remarkably vanished without a trace or explanation.

The final chapter in this regulatory saga opened in January 1993, when the then Attorney General signed a final rule (hereinafter "January 1993 Rule") that essentially reiterated the January 1990 Interim Rule overruling Chang. The January 1993 Rule took explicit account of the comments previously received concerning the January 1990 Interim Rule and then amended the regulations in essentially the same way as they had been amended by the January 1990 Interim Rule. Included in the explanatory comments to the January 1993 Rule is the statement that "[o]ne effect of this rule is to supersede . . . Matter of Chang."

The January 1993 Rule, signed by the Attorney General in the waning days of the Bush Administration, was sent to the Federal Register, where it was made available for public inspection and scheduled for a January 25 publication. President Clinton was inaugurated on January 22. Immediately thereafter, his proposed Director of the Office of Management and Budget issued a directive prohibiting publication of any new regulations not approved by an agency head appointed by President Clinton. This directive further ordered that all regulations previously submitted for publication be withdrawn from the office of the Federal Register pending approval by a Clinton-appointed agency head. Pursuant to this directive, the Acting Assistant Attorney General sent a memorandum to the Office of the Federal Register requesting the withdrawal of, among others, the January

1993 Rule. Acting on this request, officials at the Office of the Federal Register withdrew the January 1993 Rule from the Federal Register. It has not been resubmitted or published.

3. Proceedings to Date

The filing of the petition, by itself, did not halt INS deportation and exclusion proceedings against petitioner. Accordingly, soon after the filing of the petition, petitioner filed a request for immediate and preliminary injunctive relief in this Court.

. . .

III.

Analysis of the questions presented here properly begins with an elucidation of the well-established principle that an agency's consistent interpretation of its statute or regulations is entitled to judicial deference. See *Chevron U.S.A. v. Natural Resources Defense Council,* 467 U.S. 837, 843–44, 104 S.Ct. 2778, 2782–83, 81 L.Ed.2d 694 (1984); *Ford Motor Credit Co. v. Milhollin,* 444 U.S. 555, 566–67, 100 S.Ct. 790, 797–98, 63 L.Ed.2d 22 (1980). This principle, put another way, holds that "[a] court may not substitute its own construction of a statutory provision for a reasonable interpretation made by the administrator of an agency." *Chevron,* 467 U.S. at 844, 104 S.Ct. at 2782. The rationale behind the *Chevron* principle is the notion that, within limits, Congress is entitled to delegate certain policy choices to agencies or Executive departments presumed to possess the pertinent expertise. Thus, the *Chevron* principle of judicial deference is "but a shorthand way of saying that the judiciary is duty bound to respect the original choice of the political branches in vesting authority in an agency to interpret and enforce a statute." *Continental Air Lines Inc., v. Dep't of Transp.,* 843 F.2d 1444, 1454 (D.C.Cir.1988). In this context, judicial deference to an agency's interpretation of its own statutes and regulations can be viewed as one aspect of the intricate choreography that maintains the appropriate balance of power among the three co-equal branches of government. This choreography insures that, in the dance of governance, no branch leads too much or steps on the toes of the other branches.

But significantly, there are important limits to the notion of judicial deference. First, deference is appropriate only when an agency or department interprets its own rules and regulations. See, e.g., *Chevron,* 467 U.S. at 844. Only in this event is there any validity to the assumption that underlies judicial deference, namely a congressional intent to delegate certain policy choices to expert independent agencies or to the Executive Branch. Equally evident is that deference is inappropriate where the department's or agency's interpretation is contrary to the plain language of the relevant statute or regulation. See, e.g., *Bureau of Alcohol, Tobacco and Firearms v. Federal Labor Relations Auth.,* 464 U.S. 89, 98 n. 8., ... ("[D]eference is constrained by our obligation to honor the clear meaning of a statute, as revealed by its language, purpose and history."). And, central to this dispute, deference is appropriate only where an agency's interpretation of its own statutes and regulations has been consistent. See, e.g., *Allen v. Bergland,* 661 F.2d 1001, 1004 (4th Cir.1981), ... As the Supreme Court has noted, "an agency interpretation of a relevant provision which conflicts with the agency's earlier interpretations is entitled to considerably less deference than a consistently held agency view." *I.N.S. v. Cardoza-Fonseca,* 480 U.S. 421, 446 n. 30, ... Faced with conflicting administrative interpretations, courts should not engage in "blind adherence" to an agency's position. *United Transp. Union v. Dole,* 797 F.2d 823, 829 (10th Cir.1986). To hold otherwise and defer to inconsistent agency interpretations would create a scheme of statutory construction based not on a government of laws, but rather on a government of "who was most recently elected."

IV.

The record discloses no fewer than nine inconsistent administrative pronouncements regarding the ability of aliens to seek asylum, pursuant to 8 U.S.C. §1101(a)(42)(A), based on opposition to a foreign government's coercive population control policies.

. . .

In sum, on the question of statutory interpretation at bar, there is a cacophony of administrative voices, each singing a different tune in a different key. Deference to one voice or one tune in these circumstances is unwarranted. Given this and given the responsibilities of courts under the APA to set aside agency actions contrary to law, this Court must now consider, independently of past administrative interpretations of §1101(a)(42)(A), whether that statute sanctions asylum in the circumstances at bar.

V.

To be eligible for asylum under the Act, an alien must be statutorily classified as a "refugee" under 8 U.S.C. §1158(a). *Huaman-Cornelio v. Bd. of Immigration Appeals,* 979 F.2d 995, 999 (4th Cir.1992). A refugee is any person who is unable or unwilling to return to his or her country "because of persecution or a well-founded fear of persecution on account of race, religion, nationality, membership in a particular social group, or political opinion. . . ." 8 U.S.C. §1101(a)(42)(A) (1993); see *M.A. A26851062 v. I.N.S.,* 899 F.2d 304, 307 (4th Cir.1990) (en banc). The standard used to determine whether an individual has "well-founded fear of persecution" is a "reasonable person test." *Huaman-Cornelio,* 979 F.2d at 999, citing M.A., 899 F.2d at 311. An individual seeking asylum under the "reasonable person" standard must show (i) that a reasonable person in the circumstances would fear persecution if he or she were returned to his or her native country and (ii) that the fear has "some basis in the reality of the circumstances" and is validated with "specific, concrete facts." *Huaman-Cornelio,* 979 F.2d at 999, citing M.A., 899 F.2d at 311 (citations omitted).

A generalized fear of persecution is not sufficient to establish eligibility for asylum. As the Fourth Circuit has noted, "[e]ven aliens with a well-founded fear of persecution supported by concrete facts are not eligible for asylum if those facts indicate only that the alien fears retribution over purely personal matters or general conditions of upheaval and unrest." *Huaman-Cornelio,* 979 F.2d at 1000 (contention that group in Peru might conceivably harm petitioner after labeling him a traitor is not sufficient to establish eligibility for asylum absent concrete evidence that group had so labeled petitioner). Accordingly, petitioner cannot make out a valid claim for asylum by contending that the current PRC government is generally repressive, or by merely contending that he disagrees with a particular government policy. Rather, petitioner must show that he fears persecution stemming from one of the five categories of persecution enumerated in the Act. Petitioner must further show that he fears particularized persecution directed at him personally on the basis of his race, religion, nationality, membership in a particular social group, or political opinion. See *Huaman-Cornelio,* 979 F.2d at 999–1000.

Neither the INA nor the Refugee Act specifically address whether asylum eligibility can be based upon an individual's fear of persecution stemming from that individual's opposition to a government's coercive population control practices. Thus, the inquiry in the case at bar must proceed in two stages. First, the Court must determine whether petitioner's opposition to coercive population control practices in the PRC constitutes a "political opinion" within the meaning of 8 U.S.C. §1101(a)(42)(A). Next, the Court must decide whether petitioner has a particularized, well-founded fear of persecution based on this purported political opinion.

The heart of petitioner's asylum claim is the contention that his opposition to the PRC's coercive population control policies constitutes a "political opinion" within the meaning of the Act. No definition of the phrase "on account of political opinion" appears in the Act or its legislative history. See *Perlera-Escobar v. Executive Office for Imm.,* 894 F.2d 1292, 1296 (11th Cir.1990); *Campos-Guardado v. I.N.S.,* 809 F.2d 285, 290 (5th Cir.), cert. denied 484 U.S. 826, 108 S.Ct. 92, 98 L.Ed.2d 53 (1987). Yet, there can be little doubt that the phrase "political opinion" encompasses an individual's views regarding procreation. To begin with, "political" is commonly defined as "of or pertaining to exercise of rights or privileges. . . ." BLACK's LAW DICTIONARY 1158 (6th ed. 1991). And it is settled that the right to bear children is "one of the basic civil rights of man." *Skinner v. Oklahoma,* 316 U.S. 535, 541, 62 S.Ct. 1110, 1113, 86 L.Ed. 1655 (1942). Specifically, the fundamental right to procreate is protected by "penumbras" emanating from the Bill of Rights. See *Griswold v. Connecticut,* 381 U.S. 479, 484–86, 85 S.Ct. 1678, 1681–83, 14 L.Ed.2d 510 (1965); *Roe v. Wade,* 410 U.S. 113, 154–56, 93 S.Ct. 705, 727–29, 35 L.Ed.2d 147 (1973). Indeed, "[t]he decision of whether or not to beget or bear a child is at the heart of [a] cluster of constitutionally protected rights." *Carey v. Population Serv. Int'l.,* 431 U.S. 678, 685, 97 S.Ct. 2010, 2016, 52 L.Ed.2d 675 (1977). While the right to procreate is not absolute, intrusions upon this fundamental right are looked upon with disfavor. See, e.g., *Carey,* 431 U.S. at 687, 97 S.Ct. at 2017 ("[t]he teaching of Griswold is that the Constitution protects individual decisions in matters of childbearing from unjustified intrusion by the State."). Involuntary sterilization, in particular, has been viewed as an egregious infringement on the fundamental right to procreate. See *Skinner,* 316 U.S. at 541, 62 S.Ct. at 1113 (invalidating state statute allowing for involuntary sterilization of habitual offenders). As Justice Douglas noted in *Skinner:*

> [t]he power to sterilize, if exercised, may have subtle, far-reaching and devastating effects. In evil or reckless hands, it can cause races or types which are inimical to the dominant group to wither and disappear. There is no redemption for the individual whom the law touches. Any experiment which the State conducts is to his irreparable injury. He is forever deprived of a basic liberty. *Skinner,* 316 U.S. at 541, 62 S.Ct. at 1113.

Because the right to make procreational decisions is a basic liberty right protected under the Bill of Rights, it is, in that respect, analogous to other fundamental rights that are well-recognized as legitimate grounds for asylum, such as the freedom of religion and freedom of speech. Further, it is beyond dispute that the expression of one's views regarding issues related to the right to procreate is "political." See, e.g., *Planned Parenthood of Southeastern Pa. v. Casey,*—U.S. —, —, 112 S.Ct. 2791, 2815, 120 L.Ed.2d 674 (1992) (noting that part of the Court's hesitation to overrule *Roe v. Wade* stemmed from belief that "whatever the premises of opposition may be, only the most convincing justification under accepted standards of precedent could suffice to demonstrate that a later decision overruling the first was anything but a surrender to political pressure . . . "). In addition, opposition to certain aspects of procreative rights and privileges may involve the exercise of protected political rights and privileges. As the right to procreate, and therefore petitioner's expression of this right, is a fundamental right analogous to other fundamental rights that may support an asylum claim based on "persecution on the basis of political opinion," petitioner's opposition to the PRC's population control policies constitutes a "political opinion" within the meaning of §1101(a)(42)(A).

This is not to say that a citizen of the PRC, or indeed of any country, may establish asylum eligibility merely by pointing to some right guaranteed in the United States Constitution that is not guaranteed in his or her respective country. And courts interpreting §1101(a)(42)(A) should not "make immigration decisions based on [their] own implicit approval or disapproval of U.S. foreign policy and the actions of other nations." *M.A. v. I.N.S.,* 899 F.2d 304, 313 (4th Cir. 1990). Similarly, to rule here contrary to *Chang* merely due to disagreement on policy grounds with the BIA's conclusion "would transform the political asylum process from a method of individual sanctuary left largely to the political branches into a vehicle for foreign policy debates in the courts." M.A., 899 F.2d at 313. It would indeed be an infringement upon the territory of the political branches to deem the PRC's population control policies evil, immoral, or the like and to conclude, based on personal repugnance to the PRC's policies, that asylum is warranted for those opposed to such practices. It is not, however, an infringement upon the foreign policy territory of the political branches to conclude that an individual's views in opposition to a government's official policy on population control and family planning, especially when such policies involve coerced sterilization and abortion, are "political" within the meaning of 8 U.S.C. §1101(a)(42)(A).

But the inquiry cannot end here, for it is not enough that petitioner holds a "political opinion" within the meaning of 8 U.S.C. §1101(a)(42)(A). Rather, in order to establish eligibility for asylum based on a well-founded fear of persecution, petitioner must have expressed an "overt manifestation of a political opinion." *De Valle v. I.N.S.*, 901 F.2d 787, 797 (9th Cir.1990), citing *Bolanos-Hernandez v. I.N.S.*, 767 F.2d 1277, 1287 (9th Cir. 1984). Yet, an "overt manifestation" of a political opinion does not require that an individual have participated in demonstrations or political marches, have made political speeches, or the like. Rather, petitioner may show persecution on the basis of political opinion by showing that: (i) there is a significant relationship between the victim (namely petitioner) and the persecutor; and, (ii) that petitioner has engaged in sufficiently conscious and deliberate decisions or acts which attribute certain political opinions to plaintiff. *De Valle,* 901 F.2d at 791, citing *Desir v. Ilchert,* 840 F.2d 723, 728 (9th Cir. 1988).

There can be no question that petitioner has made an "overt manifestation" of his opposition to the PRC's "one couple one child" policy, and that petitioner has been persecuted for expressing this opposition. Petitioner and his wife openly expressed their opposition to the PRC's population control policies by refusing to comply with sterilization orders and by fleeing from their home village after receiving government sterilization notices. And the government, after learning that petitioner and his wife had fled, confiscated the personal property of petitioner and his wife and destroyed the couple's living quarters. It simply defies logic to contend that these governmental actions do not amount to persecution.

. . .

Petitioner in the instant case is not challenging the mere implementation of the PRC's "one couple one child policy." Rather, he is contending that his opposition to the policy, even if the policy is not viewed as inherently "persecutive" per *Chang,* led to a situation where the government directly persecuted him and his family as a result of his opposition to the policy. Petitioner's testimony, deemed credible by the immigration judge, makes clear that petitioner has met the threshold requirement of showing that he faces a "well-founded fear of persecution" for expressing his "political opinion" regarding the PRC's coercive population control measures.

Again, it is worth emphasizing that this decision does not derive from any of the Court's personal views. Rather, the Court merely determines that an individ-

ual's expression of his or her views in opposition to a country's coercive population control measures may constitute a "political opinion" within the meaning of
8 U.S.C. §1101(a)(42)(A). And, under the specific facts of this case, petitioner has
shown that he faces particularized persecution because of his opposition to the
PRC's population control practices, and thus has established prima facie eligibility for asylum. In essence, then, petitioner is one of the "huddled masses . . . yearn-
ing to be free" who has established statutory eligibility for asylum, and it is now
within the discretion of the Attorney General either to grant or deny petitioner's
specific asylum request. 8 U.S.C. §1158(a); see M.A., 899 F.2d at 307.

Questions, Materials, and Suggestions for Further Study

Guo Chun Di v. Carroll

The *Guo* case raises fundamental questions about population growth, within the
United States and abroad and about immigration. In our introduction to this case we
have cited the important early works of Ehrlich and The Club of Rome. Since those
works were written in the early 1970s, many works have been written on population
growth. Paul and Ann Ehrlich, *The Population Explosion* (New York: Simon & Schuster,
1990); Barry Commoner, *Making Peace With the Planet* (New York: Pantheon, 1990);
and Garrett Hardin, *Living Within the Limits* (Oxford: Oxford University Press, 1993).

The central debate over population growth has been whether increased economic
growth in developing nations would stem the tide of population increase, Julian
Simon, *Population Matters* (New Brunswick, N.J.: Transaction Publishers, 1990), or
whether access to birth control was also needed, Robert Cassen, et al., *Population and
Development: Old Debates, New Conclusions* (New Brunswick, N.J.: Transaction
Publishers, 1994).

Even as this debate continues, three other major debates have arisen. First there is
the debate about whether population growth has contributed to environmental
abuses at all or whether the damage arises from other causes (e.g., imbalances of
power, problems of food distribution). See Kingley Davis and Mikhail S. Bernstein,
eds., *Resources, Environment and Population: Present Knowledge, Future Options*
(Oxford: Oxford University Press, 1991). Second, women in many parts of the world
have raised questions as to whether the effort at the worldwide promotion of birth
control has been at the expense of womens' reproductive health. See Laurie Mazur,
ed, *Beyond the Numbers* (Washington, D.C.: Island Press, 1994). Third is the question
of whether the draconian measures of birth control adopted by nations such as
China and India violate universal human rights. Jack Donnelly, *Universal Human
Rights in Theory and Practice* (Ithaca: Cornell University Press, 1989).

In the *Guo* case, some of these same issues arise in the context of immigration.
Immigration is a central aspect of population growth on a worldwide basis and in the

United States. The question of who—and how many—should be admitted to the United States has become a central political issue for the twentieth century. See Georg Borjas, *Friends or Strangers? The Impact of Immigrants on the U.S. Economy* (New York: Basic Books, 1990); and George Simcox, ed., *U.S. Immigration in the 1980s: Re-Appraisal and Reform* (Boulder, Colo.: Westview Press, 1988).

9

Fundamental Causes

The International Market Economy

Case Study:
Dow Chemical v. Alfaro

The years between 1975 and 1995 saw a revolution in the way firms do business. The importance of the "global economy" is symbolized every two years as the leaders of the major trading powers—the G-7—gather to meet and discuss international trade issues. Just as Japan, Singapore, Hong Kong, and China have risen in our consciousness to rival England, France, Italy, and Germany, now Mexico, Brazil, Malaysia, India, and Russia must be considered both as market opportunities and as potential rivals by virtually every manufacturer in the United States. The North American Free Trade Agreement (NAFTA), the General Agreement on Trade and Tariffs (GATT), and a host of less significant trade treaties are now the stuff of everyday newspapers; auto dealers on Main Street are as knowledgeable of international politics and policies as bond traders on Wall Street.

One consequence of this explosion of global trade has been a concern over its effects on the environment. Perhaps the two most potent arguments against NAFTA, carried out in 1994, were the effects of job loss in the United States and the effect on the environment along the Texas-Mexico border. That international trade and commerce brings international problems is a truism. In the environmental realm, these problems arise primarily because of the different standards that must be met by producers in different countries. Manufacturers in countries with comparatively stringent environmental regulations must spend more money during the manufacturing process to meet those standards and must therefore charge more for their products if they are to remain profitable. Whereas it seems as though their competition in countries with comparatively lax environmental standards or regulations receive what amounts to an uncompetitive boon from their governments; in effect, a governmental subsidy ultimately paid for in health problems by the populace.

The case we have chosen to illustrate these problems may seem arcane at first, but it goes to the heart of the matter: Just whose laws will govern an international entity? Imagine, for a moment, that you have become the chief executive officer of a large United States manufacturer. Your firm is incorporated in one of the fifty United States and, as such, must meet the legal requirements of that state: The company is subject to laws of its home state and to the laws of the states in which it carries out its business, including the laws governing who can sue it, for what reasons, and for how much. You wish to establish a subsidiary (another, separate, but wholly owned entity) in another country. Naturally, that entity will be governed by the laws of its country or state of incorporation regardless of who owns it. Our laws do not permit an injured worker to sue the parent company if the subsidiary is solvent, but suppose that is not the case in this particular country. An injured foreign worker may be able to go to court in that country and file suit against the United States-based parent company for an injury occurring in another country, at a company that, although owned by the United States entity, was managed by locals in full compliance with local laws and regulations. Now imagine a different set of facts: Someone in that foreign state is injured and, under the laws of the foreign state, the worker cannot sue the firm for damages for this particular injury, but under the laws of the parent company's state of incorporation, such suits are not only allowed but relatively simple to bring to court. In a nutshell, this is the situation in *Alfaro*. But the issue is far more complex even than what was just described. Reverse the countries: Imagine that you are a foreign corporation thinking of setting up shop in the United States. What would be your reaction to situations such as those arising in *Alfaro?* At home you might be virtually immune from suits that are extremely easy to bring, even encouraged, in the United States.

To apply this situation to environmental law, let's suppose that you grow citrus products and wish to export your citrus to a foreign country, but that foreign country bans your citrus because you use a fungicide in shipping your product that that country has banned for internal use as a potential health threat. If your country has an agency that has carried out numerous tests with negative (that is, no damage) results on humans, you will be upset—particularly if your citrus can get to the foreign markets more cheaply than the local product can be distributed. You would be even more upset if you were to find that not only your fungicide but *all* fungicides in use by all other citrus-raising and exporting countries have been banned by that country.

How do you complain? To whom? As an "environmentalist" you are acutely sensitive to the problems created by human ingestion of fungicides, but these citrus products must be shipped overseas and a fungicide is absolutely necessary if the crop is to make the voyage. You have argued many times among your friends for what amounts to zero tolerance of pesticides, herbicides, rodenticides, and fungicides, that even the slightest hint of damage to human health should be sufficient to ban agricultural chemicals. What argument could you make other than the obvious one: The banning of the fungicide has been done for protectionist, not for health reasons. And if the importing country could show some statistical proof to bolster its position, what then?

Those are the substantive arguments. Compared to the procedural ones, they are easy. If you decided you had a case, could prove that the other country was merely being protective of its citrus growers in banning your product, what then? Do you sue the government of the foreign country in your local county courthouse? How do you get the other country to pay attention? And suppose that you decided to attack the problem at its root—to demonstrate in the leading newspaper of that country that a major grower of citrus in that country produced terrible tasting stuff—could a non-citizen, foreign grower sue you in that same local courthouse down the street for a legitimate claim under your own state's laws that you were deliberately interfering with his business relationships, an action recognized under traditional American tort law but that might not exist in the other country, where the advertisement was published and where it had its effect?

The precise ways we have to deal with transnational problems just aren't terribly precise. There have been a number of international environmental successes (the banning of chloroflourocarbons being the most obvious example), but the failures (the destruction of the fisheries off both coasts of the United States, the Colorado River, the Aswan Dam) outnumber the successes by far. Even within the United States, border disputes between the states are always contentious, frequently intractable. At their heart, like the arguments in *Alfaro* and those in reference to our citrus grower, transnational disputes revolve around just which party has just what rights under the laws of just what jurisdiction.

And these are the simple disputes. Once we begin to ask about the rights of the citizens of one country, say Canada, to be free from the trans-border migration of pesticides from the United States, or the citizens of the United States to be free of the air emissions from Canadian smelters (unregulated, of course, by the United States' Clean Air Act), the problems proliferate unimaginably.

Dow Chemical Co.
v.
Alfaro

[786 S.W.2d 674 (Tex. 1990)]

RAY, Justice.

Domingo Castro Alfaro, a Costa Rican resident and employee of the Standard Fruit Company, and eighty-one other Costa Rican employees and their wives brought suit against Dow Chemical Company and Shell Oil Company. The employees claim that they suffered personal injuries as a result of exposure to dibro-mochloropropane (DBCP) a pesticide manufactured by Dow and Shell, which was allegedly furnished to Standard Fruit. The employees exposed to DBCP allegedly suffer several medical problems, including sterility.

Alfaro sued Dow and Shell in Harris County district court in 1984. The amended petition alleged that the court had jurisdiction under article 4678 of the Revised Statutes. Following an unsuccessful attempt to remove the suit to federal court, Dow and Shell contested the jurisdiction of the trial court almost three years after the filing of the suit, and contended in the alternative that the case should be dismissed under the doctrine of forum non conveniens. Despite a finding of jurisdiction, the trial court dismissed the case on the ground of forum non conveniens.

Section 71.031 of the Civil Practice and Remedies Code provides:

(a) An action for damages for the death or personal injury of citizen of this state, of the United States or of a foreign country may be enforced in the courts of this state, although the wrongful act, neglect or default causing the death or injury takes place in a foreign state or country, if:
   (1) a law of the foreign state or country or of this state gives a right to maintain an action for damages for the death or injury;
   (2) the action is begun in this state within the time provided by the laws of this state for beginning the action; and
   (3) in the case of a citizen of a foreign country, the country has equal treaty rights with the United States on behalf of its citizens.
      (b) All matters pertaining to procedure in the prosecution or maintenance of the action in the courts of this state are governed by the laws of this state.
      (c) The court shall apply the rules of substantive law that are appropriate under the facts of the case.

Tex. Civ. Prac. & Rem. Code Ann. §71.031 (Vernon 1986). At issue is whether the language "may be enforced in the courts of this state" of Section 711.031(a) permits a trial court to relinquish jurisdiction under the doctrine of forum non conveniens. . . .

We conclude that the legislature has statutorily abolished the doctrine of forum non conveniens in suits brought under section 71.031. Accordingly, we affirm the judgment of the court of appeals, remanding the case to the trial court for further proceedings.

Doggett, Justice, concurring.

The dissenters argue that it is inconvenient and unfair for farmworkers allegedly suffering permanent physical and mental injuries, including irreversible sterility, to seek redress by suing a multinational corporation in a court three blocks away from its world headquarters and another corporation, which operates in Texas this country's largest chemical plant. Because the "doctrine" they advocate has nothing to do with fairness and convenience and everything to do with immunizing multinational corporations from accountability for their alleged torts causing injury abroad, I write separately.

I. The Facts

Respondents claim that while working on a banana plantation in Costa Rica for Standard Fruit Company, an American subsidiary of Dole Fresh Fruit Company, headquartered in Boca Raton, Florida, they were required to handle dibromochloropropane ["DBCP"], a pesticide allegedly manufactured and furnished to Standard Fruit by Shell Oil Company ["Shell"] and Dow Chemical Company ["Dow"]. The Environmental Protection Agency issued a notice of intent to cancel all food uses of DBCP on September 22, 1977. 42 Fed. Reg. 48026 (1977). It followed with an order suspending registrations of pesticides containing DBCP on November 3, 1977. 42 Fed. Reg. 57543 (1977). Before and after the E.P.A.'s ban of DBCP in the United States, Shell and Dow apparently shipped several hundred thousand gallons of the pesticide to Costa Rica for use by Standard Fruit. The Respondents, Domingo Castro Alfaro and other plantation workers, filed suit in a state district court in Houston, Texas, alleging that their handling of DBCP caused them serious personal injuries for which Shell and Dow were liable under the theories of products liability, strict liability and breach of warranty.

Shell Oil Company is a multinational corporation with its world headquarters in Houston, Texas. Dow Chemical Company, though headquartered in Midland, Michigan, conducts extensive operations from its Dow Chemical USA building located in Houston. Dow operates this country's largest chemical manufacturing plant within 60 miles of Houston in Freeport, Texas. The district court where this lawsuit was filed is three blocks away from Shell's world headquarters, One Shell Plaza in downtown Houston.

Shell has stipulated that all of its more than 100,000 documents relating to DBCP are located or will be produced in Houston. Shell's medical and scientific witnesses are in Houston. The majority of Dow's documents and witnesses are located in Michigan, which is far closer to Houston (both in terms of geography and communications linkages) than to Costa Rica. The respondents have agreed to be available in Houston for independent medical examinations, for depositions and for trial. Most of the respondents' treating doctors and co-workers have agreed to testify in Houston. Conversely, Shell and Dow have purportedly refused to make their witnesses available in Costa Rica.

The banana plantation workers allegedly injured by DBCP were employed by an American company on American-owned land and grew Dole bananas for export solely to American tables. The chemical allegedly rendering the workers sterile was researched, formulated, tested, manufactured, labeled and shipped by an

American company in the United States to another American company. The decision to manufacture DBCP for distribution and use in the third world was made by these two American companies in their corporate offices in the United States. Yet now Shell and Dow argue that the one part of this equation that should not be American is the legal consequences of their actions. . . .

Comity—deference shown to the interests of the foreign forum—is a consideration best achieved by rejecting forum non conveniens. Comity is not achieved when the United States allows its multinational corporations to adhere to a double standard when operating abroad and subsequently refuses to hold them accountable for those actions. As S. Jacob Scherr, Senior Project Attorney for the National Resources Defense Council, has noted:

> There is a sense of outrage on the part of many poor countries where citizens are the most vulnerable to exports of hazardous drugs, pesticides and food products. At the 1977 meeting of the UNEP Governing Council, Dr. J. C. Kiano, the Kenyan minister for water development, warned that developing nations will no longer tolerate being used as dumping grounds for products that had not been adequately tested "and that their peoples should not be used as guinea pigs for determining the safety of chemicals." Comments, *U.S. Exports Banned for Domestic Use, But Exported to Third World Countries,* 6 Int'l Tr. L.J. 95, 98 (1980–81) [hereinafter "U.S. Exports Banned"].

Comity is best achieved by "avoiding the possibility of incurring the wrath and distrust of the Third World as it increasingly recognizes that it is being used as the 'industrial world's garbage can.'" Note. *Hazardous Exports From A Human Rights Perspective,* 14 Sw. U.L. Rev. 81, 101 (1983) [hereinafter "Hazardous Exports"] (quoting Hon. Michael D. Barnes [Representative in Congress representing Maryland]).

The factors announced in Gulf Oil [*Corp. v. Gilbert,* 330 U.S. 501 (1947)] fail to achieve fairness and convenience. The public interest factors are designed to favor dismissal and do little to promote the efficient administration of justice. It is clear that the application of forum non conveniens would produce muddled and unpredictable case law, and would be used by defendants to terminate litigation before a consideration of the merits ever occurs.

Public Policy and the Tort Liability of Multinational Corporations in United States Courts

The abolition of forum non conveniens will further important public policy considerations by providing a check on the conduct of multinational corporations (MNCs). See Economic Approach, 22 Geo. Wash. J. Int'l. L. & Econ. at 241. The misconduct of even a few multinational corporations can affect untold millions around the world. For example, after the United States imposed a domestic ban on the sale of cancer producing TRIS-treated children's sleepwear, American companies exported approximately 2.4 million pieces to Africa, Asia and South America. A similar pattern occurred when a ban was proposed for baby pacifiers that had been linked to choking deaths in infants. Hazardous Exports, supra, 14 Sw. U.L. Rev. at 82. These examples of indifference by some corporations towards children abroad are not unusual.

The allegations against Shell and Dow, if proven true, would not be unique, since production of many chemicals banned for domestic use has thereafter continued for foreign marketing. Professor Thomas McGarity, a respected authority in the field of environmental law, explained:

> During the mid-1970s, the United States Environmental Protection Agency (EPA) began to restrict the use of some pesticides because of their environmental effects, and the Occupational Safety and Health Administration (OSHA) established workplace exposure standards for toxic and hazardous substances in the manufacture of pesticides. . . . [I]t is clear that many pesticides that have been severely restricted in the United States are used without restriction in many Third World countries, with resulting harm to fieldworkers and the global environment. McGarity, *Bhopal and the Export of Hazardous Technologies,* 20 Tex. Int'l L.J. 333, 334 (1985) (citations omitted).

By 1976, "29 percent, or 161 million pounds, of all the pesticides exported by the United States were either unregistered or banned for domestic use." McWilliams, *Tom Sawyer's Apology: A Reevaluation of United States Pesticide Export Policy,* 8 Hastings Int'l & Compl. L. Rev. 61, 61 & n.4 (1984). It is estimated that these pesticides poison 750,000 people in developing countries each year, of which 22,500 die. Id. at 62. Some estimates place the death toll from the "improper marketing of pesticides at 400,000 lives a year." Id. at 62 n.7.

Some United States multinational corporations will undoubtedly continue to endanger human life and the environment with such activities until the economic consequences of these actions are such that it becomes unprofitable to operate in this manner. At present, the tort laws of many third world countries are not yet developed. *An Economic Approach,* supra, 22 Geo. Wash. J. Int'l L. & Econ. at 222–23. Industrialization "is occurring faster than the development of domestic infrastructures necessary to deal with the problems associated with industry." *Exporting Hazardous Industries,* supra, 20 Int'l L. & Pol. at 791. When a court dismisses a case against a United States multinational corporation, it often removes the most effective restraint on corporate misconduct. See *An Economic Approach,* supra, 22 Geo. Wash. J. Int'l L. & Econ. at 241.

The doctrine of forum non conveniens is obsolete in a world in which markets are global and in which ecologists have documented the delicate balance of all life on this planet. The parochial perspective embodied in the doctrine of forum non conveniens enables corporations to evade legal control merely because they are transnational. This perspective ignores the reality that actions of our corporations affecting those abroad will also affect Texans. Although DBCP is banned from use within the United States, it and other similarly banned chemicals have been consumed by Texans eating foods imported from Costa Rica and elsewhere. See D. Weir & M. Schapiro, *Circle of Poison* 28–30, 77, 82–83 (1981). In the absence of meaningful tort liability in the United States for their actions, some multinational corporations will continue to operate without adequate regard for the human and environmental costs of their actions. This result cannot be allowed to repeat itself for decades to come.

GONZALEZ, Justice, dissenting.

Under the guise of statutory construction, the court today abolishes the doctrine of forum non conveniens in suits brought pursuant to section 71.032 of the Civil Practice and Remedies Code. This decision makes us one of the few states in the Union without such a procedural tool, and if the legislature fails to reinstate this doctrine, Texas will become an irresistible forum for all mass disaster lawsuits. See generally, Note, *Foreign Plaintiffs and Forum Non Conveniens: Going Beyond Reyno,* 64 Tex. L. Rev. 193 (1985). "Bhopal"-type litigation, with little or no connection to Texas, will add to our already crowded dockets, forcing our residents to wait in the corridors of our courthouses while foreign causes of action are tried. I would hold that Section 71.031 of the Texas Civil Practice and Remedies Code *does not* confer upon foreign litigants an *absolute right* to bring suit in Texas. Because I believe that trial courts have the inherent power to apply forum non conveniens in appropriate cases, I would provide guidelines and set parameters for its use. I would thus modify the judgment of the court of appeals and remand the cause to the trial court for further proceedings.

This cause of action arose in Costa Rica where certain Costa Rican agricultural workers suffered injuries allegedly as a result of exposure to a pesticide manufactured by the defendants. The injured workers are seeking to enforce in Texas courts claims for personal injuries that occurred in Costa Rica. Several suits involving many of the same plaintiffs and essentially the same defendants have previously been filed in the United States and then dismissed on forum non conveniens grounds. . . .

In conclusion, I have no intent, much less "zeal," to implement social policy as Justice Doggett charges. That is not our role. It is clear that if anybody is trying to advance a particular social policy, it is Justice Doggett. I admire his altruism, and I too sympathize with the plight of the plaintiffs. However, the powers of this court are well-defined, and the sweeping implementations of social welfare policy Justice Doggett seeks to achieve by abolishing the doctrine of forum non conveniens are the exclusive domain of the legislature.

Questions, Materials, and Suggestions for Further Study

Dow Chemical v. Alfaro

The *Alfaro* case gives the reader a brief glimpse of some of the problems created by multinational corporations. What arose in *Alfaro* as a worker-health issue reverberates as well in issues of international pollution. During the past quarter century, an expanding regime of international environmental law has emerged. See L. Guruswamy, Sir Geoffrey Palmer, and Burns Weston, *International Environmental Law and World Order* (St. Paul: West Publishing Co., 1994). Much of the literature emphasizing the interconnectedness of environmental problems has arisen since the original 1970's perspective of the world as a "spaceship" and J. E. Lovelock's vision of our world as *gaia*, a self-regulating, quasi-sensate organism. These exotic metaphors are one way of describing the international effects of oil spills, global warming, and migrating acid rain and nuclear fallout. Perhaps the sign of true awareness of the international environmental problems came with the 1992 writing of *A Green History of the World* (Clive Ponting, *A Green History of the World* [New York: St Martin's Press, 1992]).

The political benchmark of the international environmental movement was the U.N. Stockholm conference held in 1972 (see W. Rowland, *The Plot to Save the World* [Toronto: Clark Irwin and Co., 1973]. The conceptual framework for the conference was set forth in Barbara Ward and Rene Dubos's best-seller, *Only One Earth* (Harmondsworth, England: Penguin, 1972). The Stockholm conference marked the beginning of the worldwide environmental movement. See J. McCormick, *The Global Environmental Movement* (London: Belhaven Press, 1989). The first concerns of the movement were population growth (S. Johnson, *World Population and the United Nations* [Cambridge: Cambridge University Press, 1987]); pollution in a variety of nations, (H. Jeffrey Leonard, *Pollution and the Struggle for World Product* [Cambridge, Engl. and New York: Cambridge University Press, 1988]), specifically marine pollution, (P. Haas, *Saving the Mediterranean: The Politics of International Environmental Cooperation* [New York: Columbia University Press, 1990]; McGonigle and Zacher, *Pollution, Politics and International Law: Tankers at Sea* [Berkeley: University of California Press, 1979]); and acid rain, (M. E. Wilcher, *The Politics of Acid Rain* [Brookfield, Vt.: Avebury, 1989]).

This first stage of international environmentalism has been replaced by a second stage of more worrisome global concerns. Central issues now have become the threats to the stratospheric ozone layer (R. Benedick, *Ozone Diplomacy* [Cambridge, Mass.: Harvard University Press, 1991]), world climate changes (World Meteorological Organization/UNEP *Climate Change: The IPCC Scientific Assessment,* [Cambridge: Cambridge University Press, 1990]), and threats to world biodiversity (E. Wilson, *The Diversity of Life* [Cambridge, Mass.: Belknap, 1992]).

As a consequence, there has been a new preoccupation with international environmental politics, (Tony Breton, *The Greening of Machiavelli* [Philadelphia: Earthscan Publications, 1994]) and the building of new international environmental institutions (L. Caldwell, *International Environmental Policy, Emergence and Dimensions,* [Durham, N.C.: Duke University Press, 1990], P. Haas, R. Keohave, and M. Levy, *Institutions for the Earth* [Cambridge, Mass.: MIT Press, 1993]).

10

Fundamental Causes

Consumerism

Case Study:
Nicolle-Wagner v. Deukmejian

In his or her wildest dreams, no anti-environmentalist, regardless of how perverse or astute, could even begin to imagine the *Deukmejian* case. And no case could ever have sprung from purer motives. The supporters of California's Proposition 65, the Safe Drinking Water and Toxic Enforcement Act of 1986, intended to provide a mechanism that would inform consumers whether the food they ingested contained carcinogenic or teratogenic chemicals. On the face of it, Proposition 65 stands as the proud culmination of a crusade against pesticides and chemicals that has been carried out since at least 1960. Beginning with Rachel Carson's *Silent Spring*, published in 1962, the chemical industry in the United States has been roundly criticized for the negative health effects (some proven, others asserted) their products cause in ecosystems, animals, and humans.

It will very quickly become clear that *Nicolle-Wagner v. Deukmejian* really has to do with definitions. And it is easy enough to see why. Although on its face, Proposition 65 has an unusually clear mandate ("Thou shalt label foods containing carcinogens or the growth and production of which entailed their use"), the question remains whether the statute really means what it says. What, for example, should one do about naturally occurring carcinogens?

Many naturally occurring chemicals that appear in our food and water are both carcinogenic and teratogenic. Although the primary focus of attention in our society since the 1960s has been on the potentially dangerous nature of pesticides, recent studies have suggested that some of the chemicals naturally produced by plants themselves are potentially more lethal than many synthetic pesticides, as are the metals that we ingest in some quantities with virtually all of our food. Many of these metals are essential to health in specific quantities, but toxic in others.

The issue in the *Deukmejian* case is whether a product containing a given chemical must be labeled solely because the chemical has been put into the product in some way by humans. The proposition does not seem to require the labeling of products in which the very same chemical appears in equal, or even greater, quantities, if it occurs "naturally." To face the issue squarely and phrase it barely raises serious questions about the initial proposition and its supporters. Assuming that a chemical is a chemical is a chemical, what kind of sense does it make to label the one product but not the other? The assumption behind the statute is that consumers, operating on the basis of increased knowledge, will be better able to make intelligent decisions about the food they ingest. One might ask whether experience bears out the practicality of the chosen approach: There is considerable doubt that consumers even read existing labels; and if that is the case, they are unlikely to read new ones. And won't labeling all products just result in arguments over specific labeling practices (size of labels, type of fonts, size of type, color of warning, etc.)?

There are other related categories and similar issues as well. What of labeling a product in which the amount of the offending chemical has actually been reduced by human action to levels lower than in its naturally occurring state? Is the reduction of naturally occurring chemicals a change that should require labeling? It certainly should if the purpose is to inform the consumer of what he or she is purchasing. Suppose that in the processing of a food, naturally occurring levels of a given chemical are entirely removed in one step but replaced at natural levels in another step (as, say, flavor enhancers)? Does it make much sense to label that product? An interesting exercise might be to devise labels for products that have either not been processed at all or, having been processed, contain less concentrated levels of certain chemicals or different, less lethal ones, entirely.

Proposition 65 is not far away, as is demonstrated by the furor over BST (Bovine Somatotropin), or BGH Bovine Growth Hormone). This recently developed hormone appears to have no real effect on cows at all except that it increases milk production dramatically; although the hormone increases lactation, it does not appear in the milk.

BST is not just a bovine lactation inducer. It's a cultural Rorschach test. Why the chemical companies that produce it think it's a wonderful product is easy enough to understand. But there is a strong, almost visceral, reaction among many consumers and environmental activists against the use of BST; these people see the marketing of BST as yet another example of the unchecked growth in power of the chemical industry. For them, BST is, in the most complete way possible, an "unnatural" product, pure manipulation, generated by chemical companies solely to meet a need that never existed in the natural world. Agree with it or not, the reaction is understandable as an example of the belief that control of our environment, extending even to the foods we eat and the milk we drink, eludes us. It reminds us that there are forces controlling our lives (big government, big business) over which we seem to have lost control.

There are those (significant numbers), of course, who don't see what all the fuss is about, seeing BST as just another in a long line of agricultural chemicals, no more or less important than any artificial fertilizer. To these people, seeing themselves as "rational" or "scientific," the objectors to BST behave rather like adherents of a religion: As with all statements of religious belief, the objections are understood after a fashion, respected for what they are, but essentially not comprehended. Of course, to those who object to BST, the self-identified "rationalists" or "scientific" thinkers appear to be equally religious in this same sense. This same tendency to talk at respectful cross-purposes, like advocates of positions based upon religious belief, is a common one in many environmental disputes.

As happens with virtually all environmental issues, there are those people who use their opposition to BST as a publicly acceptable cover to advance other social or political agendas; as a weapon in another battle entirely. Many of BST's opponents claim that it will lead to the downfall of the family farm because it will increase the commercial milk supply available to the general public; many of its adherents claim that BST will be a boon to the farmer because it will increase the milk supply of that individual farmer's cows. Neither of these adversaries (and certainly not BST's manufacturer) go to the trouble of pointing out that the United States already has more than enough milk, that only eight years ago the country was so awash in milk and milk products that the federal government paid dairy farmers to slaughter their milk cows to reduce the supply, that the unsupported cost of milk at current levels of supply would be pennies a gallon, and that BST simply aggravates the problem.

Our reactions to the food we eat have never been rational. We have all lived through culturally determined fads and phases: For one generation, proteins and fats were thought essential, two generations later, proteins are seen as less important than carbohydrates. Purchasing and ingesting food are just other forms of consumption, like buying automobiles, electronics, clothes, or any number of other material goods. Eating is a social activity governed by social norms, even fads, as any look at models' bodies, waxing and waning through the centuries in painting and photography, will instantly show.

Bryan NICOLLE-WAGNER,
Plaintiff and Appellant

v.

George DEUKMEJIAN, et al.,
Defendants and Respondents

Court of Appeal, Second District
May 24, 1991
[281 Cal.Rptr 494; 230 Cal.App.3d 652]

GRIGNON, Associate Justice.

This appeal concerns the Safe Drinking Water and Toxic Enforcement Act of 1986 (Proposition 65), enacted by the voters of this state during the 1986 general elections. At issue is whether a regulation promulgated by the Health and Welfare Agency pursuant to the Act conflicts with the language of the Act and whether that regulation is reasonably necessary to effectuate the purposes of the Act. . . .

Facts and Procedural Background

Proposition 65 was a ballot measure entitled, "Restrictions on Toxic Discharge into Drinking Water; Requirement of Notice of Persons' Exposure to Toxics." Its purpose was to identify chemicals known to cause cancer or birth defects, and to prevent exposure to those chemicals through our water supplies, in the workplace, and by other means. Passage of Proposition 65 added sections 25249.5 through 25249.13 to the Health and Safety Code, effective January 1, 1987. Section 25249.5 is a prohibition on contaminating drinking water with chemicals known to cause cancer or reproductive toxicity. Section 25249.6 requires a "clear and reasonable" warning before one may lawfully expose a person to chemicals which are known to cause cancer or reproductive toxicity. That section provides: "[N]o person in the course of doing business shall knowingly and intentionally expose any individual to a chemical known to the state to cause cancer or reproductive toxicity without first giving clear and reasonable warning to such individual, except as provided in section 25249.10." On or before March 1, 1987, the Governor was charged with the duty to publish a list of chemicals known to the state to cause cancer or reproductive toxicity. In 1988, almost 300 chemicals were on the list. Section 25249.12 provides that the Governor shall designate a "lead agency to implement the provisions of Proposition 65. That lead agency is empowered to adopt and modify regulations, standards, and permits, as necessary, in order to conform with and implement the purposes of the initiative statute. The Governor designated the Health and Welfare Agency (the "Agency") as the "lead agency" for purposes of Proposition 65.

On April 29, 1987, a petition was submitted to the Agency by 20 different groups, including amicus curiae herein, the Grocery Manufacturers of America, Inc. That petition sought to exempt from the section 25249.6 "clear and reasonable" warning requirement all food products which comply with certain federal safety regulations. The petition included a compilation of the extent to which various food products contain naturally occurring carcinogens or reproductive toxins. The compilation lists over 300 types of foods which, according to the 16 referenced scientific articles, contain some amount of listed chemicals such as arsenic, chromium, lead, selenium, nickel, cadmium, benzene, benz(a)pyrene, or benz(a)anthracene. Some of these chemicals, like arsenic, selenium, nickel, and cadmium are essential for human nutrition at low levels. In addition, the petition emphasized that some food products contain a naturally occurring carcinogen, aflatoxin, despite existing regulatory efforts. Aflatoxin is a mold that grows in grains and peanuts in storage. It is produced by two common fungi, Aspergillus flavus and A. parasiticus. The federal government has established an "acceptable level" for aflatoxin.

The Agency issued a notice of proposed rulemaking and conducted a public hearing concerning a regulation to exempt from the warning requirement all naturally occurring chemicals in food products which have been identified as causing cancer or birth defects pursuant to section 25249.8. Various draft and emergency regulations were proposed. Effective July 8, 1988, the final regulation became effective. (Cal.Code Regs., tit. 22, § 12501, div. 2 pt. 2, ch. 3.)

Section 12501 provides that, "[h]uman consumption of a food shall not constitute an 'exposure' for purposes of Health and Safety Code section 25249.6 to a listed chemical in the food to the extent that the person responsible for the contact can show that the chemical is naturally occurring in the food. A chemical is considered "naturally occurring" if "it is a natural constituent of a food, or if it is present in a food solely as a result of absorption or accumulation of the chemical which is naturally present in the environment in which the food is raised, or grown, or obtained. . . ." The chemical is not naturally occurring to the extent that it is the result of any human activity or failure to observe "good agricultural or good manufacturing practices," such as the "addition of chemicals to irrigation water applied to soil or crops." Even where the chemical is a naturally occurring one, the regulations require that the producer, manufacturer, distributor, or holder of food at all times utilize measures to reduce that chemical to the lowest level currently feasible.

Following the adoption of section 12501, plaintiff filed, on October 6, 1989, a first amended complaint for declaratory and injunctive relief against the Governor of the State of California, the Secretary of the Health and Welfare and his Deputy Secretary ("defendants"), seeking a determination that the regulation is unlawful. Plaintiff contends that Proposition 65 created no categorical exemption for naturally occurring carcinogens or naturally occurring reproductive toxins, which are as threatening to health as man-made toxins. Plaintiff maintains that there is no scientific basis for distinguishing between man-made and naturally occurring substances and that Proposition 65 did not sanction such distinctions.

. . .

The only issue contested in the court below was whether section 12501 was in conflict with Health and Welfare Code sections 25249.5 et seq., or was not reasonably necessary to effectuate the statutory purpose of those sections. Following a hearing on July 10, 1990, defendants' motion was granted and plaintiff's motion was denied. Judgment was entered against plaintiff and in favor of defendant on September 17, 1990. Plaintiff's timely appeal followed.

Discussion

. . .

Plaintiff contends that the Agency regulation is in conflict with the statute, because the statute regulates all chemicals which are known to the state to cause cancer or reproductive toxicity and makes no exception for naturally occurring chemicals. Defendants contend, on the other hand, that while it is true that the statute purports to regulate all listed chemicals, warnings are required only when a business "exposes" an individual to a listed chemical. The term "exposes" is not defined by the statute and, therefore, the defendants argue that the Agency may define the term in order to implement the statute and its purposes.

Our determination rests on whether the Agency's definition of exposure conflicts with the statute or its purposes. Proposition 65, and the corresponding sections of the Health and Welfare Code, are silent on the subject of naturally occurring carcinogens and reproductive toxins. We must search then, for whatever more subtle expressions of the electorate's intent may exist in the language of the statute, as well as the ballot arguments both for and against the Proposition. Those sources indicate that Proposition 65 sought to regulate toxic substances which are deliberately added or put into the environment by human activity. The controlling language of the Proposition, now Health and Welfare Code section 25249.6, provides that "no person in the course of doing business shall knowingly and intentionally expose any individual," thereby suggesting that some degree of culpable human activity is required.

Of course, one could argue that furnishing foods to consumers which are known to contain naturally occurring carcinogens or reproductive toxins might constitute a "knowing and intentional" exposure of individuals to the chemicals. However, the ballot argument in favor of Proposition 65 explains that "[Proposition 65] will not take anyone by surprise. [It] applies only to businesses that know they are putting one of the chemicals out into the environment. . . ." A chemical is not "put" into the environment if it is naturally occurring in, for example, fruits and vegetables.

The ballot argument against Proposition 65 also includes strong language indicating that naturally occurring substances are not intended to be controlled by the proposed statute: "The simple scientific fact of the matter is that manmade carcinogens represent only a tiny fraction of the total carcinogens we are exposed to, most of which are natural substances such as tobacco, alcohol, and chemicals in green plants. Significant amounts of manmade carcinogens are highly regulated in California under the most stringent laws in the United States. This initiative will result in chasing after trivial amounts of manmade carcinogens at enormous cost with minimal benefit to our health."

To be sure, one could find some support for plaintiff's position that no exemption for naturally occurring chemicals was intended, based on the absence of such distinctions in both the general language of the Proposition and in the specific definition of the substances proposed to be controlled. The ballot Proposition itself stated, by way of introduction, that: "[t]he people of California find that hazardous chemicals pose a serious threat to their health and well-being, that state government agencies have failed to provide them with adequate protection and that these failures have been serious enough to lead to investigations by federal agencies of the administration of California's toxic protection programs. The people therefore declare their rights: ... (b) To be informed about exposures to chemicals that cause cancer, birth defects, or other reproductive harm." Similarly, the list of chemicals to be controlled is defined in the Proposition as "those chemicals known to the state to cause cancer or reproductive toxicity" and makes no distinction between man-made and naturally occurring substances.

Thus, although some language may be found in the Proposition and ballot arguments which both supports and refutes plaintiff's position that naturally occurring toxins are subject to the initiative statute, we are persuaded, on balance, that the better view is that the electorate did not intend naturally occurring substances to be controlled by Proposition 65. Use of terms such as "knowingly and intentionally" and "putting" imply that culpable human conduct which results in toxins being added to the environment is the activity to be controlled. The opponents of the initiative expressly indicated that only "man-made" substances would be regulated. We find that section 12501 is consistent with the governing statutes.

Does the Regulation Reasonably Effectuate the Statutory Purpose?

We also find that substantial evidence was presented that the regulation reasonably effectuates the statutory purpose. (Gov.Code, §11350, subd. (b)) Evidence was presented at the public hearings on this regulation, and was made part of the original petition for the proposed regulation, that most food products contain at least trace amounts of carcinogens and reproductive toxins which appear on the Governor's list. The administrative record also includes commentary regarding the paucity of scientific data regarding the risks posed by exposure to such naturally occurring substances. We all presume, to some extent, that foods that have been eaten for thousands of years are healthful, despite the presence of small amounts of naturally occurring toxins. Were these substances not exempted from section 25249.6's warning requirements, the manufacturer or seller of such products would bear the burden of proving, under subdivision (c) of Health and Welfare Code section 10, that the exposure poses no "significant risk" to individuals. The administrative record in this matter indicates that such evidence largely does not exist. Thus, grocers and others would be required, in order to avoid liability under these statutes, to post a warning label on most, if not all, food products. The Agency's Final Statement of Reasons for section 12501 includes the observation that the "[a]bsence of such an exemption could unnecessarily reduce the availability of certain foods or could lead to unnecessary warnings, which could distract the public from other important warnings on consumer products." Since one of the principal purposes of the statutes in question is to provide "clear and reasonable warning" of exposure to carcinogens and reproductive toxins, such warnings would be diluted to the point of meaninglessness if they were to be found on most or all food products.

The Final Statement of Reasons also provides that the rationale for this special treatment for foodstuffs is the historical desire to preserve naturally occurring foods in the American food supply, despite the presence in those foods of small amounts of potentially deleterious substances, as well as to recognize the general safety of unprocessed foods as a matter of consumer experience. This exemption, therefore, will further the statutory purpose in safeguarding the effectiveness of warnings which are given, and in removing from regulatory scrutiny those substances which pose only an "insignificant risk" of cancer or birth defects, within the meaning of the statute.

The regulation is also narrowly drawn. It is applicable only to naturally occurring chemicals in foodstuffs and not other products, such as pharmaceuticals and cosmetics. It takes pains to define "naturally occurring" in such a fashion so as to preclude chemicals which are in whole or in part the product of human activity. Thus, a chemical is "naturally occurring" only if it is a natural constituent of food or if it is present solely as a result of the absorption or accumulation of chemicals which are naturally present in the environment. Even if a chemical occurs naturally in a food, it is not deemed to be "naturally occurring," under the regulation, to the extent it is avoidable by good agricultural or manufacturing techniques. Natural contaminants must be reduced to the "lowest level currently feasible."

Conclusion

We hold that the actions of the Health and Welfare Agency in promulgating Section 12501 were not arbitrary or capricious, or lacking in evidentiary support, and that the Agency considered all relevant factors. We further hold that the regulation is the product of the Agency's rational analysis of those factors, and that it is not in conflict with and reasonably promotes the statutory purposes of Proposition 65.

AFFIRMED.

Questions, Materials, and Suggestions for Further Study

Nicolle-Wagner v. Deukmejian

The California law in the *Deukmejian* case seeks to regulate the consumption process in order to prevent the harm that is perceived to be created by the use of toxic chemicals in the production, primarily, of food. The law is based upon the assumption that it is our habits of consumption that contribute to this harm. The proposition assumes that it is our consumption habits that give rise indirectly to the ingestion of the chemicals and that educating the public to shun the toxics will result in the improved general health of the populace at large.

Thus, the *Deukmejian* case raises more general questions about the role that overconsumption and affluence may have had in producing what we now identify as our environmental problems than would at first appear. Attacks on what some have labeled our "affluent society" as a source of pollution view the massive production and consumption of goods of all kinds (not merely the smattering of products at issue in *Deukmejian*) as the principal sources of the extreme waste in our society that leads to pollution. In light of the greater pollution seen in the demonstrably nonaffluent societies of Eastern Europe and of China, however, others might question the connection.

In 1958, John Kenneth Galbraith portrayed the United States as "the affluent society" in a book of the same name (Cambridge: Houghton-Mifflin Co.). According to Galbraith, this affluence resulted in our failure to attend to our public needs, including, but not limited to, public pollution. Galbraith posed the question of whether our consumer-created affluence and pollution were not intertwined, essential aspects of American life. Echoing a tradition of thought extending from Marx, Simmel, Weber, Tawney, and Veblen, this theme has recently been picked up by authors who continue to examine the way of life in our modern consumption-oriented society. Paul Wachtel, *The Poverty of Affluence* (St. Paul: New Society Publishers, 1989). What these modern authors seek to demonstrate is that our commitment to high levels of consumption is a far more integral part of our psyches than most of us are willing to admit. See Eugene Linden, *Affluence and Discontent* (New York: Viking Press, 1979); Mary Douglas and Baron Isherwood, *The World of Goods* (New York: W. W. Norton & Co., 1979); Robert Bocock, *Consumption* (London: Routledge, 1993).

Recognizing the subtlety and depth of our affluent lifestyle raises the question about what our basic needs may be. See Christopher Berry, *The Idea of Luxury* (Cambridge: Cambridge University Press, 1994); Patricia Spingborg, *The Problem of Human Needs and the Critique of Civilization* (London: George Allen & Unwin, 1981).

There have been at least five responses to the vision of the affluent society and its attendant environmental problems. First, some have urged a return to what they refer to as "the simple life." See Helen and Scott Nearing, *Living the Good Life* (New York: Schoken Books, 1970); Vernard Eller, *The Simple Life* (Grand Rapids, Mich.: William Eerdmans Publishing Co., 1973); Warren Johnson, *Muddling Through Frugality* (San Francisco: Sierra Club Books, 1978). Other writers have urged a no-growth or stationary state society. For example, see Herman Daly, *Steady-State Economics*, 2d ed. (Washington, D.C.: Island Press, 1991); Herman Daly and John Cobb, *For the Common Good* (Boston: Beacon Press, 1989).

A third group sought to reintroduce the notion of the value of leisure as opposed to constant production in our society. See Tibor Scitovsky, *The Joyless Economy* (Oxford: Oxford University Press, 1992); Steffan Linde, *The Harried Leisure Class* (New York: Columbia Press, 1970); Michaly Csikszentmihali, *Flow: The Psychology of Optimal Experience* (New York: Harper & Row Publishers, 1990); and Josef Pieper, *Leisure: The Basis of Culture* (New York: Pantheon Books, Inc., 1955).

More focused solutions may be the adoption of "green marketing" schemes, by which products are labeled as environmentally friendly (Theodore Panaiotov, *Green Markets: The Economics of Sustainable Development* [San Francisco: I.C.S. Press, 1993]). These green marketing schemes would, much like the proposition in the

Deukmejian case, label products that contain toxics or that are produced with, or result in, toxic pollution. The consumer would then have a legitimate choice: whether to purchase products that are "more" or "less" environmentally friendly. A fifth, and final, approach would be to rely upon consumption taxes, which discourage the purchase of some goods (U.S. General Accounting Office, *Tax Policy: Choosing Among Consumption Taxes* [Washington, D.C.: U.S. Government, 1987]).

Part 4

Law as a Means of Attaining Environmental Ideals

The proper relationship between law and ideals has been argued from time immemorial. Some laws, such as our detailed tax code, appear to illustrate the glories to be attained through the rigorous application of arithmetic; sterile exercises devoid of any form of ideals. Other laws, among them those that have attempted to enforce one segment of the population's notion of ideals upon the rest of the populace, such as prohibition statutes, have been notorious failures. And still others, like traffic laws, seem little more than necessary accommodations that simplify and regularize the tedious task of getting along with our fellow citizens. Parking regulations may be more necessary to civilization in the long run than the abstract ideals of equitable apportionment of available resources, which is the basis for those very parking regulations. Yet the detailed provisions of the tax code can ultimately be traced to morally based notions of who should be taxed how much, and the failure of prohibition does not mean that all morally based legislation is doomed, as the civil rights activists of the 1960s accurately foresaw. As the laws against murder suggest, morality does seem to have something to do with law, but determining precisely what that relationship might be is no easy task.

Legislators almost never seem to deal with ideals; they need disasters. Environmental laws arise initially out of particular incidents, such as the Santa Barbara oil spill of 1960, the DDT problem dramatized in the 1960s by Rachel Carson in *Silent Spring,* and the *Exxon Valdez* oil spill. The recognition that these incidents and the problems accompanying them were serious contributed to a social movement imbued with numerous ideals that were delineated by various leaders and writers. Lester Brown, in his portent of the threat of hazardous wastes, argued that we need to protect human health. Supreme Court Justice William O. Douglas argued for a Wilderness Bill of Rights to protect the rights of Nature. Nature writers from Thoreau to Joseph Sax have appealed to the recreative role of Nature, perhaps most clearly expressed visually in the photographs of Ansel Adams.

153

Environmental ideals are a dime a dozen. Some are rooted in our history and traditions, others are the inventions of clever "talking heads." The more thoughtful attempts include formulations by writers like Garrett Hardin, who wishes to preserve the concept of the "commons"—an ideal of shared resources modeled on the shared common ground of colonial America. Others, like the economist Barry Commoner, wish to protect the cycles of Nature from the disruptions of the modern petrochemical manufacturing complex. Some environmental writers view the entire planet as a self-adjusting ecosystem that they have named Gaia after the Greek goddess of the earth. Whether the appeal is for the protection of future generations, the maintenance of the environment in public trust, the promotion of environmentally sensitive lifestyles, or the development of a recycling, conservation-oriented society—these approaches all reflect ideals that carry implications for environmental law.

Many of these ideals overlap and require clarification. This exercise is more than academic because, once incorporated into laws, ideals affect every one of us, including those of us who disagree with them. When, for example, the ideal of conservation leads to sustained-yield forestry practices, the price and availability of timber along with the number of acres of wilderness are affected. Because environmental ideals are not shared by all those inconvenienced by them and because their implementation can affect some of us beneficially and others adversely, they contain what some call "essentially contested concepts," which give rise to endless disputes. The arena in which the necessary clarification initially takes place is the legislature. When Congress passed the Clean Air Act, for example, it made a policy decision to allow a certain amount of pollution by distinguishing between primary (or health-related) and secondary (or welfare-related) criteria. Congress was defining clean air and ranking its various uses. This procedure makes a great deal of sense. In an industrial society, a certain amount of pollution may be inevitable. If this sort of ranking must be done, perhaps a representative body, which we all had a part in electing, should do it. Perhaps no one is better qualified than our representative institutions to set environmental policy.

But there are alternative approaches and arenas as well. As part of the process of becoming incorporated into laws, all ideals become compromised. One could argue that the legislative process is so oriented toward compromise that no lasting, significant environmental decision could possibly be made through its mechanism. One senator or representative may horse-trade with another; as a result, the allowable level of asbestos may be changed, or a statistically certain number of carcinomas may be accepted so that a dam or a highway can be built.

Statements of ideals and environmental values are notoriously vague, and the initial legislative or constitutional expression of these values may be equally ambiguous. To say that we all have a "right to a decent environment" is one thing; it is quite another to figure out what that statement actually means, as Mr. Tanner discovered (see Chapter 3). By itself the statement has no meaning, but when an environmentalist invokes it during a specific conflict between environmental and other values, the resulting legal decision helps establish a definition of that value, which will apply in future court conflicts over the same issue.

General legislative mandates are frequently made precise, given a local habitation and a name, in the arena of the court. It is in the court that the definitions are further honed. The four cases in Part 4 were chosen to illustrate the process by which environmental ideals become incorporated into law and the process by which those statements of law are further refined by the courts. We have chosen cases that express four of the almost infinite number of possible environmental ideals: the equitable distribution of property rights and liabilities; the idea that we should approach nature as nonexploitative stewards rather than as developers; the notion of providing the abstraction "Nature" with a voice in the courtroom; and the conservation of resources for future generations.

11

Environmental Ideals

Equitable Distribution of Rights and Liabilities

Case Study: *East Bibb Twiggs v. Macon Bibb County Planning and Zoning Commission*

Although one can argue whether the power to tax is the power to destroy, there is no doubt that the power to zone is the power to discriminate: Discrimination is its entire purpose. Zoning discriminates between residential, commercial, and manufacturing uses, between various types of residences (single family homes versus apartment buildings, one acre zones versus tract lots), and various types of commercial enterprises (campus style corporate headquarters versus convenience stores) and manufacturers (steel mills versus computer chip manufacturers). One difficulty with zoning was best summed up by Justice Oliver Wendell Holmes, who is alleged to have said that one has to read the law as one would a bad man. Zoning's strictures on land use can also be used to discriminate between and among favored and disfavored individuals or groups of individuals, which is decidedly *not* its purpose. To discriminate among land uses is a legitimate zoning function; to discriminate among individuals independent of that land use is not. But occasionally, to do one is to do the other, and it is in the different forms and meanings of "discrimination" that the *East Bibb* case arises.

The problem that frequently arises with zoning regulations is determining the intent behind the legislation, the zoning ordinance itself. The state court before which a zoning challenge is brought examines the local zoning regulation strictly, trying to ensure that land use and only land use is being controlled.

To better understand the argument in the *East Bibb* case, we must go back to the period immediately following World War II, extending through the affluent 1950s and 1960s. The end of World War II saw the rise of the automobile, unheard of affluence, and increased mobility for nearly all classes in U.S. society. During this period the suburbs sprouted and the commuting public was born. At the same time, tremendous demographic pressures were increasing urban density. As a result, the value and cost of suburban housing increased. Almost inevitably, as suburbs grew ever outward, the innermost urban areas—those that had profited by the earlier growth—fell victim to urban blight and decay. As the waves of suburbanization spread outward from the central cities, rural communities cast about for ways to allow just enough development to increase property values, yet to preserve intact their distinctive local character. They found the weapon they needed in zoning, which use they attempted to evolve from a device used to control development into a means of establishing enclaves of specific social and economic status. By limiting the housing options available under a zoning plan, the community could control the economic status of its residents. By not allowing rental property or multiple-family dwellings, by requiring large minimum lot sizes, and by totally excluding mobile homes, for example, zoning regulations would ensure that only a particular economic group of people—those whom the neighbors would regard as "the right sort"—could live in a municipality; others would be excluded.

"Exclusionary zoning" took an almost infinite number of forms directed at engineering not merely population density but also population growth and even social selection. In 1975, the New Jersey Supreme Court declared that one such set of ordinances violated the state constitution. No more, Justice Hall wrote, could a New Jersey community limit itself to one social class:

> We conclude that every such municipality must, by its land-use regulations, presumptively make realistically possible an appropriate variety and choice of housing. More specifically, presumptively it cannot foreclose the opportunity of the classes of people mentioned for low and moderate income housing and in its regulations must affirmatively afford that opportunity at least to the extent of the municipality's fair share of the present and prospective regional need thereof (*So. Burlington C. NAACP v. Township of Mount Laurel*, 336 A2d 713, 724 [NJ 1975]).

Judge Hall's decision, arguably the single most influential land-use decision in the last three decades, placed a regional, not merely local, obligation on communities. Somewhere in the region, the decision suggests, there must be adequate facilities for people of all economic levels.

This landmark decision, the importance of which has spread far beyond New Jersey, was discussed in conjunction with the *Ramapo* decision in the first edition of *Green Justice*. Judge Hall dealt adequately with the "typical" pattern of exclusionary zoning: zoning intended to keep one class of people *out* of a neighborhood. The question arising in *East Bibb*, although related, is different: What of zoning that restricts clearly negative activities to one or a certain number of identifiable zones, and, further, what if those zones either are or are becoming more and more occupied by members of an identifiable ethnic or social class?

Situations such as arise in *East Bibb* present one problem with an almost infinite number of facets: Arguably, for landowners currently residing in the zone and who purchased their property prior to the owners having decided to open a landfill, there will be a loss of property values (one could also ask whether their property tax rates will accurately reflect this diminution in value, although that's another story). It can be argued that future residents of a zone having a landfill will most likely have a lower annual income than those in other zones, since property values will be lower. Residents of a zone containing a landfill will almost certainly pay less for their houses than residents of other zones. Arguably, those with lower incomes will be social minorities. Arguably, this discrepancy between zones, in which they reflect social/economic status, will increase over time as the difference in property values between zones increases because of the landfill. And arguably, the result will be a ghetto.

The crucial question is whether or not placing the landfill where they did reflects a bias on the part of the community, as reflected in the zoning authorities, the community's elected representatives. On the one hand, the community can hardly refuse a landowner the right to open a landfill if that particular use is authorized by the ordinance. On the other hand, the community cannot decide on a whim to plunk a landfill down in one of the "poorer" sections of town just because it's convenient and the residents are not politically active in comparison to those in other, more affluent, neighborhoods. If there were no legitimate reason for placing a landfill in a less-affluent neighborhood, the action would most likely be considered unconstitutional discrimination.

The *East Bibb* case is only one of the more tendentious of a new category of cases arising in the environmental context. These cases all concern the relationship between those who benefit from the environmental movement in terms of cleaner, more pleasant surroundings and those who don't, who believe that they have been discriminated against on racial, ethnic, or social grounds. There are some reasons not to dismiss their claims out of hand. As we mentioned in the introduction to Part 4, the very definition of "environment" as we use it in environmental law may be disguising a class bias: Our concerns are with the preservation of amenities in the rural and suburban "environment," not with reducing or eliminating such negative urban phenomena as drugs, gangs, malnutrition, and infant mortality. Certainly a legitimate question to ask is whether a society that spends millions of dollars on cleaning up a former waste site so that the cancer risk is less than 1 per 1,000,000 might not be better advised to save an entire human being for each $1,000 spent on prenatal care, nutrition, and education.

Just what elements of all these dilemmas should be considered? By whom should they be considered? Just what weight should they be given? And what sort of showing should a party have to make if he or she is to claim discriminatory intent on the part of decisionmakers? These are all questions that arise in the reading of *East Bibb* and that the student should be ready to deal with. If we believe that "environmental justice is our goal" and that our specific objective is to provide for an "environmentally just society," it must be just for all. Attaining that goal, and achieving that objective may require changes in our attitudes toward both our environmental goals and the society within which they are attained.

EAST BIBB TWIGGS
NEIGHBORHOOD ASSOCIATION
et al., Plaintiffs
v.
MACON-BIBB COUNTY PLANNING
AND ZONING COMMISSION
et al., Defendants

United States District Court,
Middle District of Georgia
February 16, 1989
[706 F. Supp. 880]

OWENS, Chief Judge.

This case involves allegations that plaintiffs have been deprived of equal protection of the law by the Macon-Bibb County Planning & Zoning Commission ("Commission"). Specifically, plaintiffs allege that the Commission's decision to allow the creation of a private landfill in census tract No. 133.02 was motivated at least in part by considerations of race. Defendants vigorously contest that allegation. Following extensive discovery by the parties, this court conducted a nonjury trial on October 4–5, 1988. The parties were permitted to supplement the record following the conclusion of the trial. Based upon a thorough examination of the file and careful consideration of both the evidence submitted and arguments offered during the trial, the court now issues the following ruling.

Facts

On or about May 14, 1986, defendants Mullis Tree Service, Inc. and Robert Mullis ("petitioners") applied to the Commission for a conditional use to operate a non-putrescible waste landfill at a site bounded at least in part by Davis and Donnan Davis Roads. The property in question is located in census tract No. 133.02, a tract containing five thousand five hundred twenty-seven (5,527) people, three thousand three hundred sixty-seven (3,367) of whom are black persons and two thousand one hundred forty-nine (2,149) of whom are white persons. The only other private landfill approved by the Commission is situated in the adjacent census tract No. 133.01, a tract having a population of one thousand three hundred and sixty-nine (1,369) people, one thousand forty-five (1,045) of whom are white persons and three hundred twenty (320) of whom are black persons. That site was approved as a landfill in 1978. The proposed site for the landfill in census tract No. 133.02 is zoned A-Agricultural, and the parties are in agreement that property so zoned is eligible for the construction of and subsequent operation as a landfill of this type.

On May 27, 1986, the Commission conducted a hearing on petitioners' application for a conditional use. Evidence was presented by petitioners, and certain individuals expressed various concerns about the location of the landfill in this area. The Commission deferred the decision on petitioners' application pending input from the City of Macon and the County of Bibb regarding the location of a landfill on the proposed site.

By letters dated June 5, 1986, and June 10, 1986, respectively, the County and the City responded to invitations from the Commission to participate in the evaluation of the instant application and to participate in the development of a procedure by which the City and the County actively participate in the evaluation of future applications for landfills. The Bibb County Board of Commissioners, through its Chairman, Mr. Emory Green, while expressing its appreciation for and accepting the Commission's offer to participate, stated that the Commission had full authority to act on any such application and that any suggestion or recommendation offered by the County Commission would be for "informational" purposes only. The City, through Mayor George Israel, applauded the Commission's suggestion that a procedure be developed, but it had "no comment" regarding the specific project in question in that the project was located outside the Macon city limits. During this exchange of letters, the Environmental Protection Division ("EPD") of the Georgia Department of Natural Resources informed Mr. Mullis by letter dated May 30, 1986, that the proposed site was acceptable for disposal of non-putrescible waste.

The Commission reconvened on June 23, 1986, to consider petitioners' application. Petitioners were present and were represented by Mr. Charles Adams. Approximately one hundred fifty (150) individuals opposed to the landfill attended the Commission meeting. Numerous statements were made, and various opinions were offered. Included among those reasons offered in opposition to the landfill were the following: (1) threat to the residential character of the neighborhood; (2) devaluation of the residents' property; (3) danger to the ecological balance of the area; (4) concern regarding the possible expansion of the landfill into a public dump; (5) hazards to residents and children from increased truck traffic; and (6) dissatisfaction with the perceived inequitable burden borne by the East Bibb Area in terms of "unpleasant" and "undesirable" land-uses.

Mr. Mullis and his representative, Mr. Adams, emphasized the need for an additional landfill and championed the free enterprise system as the appropriate developer and manager of such sites. They relied upon the reports supplied by Tribble & Richardson, Inc., an engineering concern with vast experience in examining proposed landfill sites, and upon the EPD's approval of the site. Petitioners further emphasized that the landfill would be managed pursuant to the existing regulations and under close supervision of the EPD.

After hearing the views of numerous individuals, the Commission voted to deny the application. The stated reasons were as follows: (1) the proposed landfill would be located adjacent to a predominantly residential area; (2) the increase in heavy truck traffic would increase noise in the area; and (3) the additional truck traffic was undesirable in a residential area. See Commission letter dated June 30, 1986.

Pursuant to a request from petitioners through both Tribble & Richardson and Mr. Charles Adams, the Commission voted on July 14, 1986, to rehear petitioners' application. The rehearing was conducted on July 28, 1986. Applicant Robert Mullis and his representatives addressed numerous concerns which had been previously raised by citizens opposed to the landfill and by members of the Commission. Specifically, Mr. Mullis informed those present that he had met all of the existing state, city, county and planning and zoning commission requirements for the approval of a permit to operate a landfill. He also reiterated that the site had been tested by engineers and that it had been found geologically suitable for a landfill. He explained that burning, scavenging, open dumping and disposal of hazardous wastes would be strictly prohibited, and he advised that this landfill would be regulated and inspected by the EPD. Mr. Mullis and Mr. Hodges of Tribble & Richardson pointed out that the site entrance would be selected by the EPD and that such selection would be subject to approval by the Commission. Mr. Mullis assured those present that the site would be supervised at all times. Finally, Mr. Mullis informed the Commission and the other participants that the buffer zone would be increased an additional fifty (50) feet, from one hundred (100) feet to one hundred fifty (150) feet, in those areas where the landfill site adjoined residences. Also included in the record was a letter dated July 16, 1986, in which Mr. Mullis stated that there existed only five residences continguous [sic.] to the proposed landfill site and only twenty-five houses within a one mile radius of the site.

The citizens opposing the landfill voiced doubts about the adequacy of the buffer zone and the potential health threats from vermin and insects. Concerns were expressed regarding the impact the landfill might have upon the water in the area in that many of the residents relied upon wells for their household water. Certain of the participants questioned whether the residents of this area were subject to the same considerations afforded residents in other areas of the city and county when decisions of this nature were made.

When the above-mentioned allegations of unfairness were raised by opponents to the landfill, Commission Chairperson Dr. Cullinan expressed concern regarding that perception. He stated as follows:

I'm interested in your comments about manipulations and information may have been passed subrosa in some way. I'm interested in that because I think government and ultimately democracy functions on the legitimacy of its purpose and if people don't have faith in their institutions, the system won't work. They may not like all of the decisions that government institutions make, but I would feel badly if they thought that there was some sort of conspiracy afoot and I can tell you that I received a number of calls before and after my own meanderings through that land and I received no calls from big corporate people asking me to vote a particular way. Although, I did receive numerous calls from people in the area. Although, I can't speak for the other commissioners feeling is that their experiences are similar to mine. I think that the record should show to the best of this chairman's knowledge there is not manipulations or conspiracies afoot and if you have such information I would be interested in having it entered into the record. Defendant's Exhibit D-P & Z 3, Transcript of July 28, 1986, Hearing.

Dr. Cullinan further stated that "anything that I have any knowledge of will be in the record. We're not going to let vague charges of conspiracy go unchallenged here. We want this Board to be a legitimate Board and speak to the will of all of the people . . . . " Id.

At the conclusion of the discussion, the Commission deliberated and voted. The Commission approved the application subject to the following conditions: (1) approval by the county engineer; (2) approval or permits from all applicable state and federal agencies; (3) restriction on dumping of all but non-putrescible materials; and (4) review and approval by the Commission of the final site plan. See Commission Letter dated August 1, 1986.

On November 10, 1986, the Commission approved the final site plan for the landfill. On November 20, 1986, the EPD issued a permit to Mullis Tree Service conditioned upon the permitee [sic.] complying with the following conditions of operation:

1. No hazardous or putrescible waste shall be deposited at the landfill.
2. Materials placed in the landfill shall be spread in layers and compacted to the least practical volume.
3. A uniform compacted layer of clean earth cover not less than one (1) foot in depth shall be placed over all exposed waste material at least monthly or more frequently as may be determined by the division.
4. The disposal site shall be graded and drained to minimize runoff onto the landfill . . . to drain water from the surface of the landfill.
5. The landfill shall be operated in such manner as to prevent air, land, or water pollution, public health hazards or nuisances.
6. Access to the landfill shall be limited to authorized entrances which shall be closed when the site is not in operation.
7. Suitable means shall be provided to prevent and control fires. Stockpiled soil is considered to be the most satisfactory fire fighting material.

8. The Design and Operational Plan submitted by the permittee and approved by the Division for this landfill is hereby made a part of this permit and the landfill shall be operated in accordance with the plan.
9. This permit shall become null and void one year from the effective date if the permitted disposal operation has not commenced within one year from the effective date.

Discussion

"To prove a claim of discrimination in violation of the Equal Protection Clause a plaintiff must show not only that the state action complained of had a disproportionate or discriminatory impact but also that the defendant acted with the intent to discriminate." *United States v. Yonkers Board of Education,* 837 F.2d 1181, 1216 (2nd Cir. 1987), cert. denied,—U.S.—, 108 S.Ct. 2821,100 L.Ed.2d 922 (1988); see *Washington v. Davis,* 426 U.S. 229, 96 S.Ct. 2040, 48 L.Ed.2d 697 (1976); *E & T Realty v. Strickland,* 830 F.2d 1107 (11th Cir. 1987), cert. denied,—U.S., 108 S.Ct. 1225, 99 L.Ed.2d 425 (1988). A plaintiff need not establish that "the challenged action rested solely on racially discriminatory purposes. Rarely can it be said that a legislature or administrative body operating under a broad mandate made a decision motivated solely by a single concern, or even that a particular purpose was the 'dominant' or 'primary' one." *Village of Arlington Heights v. Metropolitan Housing Development Corp.,* 429 U.S. 252, 265, 97 S.Ct. 555, 563, 50 L.Ed.2d 450, 464–65 (1977). "Determining whether invidious discriminatory purpose was a motivating factor demands a sensitive inquiry into such circumstantial and direct evidence of intent as may be available." Id. at 266, 97 S.Ct. at 564, 50 L.Ed.2d at 465. Considerations include the following: (1) the impact of the official action—whether it bears more heavily on one race than upon another; (2) the historical background of the decision; (3) the specific sequence of events leading up to the challenged decision; (4) any departures, substantive or procedural, from the normal decision-making process; and (5) the legislative or administrative history of the challenged decision. Id. at 266–68, 97 S.Ct. at 564–65, 50 L.Ed.2d at 465–66.

Having considered all of the evidence in light of the above-identified factors, this court is convinced that the Commission's decision to approve the conditional use in question was not motivated by the intent to discriminate against black persons. Regarding the discriminatory impact of the Commission's decision, the court observes the obvious—a decision to approve a landfill in any particular census tract impacts more heavily upon that census tract than upon any other. Since census tract No. 133.02 contains a majority black population equalling roughly sixty percent (60%) of the total population, the decision to approve the landfill in census tract No. 133.02 of necessity impacts greater upon that majority population.

However, the court notes that the only other Commission approved landfill is located within census tract No. 133.01, a census tract containing a majority white population of roughly seventy-six percent (76%) of the total population. This decision by the Commission and the existence of the landfill in a predominantly white census tract tend to undermine the development of a "clean pattern, unexplainable on grounds other than race. . . ." *Village of Arlington Heights,* 429 U.S. at 266, 97 S.Ct. at 564, 50 L.Ed.2d at 465.

Plaintiffs hasten to point out that both census tracts, Nos. 133.01 and 133.02, are located within County Commission District No. 1, a district whose black residents compose roughly seventy percent (70%) of the total population. Based upon the above facts, the court finds that while the Commission's decision to approve the landfill for location in census tract No. 133.02 does of necessity impact to a somewhat larger degree upon the majority population therein, that decision fails to establish a clear pattern of racially motivated decisions.

Plaintiffs contend that the Commission's decision to locate the landfill in census tract No. 133.02 must be viewed against an historical background of locating undesirable land-uses in black neighborhoods. First, the above discussion regarding the two Commission approved landfills rebuts any contention that such activities are always located in direct proximity to majority black areas. Further, the court notes that the Commission did not and indeed may not actively solicit this or any other landfill application. The Commission reacts to applications from private landowners for permission to use their property in a particular manner. The Commissioners observed during the course of these proceedings the necessity for a comprehensive scheme for the management of waste and for the location of landfills. In that such a scheme has yet to be introduced, the Commission is left to consider each request on its individual merits. In such a situation, this court finds it difficult to understand plaintiffs' contentions that this Commission's decision to approve a landowner's application for a private landfill is part of any pattern to place "undesirable uses" in black neighborhoods. Second, a considerable portion of plaintiffs' evidence focused upon governmental decisions made by agencies other than the planning and zoning commission, evidence of alleged discriminatory intent of the Commission.

Finally, regarding the historical background of the Commission's decision, plaintiffs have submitted numerous exhibits consisting of newspaper articles reflecting various zoning decisions made by the Commission. The court has read each article, and it is unable to discern a series of official actions taken by the Commission for invidious purposes. See *Village of Arlington Heights,* 429 U.S. at 267, 97 S.Ct. at 564, 50 L.Ed.2d at 466. Of the more recent articles, the court notes that in many instances matters under consideration by the Commission attracted widespread attention and vocal opposition. The Commission oft times was responsive to the opposition and refused to permit the particular development under consideration, while on other occasions the Commission permitted the development to proceed in the face of opposition. Neither the articles nor the evidence presented during trial provides factual support for a determination of the underlying motivations, if any, of the Commission in making the decisions. In short, plaintiffs' evidence does not establish a background of discrimination in the Commission's decisions.

"The specific sequence of events leading up to the challenged decision also may shed some light on the decisionmaker's purpose." *Village of Arlington Heights,* 429 U.S. at 267, 97 S.Ct. at 664, 60 L.Ed.2d at 466. Plaintiff identifies as the key piece of evidence in this regard a statement contained in "Action Plan for Housing," a study of the status of housing in the Macon area conducted by the Macon-Bibb County Planning and Zoning Commission. The study states that "[r]acial and low income discrimination still exist in the community." The study was issued in March of 1974, and it constitutes a recognition by the Commission that racial discrimination still existed in the Macon community in 1974. That recognition in no way implies that racial discrimination affected the decision making process of the Commission itself. Rather, the statement indicates the Commission's awareness that certain individuals and/or groups in society had yet to come to grips with the concept of equality before the law. The Commission's recognition of the situation does not constitute its adoption. Indeed, such recognition probably encourages that Commission to exercise vigilance in guarding against such unprincipled influence. The statements of the various Commissioners during their deliberations indicates a real concern about both the desires of the opposing citizens and the needs of the community in general.

In terms of other specific antecedent events, plaintiffs have not produced evidence of any such events nor has the court discerned any such events from its thorough review of the record. No sudden changes in the zoning classifications have been brought to the court's attention. Plaintiffs have not produced evidence showing a relaxation or other change in the standards applicable to the granting of a conditional use. Thus, this court finds no specific antecedent events which support a determination that race was a motivating factor in the Commission's decision.

Plaintiffs contend that the Commission deviated from its "normal procedures" in several ways. First, plaintiffs point to the Commission's efforts to encourage input from the County and the City. These efforts do not constitute evidence that "improper purposes are playing a role" in the Commission's decision. The statements of the Commissioners make clear that such efforts had their genesis in the Commission's concerns about accountability to the public for certain controversial governmental decisions and about centralized planning for the area's present and future waste disposal problems.

Plaintiffs' contentions regarding other alleged procedural irregularities, including the requirement that the Commission make certain findings of fact and that a rehearing was improperly granted, are without merit. The court has examined the Comprehensive Land Development Resolution in light of the actions taken and has been unable to identify any procedural flaws.

The final factor identified in *Village of Arlington Heights* involves the legislative or administrative history, particularly the contemporary statements made by members of the Commission. Plaintiffs focus on the reasons offered by the Commission for the initial denial of petitioners' application, i.e., that the landfill was adjacent to a residential area and that the approval of the landfill in that area would result in increased traffic and noise, and they insist that those reasons are still valid. Thus, plaintiffs reason, some invidious racial purpose must have motivated the Commission to reconsider its decision and to approve that use which was at first denied. This court, having read the comments of the individual commissioners, cannot agree with plaintiffs' arguments.

Mr. Pippinger, who first opposed the approval of the conditional use, changed his position after examining the area in question and reviewing the data. He relied upon the EPD's approval of the site and upon his determination that the impact of the landfill on the area had been exaggerated. Mrs. Kearnes, who also inspected the site, agreed with Mr. Pippinger.

Dr. Cullinan also inspected the site. After such inspection and after hearing all of the evidence, he stated that, based "on the overriding need for us to meet our at large responsibilities to Bibb County I feel that [the site in question] is an adequate site and in my most difficult decision to date I will vote to support the resolution." Transcript of July 28, 1986, Commission Meeting.

Both Dr. Cullinan and Mr. Pippinger were concerned with the problems of providing adequate buffers protecting the residential area from the landfill site and of developing an appropriate access to the site for the dumping vehicles. These concerns were in fact addressed by both the Commission and the EPD.

The voluminous transcript of the hearings before and the deliberations by the Commission portray the Commissioners as concerned citizens and effective public servants. At no time does it appear to this court that the Commission abdicated its responsibility either to the public at large, to the particular concerned citizens or to the petitioners. Rather, it appears to this court that the Commission carefully and thoughtfully addressed a serious problem and that it made a decision based upon the merits and not upon any improper racial animus.

For all the foregoing reasons, this court determines that plaintiffs have not been deprived of equal protection of the law. Judgement, therefore, shall be entered for defendants.

SO ORDERED.

Questions, Materials, and Suggestions for Further Study

East Bibb Twiggs Neighborhood Association
v. Macon-Bibb County Planning and Zoning Commission

The justice to which we refer in *Green Justice* is usefully divided into four different kinds. First, there is corrective justice, whereby a person is made whole through the award of damages or restitution. Corrective justice is discussed in Jules Coleman's *Risks and Wrongs* (Cambridge: Cambridge University Press, 1992). Corrective justice is exemplified in toxic tort cases where individuals seek damages because of harm allegedly caused by toxic substances. See Gerald Boston and M. Stuart Madden, *Law of Environmental and Toxic Torts* (St. Paul: West Publishing Co., 1994). The central issue here is, of course, what standard should be employed to determine when an individual is made whole. A second kind of environmental justice is retributive justice, where an individual is punished by fines or even imprisonment for the violation of environmental statutes, for polluting, or for taking an endangered species. An excellent general discussion of retributive justice is Jerome Michael and Mortimer Adler's *Crime, Law and Social Science* (Montclair, N.J.: Patterson Smith, 1971), which explores the different purposes of punishment. A third kind of justice is contributory justice, the obligation of individuals to contribute their fair share to the common good. The central question for contributory justice is: What is a fair share? One specific example of contributory justice is the taxation of natural resources (John Dzienkowski and Robert Peroni, *Natural Resources Taxation* [Durham, N.C.: Carolina Academic Press, 1988]).

A final kind of justice, that most commonly discussed, is distributive justice, the fair distribution of benefits and burdens of government programs. For a good general discussion of distributive justice, see Nicholas Rescher's *Distributive Justice: A Constructive Critique of the Utilitarian Theory of Distribution* (Lanham, Md.: University Press of America, 1966, reprinted in 1982). As Rescher points out, there are different standards for determining fair share distributions. For one discussion of the distribution of environmental costs and benefits, see Eugene Seskin and Lester Lowe, *Air Pollution and Human Health* (Baltimore: Johns Hopkins University Press, 1977). In the early-to-mid-1990s, increased attention has been focused upon the impact of our environmental policies on the vulnerable (see Robert Goodin, *Protecting the Vulnerable: A Reanalysis of Our Social Responsibilities* [Chicago: University of Chicago Press, 1984]), minorities, and low-income groups.

Most planning and policy analyses have focused upon the non-distributive impacts of government programs. See Michael Carley, *Rational Techniques in Policy Analysis* (London: Heinemann Educational Books, 1980). Recently, however, policy analysis in the form of equity analysis has emerged. See H. Peyton Young, *Equity in Theory and Practice* (Princeton: Princeton University Press, 1994). Young's analysis seeks to measure the degrees of different kinds of equity and inequity.

12

Environmental Ideals

Nature as Held in Public Trust

Case Study:
National Audubon Society v. Department of Water and Power of the City of Los Angeles

A legal trust is created by separating the ownership of something from its use. In a private trust, a person (the donor) places some resources (the res) in a trust to be managed according to the person's wishes by a trustee for the benefit of certain named beneficiaries. Although the trustee has title to the property, he or she does not own it and cannot use it as desired but must follow the instructions of the donor. If the trustee does not do so, or if he or she somehow squanders the assets that make up the res, the trustee can be sued by the donor (or the donor's representatives) or by the beneficiaries (or their representatives). Most of us are familiar with the term through "testamentary trusts," by which an individual leaves a certain amount of money or other property to be managed by a trustee (typically a bank) for the benefit of an heir or family member.

Such a simple explanation of the common testamentary trust hardly does justice to the protean concept behind it. One of the ideals that has come to animate the environmental movement recently is that of the public trust. Under the common law, certain natural resources, particularly tidal areas, were not owned by any one individual but were held for the purposes of public navigation, recreation, water-related commerce, and conservation. This remains true today: As the court discusses in

National Audubon Society v. Department of Water and Power of the City of Los Angeles, even the legislature may not pass laws violating this public trust.

The primary difference between the private and the public trust is the lack of a written document for the latter. One of the very few ironclad rules for the creation of a private trust is that explicit instructions must be provided for the trustee to follow in administering the trust. Since the clearest way to communicate such instructions is in writing, it has become almost axiomatic that a private trust requires a written document. But the theory behind the public trust makes a written document impossible. Presumably, the resources that make up the res were given by the creator to the government (the trustee) to be held for the people (the beneficiaries). Although this arrangement sounds fine in theory, it does not define which resources (all? some? if some, which?), which government (succeeding U.S. administrations tend to run in cycles of conservation and development), or for which people (those who bird-watch in secluded woods, those who need lumber for subsistence housing, or those who gamble on resource exploitation).

Applying the public trust doctrine to the environment was resurrected from English law and previously overlooked U.S. cases by Joseph Sax, lawyer and legal scholar. Sax urged that the common-law notion of public trust be used to check government abuse in the management of natural resources. In his review of past cases he revealed the courts' concern for public access, proper control by public agencies, general use by the citizenry of the resources, and the securing of observable public benefits, where public uses are diminished. By the early 1970s, several cases had been successfully brought under the common-law public trust doctrine. But in many states, the doctrine applied only to tidal lands, leaving valuable inland resources unprotected. Some states refused to add conservation to the list of purposes that the public trust could serve.

Then in *Defending the Environment: A Handbook for Citizen Action* (New York: Vintage Books, 1970, 1972), Professor Joseph Sax urged the passage of statutes placing environmental resources in a public trust. He drafted the Thomas J. Anderson, Gordon Rockwell Environmental Protection Act of 1970, which was passed in Michigan and several other states. This act permits members of the public to bring action in court or to intervene in administrative hearings to attempt to show that "the conduct of the defendant has or is likely to pollute, impair, or destroy the air, water, or other natural resources or the public trust therein." Many cases resulting in the successful protection of the environment have been brought under this law. In many ways it accomplishes the goals enunciated by Justice Douglas in his dissenting opinion in *Sierra Club v. Morton*, by giving the public standing to object to certain government actions that have adverse effects on natural objects or processes.

The largest city in the United States has virtually no water of its own. The development of Los Angeles, its history, its politics, and its economics have been shaped in large part by its voracious thirst. To supply this need, Los Angeles and other coastal desert cities of California have stretched a vast and intricate spiderweb of canals and aqueducts into the foothills of the Sierras, bringing the city's need for water into direct conflict with the needs of others. In California, conflicts over the uses of water are far reaching. How much water should be set aside for drinking? How much for irrigated cropland? How much for sanitary sewer systems? How much for industry? How much for mining? How much for recreation? How much for wildlife? How much can we afford to waste by evaporation as it courses through canals? And, finally when the city's supply is exhausted, how much water can it get from neighbors, especially if the neighbors do not want to give it up?

To speak of "running out" of land makes little sense to most people. When land is scarce, a market mechanism takes over and the price for land simply rises. Running out of air is likewise something people generally have a hard time identifying as a potential problem. But running out of water is a clear and understandable possibility. Water is one natural resource obviously worth preserving, yet the mechanism by which to preserve it, considering its multitude of uses, is hard to determine. One possible technique is the use of a trust.

NATIONAL AUDUBON SOCIETY et al.,
Petitioners
v.
The SUPERIOR COURT OF ALPINE COUNTY,
Respondent
DEPARTMENT OF WATER
AND POWER OF THE CITY
OF LOS ANGELES, et al.,
Real Parties in Interest

Supreme Court of California
February 17, 1983
[658 P.2d 709]

BROUSSARD, Justice.

Mono Lake, the second largest lake in California, sits at the base of the Sierra Nevada escarpment near the eastern entrance to Yosemite National Park. The lake is saline; it contains no fish but supports a large population of brine shrimp which feed vast numbers of nesting and migratory birds. Islands in the lake protect a large breeding colony of California gulls, and the lake itself serves as a haven on the migration route for thousands of Northern Phalarope, Wilson's Phalarope, and Eared Grebe. Towers and spires of tufa on the north and south shores are matters of geological interest and a tourist attraction.

. . . In 1940, however, the Division of Water Resources, the predecessor to the present California Water Resources Board, granted the Department of Water and

Power of the City of Los Angeles (hereafter DWP) a permit to appropriate virtually the entire flow of four of the five streams flowing into the lake. DWP promptly constructed facilities to divert about half the flow of these streams into DWP's Owens Valley aqueduct. In 1970 DWP completed a second diversion tunnel, and since that time has taken virtually the entire flow of these streams.

As a result of these diversions, the level of the lake has dropped; the surface area has diminished by one-third; one of the two principal islands in the lake has become a peninsula, exposing the gull rookery there to coyotes and other predators and causing the gulls to abandon the former island. The ultimate effect of continued diversions is a matter of intense dispute, but there seems little doubt that both the scenic beauty and the ecological values of Mono Lake are imperiled.

Plaintiffs filed suit in superior court to enjoin the DWP diversions on the theory that the shores, bed and waters of Mono Lake are protected by a public trust. Plaintiffs' suit was transferred to the federal district court, which requested that the state courts determine the relationship between the public trust doctrine and the water rights system, and decide whether plaintiffs must exhaust administrative remedies before the Water Board prior to filing suit. . . .

This case brings together for the first time two systems of legal thought: the appropriative water rights system which since the days of the gold rush has dominated California water law, and the public trust doctrine which, after evolving as a shield for the protection of tidelands, now extends its protective scope to navigable lakes. Ever since we first recognized that the public trust protects environmental and recreational values (*Marks v. Whitney* [1971] 6 Cal.3d 251, 98 Cal. Rptr. 790, 491 P.2d 374), the two systems of legal thought have been on a collision course (Johnson, Public Trust Protection for Stream Flows and Lake Levels [1980] 14 U.C. Davis L.Rev. 233). They meet in a unique and dramatic setting which highlights the clash of values. Mono Lake is a scenic and ecological treasure of national significance, imperiled by continued diversions of water; yet, the need of Los Angeles for water is apparent, its reliance on rights granted by the board evident, the cost of curtailing diversions substantial.

Attempting to integrate the teachings and values of both the public trust and the appropriative water rights system, we have arrived at certain conclusions which we briefly summarize here. In our opinion, the core of the public trust doctrine is the state's authority as sovereign to exercise a continuous supervision and control over the navigable waters of the state and the lands underlying those waters. This authority applies to the waters tributary to Mono Lake and bars DWP or any other party from claiming a vested right to divert waters once it becomes clear that such diversions harm the interests protected by the public trust. The corollary rule which evolved in tideland and lakeshore cases barring conveyance of rights free of the trust except to serve trust purposes cannot, however, apply without modification to flowing waters. The prosperity and habitability of much of this state requires the diversion of great quantities of water from its streams for purposes unconnected to any navigation, commerce, fishing, recreation, or ecological use relating to the source stream. The state must have the power to grant non-vested usufructuary rights to appropriate water even if diversions harm public trust uses. Approval of such diversion without considering public trust values, however, may result in needless destruction of those values. Accordingly, we believe that before state courts and agencies approve water diversions they should consider the effect of such diversions upon interests protected by the public trust, and attempt, so far as feasible, to avoid or minimize any harm to those interests.

The water rights enjoyed by DWP were granted, the diversion was commenced, and has continued to the present without any consideration of the impact upon the public trust. An objective study and reconsideration of the water rights in the Mono Basin is long overdue. The water law of California—which we conceive to be an integration including both the public trust doctrine and the board administered appropriative rights system—permits such a reconsideration; the values underlying that integration require it.

...

1. Background and History of the Mono Lake Litigation.

DWP supplies water to the City of Los Angeles. Early in this century, it became clear that the city's anticipated needs would exceed the water available from local sources, and so in 1913 the city constructed an aqueduct to carry water from the Owens River 233 miles over the Antelope-Mojave plateau into the coastal plain and thirsty city.

The city's attempt to acquire rights to water needed by local farmers met with fierce, and at times violent, opposition. . . . But when the "Owens Valley War" was over, virtually all the waters of the Owens River and its tributaries flowed south to Los Angeles. Owens Lake was transformed into an alkali flat.

The city's rapid expansion soon strained this new supply, too, and prompted a search for water from other regions. The Mono Basin was a predictable object of this extension, since it lay within 50 miles of the natural origin of Owens River, and thus could easily be integrated into the existing aqueduct system.

After purchasing the riparian rights incident to Lee Vining, Walker, Parker and Rush Creeks, as well as the riparian rights pertaining to Mono Lake, the city applied to the Water Board in 1940 for permits to appropriate the waters of the four tributaries. At hearings before the board, various interested individuals protested that the city's proposed appropriations would lower the surface level of Mono Lake and thereby impair its commercial, recreational and scenic uses.

The board's primary authority to reject that application lay in a 1921 amendment to the Water Commission Act of 1913, which authorized the board to reject an application "when in its judgment the proposed appropriation would not best conserve the public interest." . . . The 1921 enactment, however, also "declared to be the established policy of this state that the use of water for domestic purposes is the highest use of water" . . . and directed the Water Board to be guided by this declaration of policy. Since DWP sought water for domestic use, the board concluded that it had to grant the application notwithstanding the harm to public trust uses of Mono Lake.

The board's decision states "[i]t is indeed unfortunate that the City's proposed development will result in decreasing the aesthetic advantages of Mono Basin *but there is apparently nothing that this office can do to prevent it.* The use to which the City proposes to put the water under its Applications . . . is defined by the Water Commission Act as the highest to which water may be applied and to make available unappropriated water for this use the City has, by the condemnation proceedings described above, acquired the littoral and riparian rights on Mono Lake and its tributaries south of Mill Creek. This office therefore has *no alternative but to dismiss all protests based upon the possible lowering of the water level in Mono Lake and the effect that the diversion of water from these streams may have upon the aesthetic and recreational value of the Basin.*" (Div. Wat. Resources Dec. 7053, 7055, 8042 & 8043 (Apr. 11, 1940), at p. 26, italics added.)

By April of 1941, the city had completed the extension of its aqueduct system into the Mono Basin by construction of certain conduits, reservoirs at Grant and Crowley Lakes, and the Mono Craters Tunnel from the Mono Basin to the Owens River. In the 1950's, the city constructed hydroelectric power plants along the system to generate electricity from the energy of the appropriated water as it flowed downhill into the Owens Valley. Between 1940 and 1970, the city diverted an average of 57,067 acre-feet of water per year from the Mono Basin. The impact of these diversions on Mono Lake was clear and immediate: the lake's surface level receded at an average of 1.1 feet per year.

In June of 1970, the city completed a second aqueduct designed to increase the total flow into the aqueduct by 50 percent. Between 1970 and 1980, the city diverted an average of 99,580 acre-feet per year from the Mono Basin. By October of 1979, the lake had shrunk from its prediversion area of 85 square miles to an area of 60.3 square miles. Its surface level had dropped to 6,373 feet above sea level, 43 feet below the prediversion level.

No party seriously disputes the facts set forth above. However, the parties hotly dispute the projected effects of future diversions on the lake itself, as well as the indirect effects of past, present and future diversions on the Mono Basin environment.

DWP expects that its future diversions of about 100,000 acre-feet per year will lower the lake's surface level another 43 feet and reduce its surface area by about 22 square miles over the next 80 to 100 years, at which point the lake will gradually approach environmental equilibrium (the point at which inflow from precipitation, groundwater and nondiverted tributaries equals outflow by evaporation and other means). At this point, according to DWP, the lake will stabilize at a level 6,330 feet above the sea's, with a surface area of approximately 38 square miles. Thus, by DWP's own estimates, unabated diversions will ultimately produce a lake that is about 56 percent smaller on the surface and 42 percent shallower than its natural size.

Plaintiffs consider these projections unrealistically optimistic. They allege that, 50 years hence, the lake will be at least 50 feet shallower than it now is, and hold less than 20 percent of its natural volume. Further, plaintiffs fear that "the lake will not stabilize at this level," but "may continue to reduce in size until it is dried up." Moreover, unlike DWP, plaintiffs believe that the lake's gradual recession indirectly causes a host of adverse environmental impacts. Many of these alleged impacts are related to an increase in the lake's salinity, caused by the decrease in its water volume.

As noted above, Mono Lake has no outlets. The lake loses water only by evaporation and seepage. Natural salts do not evaporate with water, but are left behind. Prior to commencement of the DWP diversions, this naturally rising salinity was balanced by a constant and substantial supply of fresh water from the tributaries. Now, however, DWP diverts most of the fresh water inflow. The resultant imbalance between inflow and outflow not only diminishes the lake's size, but also drastically increases its salinity.

Plaintiffs predict that the lake's steadily increasing salinity, if unchecked, will wreck havoc throughout the local food chain. . . .

DWP's diversions also present several threats to the millions of local and migratory birds using the lake. First, since many species of birds feed on the lake's brine shrimp, any reduction in shrimp population allegedly caused by rising salinity endangers a major avian food source. . . .

The California gull is especially endangered, both by the increase in salinity and by loss of nesting sites. Ninety-five percent of this state's gull population and 25 percent of the total species population nests at the lake. (Task Force Report at p. 21.) Most of the gulls nest on islands in the lake. As the lake recedes, land between the shore and some of the islands has been exposed, offering such predators as the coyote easy access to the gull nests and chicks. In 1979, coyotes reached Negrit Island, once the most popular nesting site, and the number of gull nests at the lake declined sharply. In 1981, 95 percent of the hatched chicks did not survive to maturity. Plaintiffs blame this decline and alarming mortality rate on the predator access created by the land bridges; DWP suggests numerous other causes, such as increased ambient temperatures and human activities, and claims that the joining of some islands with the mainland is offset by the emergence of new islands due to the lake's recession.

Plaintiffs allege that DWP's diversions adversely affect the human species and its activities as well. First, as the lake recedes, it has exposed more than 18,000 acres of lake bed composed of very fine silt which, once dry, easily becomes airborne in winds. This silt contains a high concentration of alkali and other minerals that irritate the mucous membranes and respiratory systems of human and other animals. (See Task Force Report at p. 22.) While the precise extent of this threat to the public health has yet to be determined, such threat as exists can be expected to increase with the exposure of additional lake bed. DWP, however, claims that its diversions neither affect the air quality in Mono Basin nor present a hazard to human health.

Furthermore, the lake's recession obviously diminishes its value as an economic, recreational, and scenic resource. Of course, there will be less lake to use and enjoy. The declining shrimp hatch depresses a local shrimping industry. The rings of dry lake bed are difficult to traverse on foot, and thus impair human access to the lake, and reduce the lake's substantial scenic value. Mono Lake has long been treasured as a unique scenic, recreational and scientific resource . . . but continued diversions threaten to turn it into a desert wasteland like the dry bed of Owens Lake.

[Here the court reviews the procedural history of the case to date and explains that it is reviewing the summary judgment of the Alpine County Superior Court.]

2. The Public Trust Doctrine in California.

"By the law of nature these things are common to mankind—the air, running water, the sea and consequently the shores of the sea." (Institutes of Justinian 2.1.1.) From this origin in Roman law, the English common law evolved the concept of the public trust, under which the sovereign owns "all of its navigable waterways and the lands lying beneath them 'as trustee of a public trust for the benefit of the people.' (*Colberg, Inc. v. State of California ex rel Dept. Pub Works* (1967) 67 Cal.2d 408, 416, 62 Cal.Rptr. 401, 432 P.2d 3.) The State of California acquired title as trustee to such lands and waterways upon its admission to the union (*City of Berkeley v. Superior Court* (1980) 26 Cal.3d 515, 521, 162 Cal.Rptr. 327, 606 P.2d 362 and cases there cited); from the earliest days . . . its judicial decisions have recognized and enforced the trust obligation.

Three aspects of the public trust doctrine require consideration in this opinion: the purpose of the trust; the scope of the trust, particularly as it applies to the non-navigable tributaries of a navigable lake; and the powers and duties of the state as trustee of the public trust. We discuss these questions in the order listed.

(a) The Purpose of the Public Trust.

The objective of the public trust has evolved in tandem with the changing public perception of the values and uses of waterways. As we observed in *Marks v. Whitney*, supra, 6 Cal.3d 251, 98 Cal.Rptr. 790, 491 P.2d 374, "[p]ublic trust easements [were] traditionally defined in terms of navigation, commerce and fisheries. They have been held to include the right to fish, hunt, bathe, swim, to use for boating and general recreation purposes the navigable waters of the state, and to use the bottom of the navigable waters for anchoring, standing, or other purposes" . . . We went on, however, to hold that the traditional triad of uses—navigation, commerce and fishing—did not limit the public interest in the trust res. In language of special importance to the present setting, we stated that "[t]he public uses to which tidelands are subject are sufficiently flexible to encompass changing public needs. In administering the trust the state is not burdened with an outmoded classification favoring one mode of utilization over another. [Citation.] There is a growing public recognition that one of the most important public uses of the tidelands—a use encompassed within the tidelands trust—is the preservation of those lands in their natural state, so that they may serve as ecological units for scientific study, as open space, and as environments which provide food and habitat for birds and marine life, and which favorably affect the scenery and climate of the area."

Mono Lake is a navigable waterway. . . . It supports a small local industry which harvests brine shrimp for sale as fish food, which endeavor probably qualifies the lake as a "fishery" under the traditional public trust cases. The principal values plaintiffs seek to protect, however, are recreational and ecological—the scenic views of the lake and its shore, the purity of the air, and the use of the lake for nesting and feeding by birds. . . . [I]t is clear that protection of these values is among the purposes of the public trust.

(b) The Scope of the Public Trust.

Early English decisions generally assumed the public trust was limited to tidal waters and the lands exposed and covered by the daily tides. . . . [M]any American decisions, including the leading California cases, also concern tidelands. It is, however, well settled in the United States generally and in California that the public trust is not limited by the reach of the tides, but encompasses all navigable lakes and streams.

Mono Lake is, as we have said, a navigable waterway. The beds, shores and waters of the lake are without question protected by the public trust. The streams diverted by DWP, however, are not themselves navigable. Accordingly, we must address in this case a question not discussed in any recent public trust case—whether the public trust limits conduct affecting nonnavigable tributaries to navigable waterways.

This question was considered in two venerable California decisions. The first, *People v. Gold Run D. & M. Co.* (1884) 66 Cal. 138, 4 P. 1152, is one of the epochal decisions of California history, a signpost which marked the transition from a mining economy to one predominantly commercial and agricultural. The Gold Run Ditch and Mining Company and other mining operators used huge water cannon to wash gold-bearing gravel from hillsides—in the process they dumped 600,000 cubic yards of sand and gravel annually into the north fork of the American River. The debris, washed downstream, raised the beds of the American and Sacramento Rivers, impairing navigation, polluting the waters, and creating the danger that in time of flood the rivers would turn from their channels and inundate nearby lands.

Although recognizing that its decision might destroy the remains of the state's gold mining industry, the court affirmed an injunction barring the dumping. The opinion stressed the harm to the navigability of the Sacramento River, "a great public highway in which the people of the State have paramount and controlling rights." Defendant's dumping, the court said, was "an unauthorized invasion of the rights of the public to its navigation. Rejecting the argument that dumping was sanctioned by custom and legislative acquiescence, the opinion asserted that "the rights of the people in the navigable rivers of the State are paramount and controlling. The State holds the absolute right to all navigable waters and the soils under them . . . . The soil she holds as trustee of a public trust for the benefit of the people; and she may, by her legislature, grant it to an individual; but she cannot grant the rights of the people to the use of the navigable waters flowing over it. . . ."

In the second decision, *People v. Russ* (1901) 132 Cal. 102, 64 P. 111, the defendant erected dams on sloughs which adjoined a navigable river. Finding the sloughs nonnavigable, the trial court gave judgment for defendant. We reversed, directing the trial court to make a finding as to the effect of the dams on the navigability of the river. "Directly diverting waters in material quantities from a navigable stream may be enjoined as a public nuisance. Neither may the waters of a navigable stream be diverted in substantial quantities by drawing from its tributaries. . . . If the dams upon these sloughs result in the obstruction of Salt River as a navigable stream, they constitute a public nuisance."

DWP points out that the Gold Run decision did not involve diversion of water, and that in *Russ* there had been no finding of impairment to navigation. But the principles recognized by those decisions apply fully to a case in which diversions from a nonnavigable tributary impair the public trust in a downstream river or lake. "If the public trust doctrine applies to constrain fills which destroy navigation and other public trust uses in navigable waters, it should equally apply to constrain the extraction of water that destroys navigation and other public interests. Both actions result in the same damage to the public interest." (Johnson, Public Trust Protection for Stream Flows and Lake Levels (1980) 14 U.C.Davis L.Rev. 233, 257–258). . . .

We conclude that the public trust doctrine, as recognized and developed in California decisions, protects navigable waters from harm caused by diversion of nonnavigable tributaries.

(c) Duties and Powers of the State as Trustee.

In the following review of the authority and obligations of the state as administrator of the public trust, the dominant theme is the state's sovereign power and duty to exercise continued supervision over the trust. One consequence, of importance to this and many other cases, is that parties acquiring rights in trust property generally hold those rights subject to the trust, and can assert no vested right to use those rights in a manner harmful to the trust.

As we noted recently in *City of Berkeley v. Superior Court,* supra, 26 Cal.3d 515, 162 Cal.Rptr. 327, 606 P.2d 362, the decision of the *United States Supreme Court in Illinois Central Railroad Company v. Illinois,* supra, 146 U.S. 387, 13 S.Ct. 110, 36

L.Ed. 1018, "remains the primary authority even today, almost nine decades after it was decided." . . . The Illinois Legislature in 1886 had granted the railroad in fee simple 1,000 acres of submerged lands, virtually the entire Chicago waterfront. Four years later it sought to revoke that grant. The Supreme Court upheld the revocatory legislation. Its opinion explained that lands under navigable waters conveyed to private parties for wharves, docks, and other structures in furtherance of trust purposes could be granted free of the trust because the conveyance is consistent with the purpose of the trust. But the legislature, it held, did not have the power to convey the entire city waterfront free of trust, thus barring all future legislatures from protecting the public interest. The opinion declares that: A grant of all the lands under the navigable waters of a state has never been adjudged to be within the legislative power; and any attempted grant of the kind would be held, if not absolutely void on its face, as subject to revocation. The State can no more abdicate its trust over property in which the whole people are interested, like navigable waters and soils under them, . . . than it can abdicate its police powers in the administration of government and the preservation of the peace. In the administration of government the use of such powers may for a limited period be delegated to a municipality or other body, but there always remains with the State the right to revoke those powers and exercise them in a more direct manner, and one more conformable to its wishes. So with trusts connected with public property, or property of a special character, like lands under navigable waters, they cannot be placed entirely beyond the direction and control of the State." (146 U.S. pp. 453–454, 13 S.Ct. p. 118.)

. . .

The California Supreme Court endorsed the Illinois Central principles in *People v. California Fish Co.* (1913) 166 Cal. 576, 138 P. 79. California Fish concerned title to about 80,000 acres of tidelands conveyed by state commissioners pursuant to statutory authorization. The court first set out principles to govern the interpretation of statutes conveying that property: "[S]tatutes purporting to authorize an abandonment of . . . public use will be carefully scanned to ascertain whether or not such was the legislative intention, and that intent must be clearly expressed or necessarily implied. It will not be implied if any other inference is reasonably possible. And if any interpretation of the statute is reasonably possible which would not involve a destruction of the public use or an intention to terminate it in violation of the trust, the courts will give the statute such interpretation." (Id., at p. 597, 138 P. 79.) Applying these principles, the court held that because the statute in question and the grants pursuant thereto were not made for trust purposes, the grantees did not acquire absolute title; instead, the grantees "own the soil, subject to the easement of the public for the public uses of navigation and commerce, and to the right of the state, as administrator and controller of these public uses and the public trust therefor, to enter upon and possess the same for the preservation and advancement of the public uses and to make such changes and improvements as may be deemed advisable for those purposes." (Id., at pp. 598–599, 138 P. 79.)

Finally, rejecting the claim of the tideland purchasers for compensation, the court stated they did not lose title, but retained it subject to the public trust. . . . While the state may not retake the absolute title without compensation (p. 599, 138 P. 79), it may without such payment erect improvements to further navigation and take other actions to promote the public trust.

[Here the court examines two other earlier California cases.]

. . .

In summary, the foregoing cases amply demonstrate the continuing power of the state as administrator of the public trust, a power which extends to the revocation of previously granted rights or to the enforcement of the trust against lands long thought free of the trust. . . . Except for those rare instances in which a grantee may acquire a right to use former trust property free of trust restrictions, the grantee holds subject to the trust, and while he may assert a vested right to the servient estate (the right of use subject to the trust) and to any improvements he erects, he can claim no vested right to bar recognition of the trust or state action to carry out its purposes.

Since the public trust doctrine does not prevent the state from choosing between trust uses . . . the Attorney General of California, seeking to maximize state power under the trust, argues for a broad concept of trust uses. In his view, "trust uses" encompass all public uses, so that in practical effect the doctrine would impose no restrictions on the state's ability to allocate trust property. We know of no authority which supports this view of the public trust, except perhaps the dissenting opinion in *Illinois Central R. Co. v. Illinois,* supra, 146 U.S. 387, 13 S.Ct. 110, 36 L.Ed. 1018. . . .

Thus, the public trust is more than an affirmation of state power to use public property for public purposes. It is an affirmation of the duty of the state to protect the peoples' common heritage of streams, lakes, marshlands and tidelands, surrendering that right of protection only in rare cases when the abandonment of that right is consistent with the purposes of the trust.

3. The California Water Rights System.

"It is laid down by our law writers, that the right of property in water is usufructuary and consists not so much of the fluid itself as the advantage of its use." (*Eddy v. Simpson* (1853) 3 Cal. 249, 252.) Hence, the cases do not speak of the ownership of water, but only of the right to its use. . . . Accordingly, Water Code section 102 provides that "[a]ll water within the State is the property of the people of the State, but the right to the use of water may be acquired by appropriation in the manner provided by law."

Our recent decision in *People v. Shirokow* (1980) 26 Cal.3d 301, 162 Cal.Rptr. 30, 605 P.2d 859, described the early history of the appropriative water rights system in California. We explained that "California operates under the so-called dual system of water rights which recognizes both the appropriation and the riparian doctrines. (Hutchins, The California Law of Water Rights, supra, at pp. 40, 55–67.) The riparian doctrine confers upon the owner of land contiguous to a water-course the right to the reasonable and beneficial use of water on his land. The ap-propriation doctrine contemplates the diversion of water and applies to 'any tak-ing of water for other than riparian or overlying uses.' (*City of Pasadena v. City of Alhambra* (1949) 33 Cal.2d 908, 925 [207 P.2d 17], and cases there cited.) . . .

. . .

"Common law appropriation originated in the gold rush days when miners di-verted water necessary to work their placer mining claims. The miners adopted among themselves the priority rule of 'first in time, first in right,' and California courts looked to principles of equity and of real property law to adjudicate con-flicting claims. [Citations.] Thus it was initially the law in this state that a person could appropriate water merely by diverting it and putting it to use.

"The first appropriation statute was enacted in 1872 and provided for initiation of the appropriative right by the posting and recordation of notice. (Civ.Code 1411422.) The nonstatutory method retained its vitality and appropriative rights were acquired by following either procedure. [Citation.]

"Both methods were superseded by the 1913 enactment of the Water Commission Act, which created a Water Commission and provided a procedure for the appropriation of water for useful and beneficial purposes. The main pur-pose of the act was 'to provide an orderly method for the appropriation of [un-appropriated] waters.' (*Temescal Water Co. v. Dept of Public Works* (1955) 44 Cal.2d 90, 95 [280 P.2d 1]). . . . By amendment in 1923, the statutory procedure became the exclusive means of acquiring appropriative rights. . . . The provisions of the Water Commission Act, as amended from time to time, have been codified in Water Code, divisions 1 and 2. . . ."

The role of the Water Board under the 1913 act, as Shirokow indicated, was a very limited one. The only water subject to appropriation under the act was water which was not then being applied to useful and beneficial purposes, and was not otherwise appropriated. . . . Thus, appropriative rights acquired under the act were inferior to pre-existing rights such as riparian rights, pueblo rights, and prior prescriptive appropriations. . . .

. . .

In 1926, however, a decision of this court led to a constitutional amendment which radically altered water law in California and led to an expansion of the powers of the board. In *Herminghaus v. South California Edison Co.* (1926) 200 Cal. 81, 252 P. 607, we held not only that riparian rights took priority over appro-priations authorized by the Water Board, a point which had always been clear, but that as between the riparian and the appropriator, the former's use of water was not limited by the doctrine of reasonable use. . . . That decision led to a constitutional amendment which abolished the right of a riparian to devote water to unreasonable uses, and established the doctrine of reasonable use as an overriding feature of California water law. . . .

Article X, section 2 (enacted in 1928 as art. XIV, § 3) reads in pertinent part as follows: "It is hereby declared that because of the conditions prevailing in this State the general welfare requires that the water resources of the State be put to beneficial use to the fullest extent of which they are capable, and that the waste or unreasonable use or unreasonable method of use of water be prevented, and that the conservation of such waters is to be exercised with a view to the reasonable and beneficial use thereof in the interest of the people and for the public welfare. The right to water or to the use or flow of water in or from any natural stream or water course in this State is and shall be limited to such water as shall be reasonably required for the beneficial use to be served, and such right does not and shall not extend to the waste or unreasonable use or unreasonable method of use or unreasonable method of diversion of water. . . . This section shall be self-executing, and the Legislature may also enact laws in the furtherance of the policy in this section contained."

This amendment does more than merely overturn Herminghaus—it establishes state water policy. All uses of water, including public trust uses, must now conform to the standard of reasonable use. . . .

The 1928 amendment did not declare whether the in-stream uses protected by the public trust could be considered reasonable and beneficial uses. In a 1936 case involving Mono Lake, however, the court squarely rejected DWP's argument that use of stream water to maintain the lake's scenic and recreational values violated the constitutional provision barring unreasonable uses. . . . The point is now settled by statute, Water Code section 1243 providing that "[t]he use of water for recreation and preservation and enhancement of fish and wildlife resources is a beneficial use of water."

The 1928 amendment itself did not expand the authority of the Water Board. The board remained, under controlling judicial decisions, a ministerial body with the limited task of determining priorities between claimants seeking to appropriate unclaimed water. More recent statutory and judicial developments, however, have greatly enhanced the power of the Water Board to oversee the reasonable use of water and, in the process, made clear its authority to weigh and protect public trust values.

In 1955, the Legislature declared that in acting on appropriative applications, "the board shall consider the relative benefit to be derived from (1) all beneficial uses of the water concerned including, but not limited to, use for domestic, irrigation, municipal, industrial, preservation and enhancement of fish and wildlife, recreational, mining and power purposes . . . . The board may subject such appropriations to such terms and conditions as in its judgment will best develop, conserve, and utilize in the public interest, the water sought to be appropriated." (Wat.Code, § 1257.) In 1959 it stated that "[t]he use of water for recreation and preservation and enhancement of fish and wildlife resources is a beneficial use of water." (Wat.Code, § 1243.) Finally in 1969 the Legislature instructed that "[i]n determining the amount of water available for appropriation, the board shall take into account, whenever it is in the public interest, the amounts of water needed to remain in the source for protection of beneficial uses." (Wat.Code, § 1243.5.)

. . .

Thus, the function of the Water Board has steadily evolved from the narrow role of deciding priorities between competing appropriators to the charge of comprehensive planning and allocation of waters. This change necessarily affects the board's responsibility with respect to the public trust. The board of limited powers of 1913 had neither the power nor duty to consider interests protected by the public trust; the present board, in undertaking planning and allocation of water resources, is required by statute to take those interests into account.

4. The Relationship Between the Public Trust Doctrine and the California Water Rights System.

As we have seen, the public trust doctrine and the appropriative water rights system administered by the Water Board developed independently of each other. Each developed comprehensive rules and principles which, if applied to the full extent of their scope, would occupy the field of allocation of stream waters to the exclusion of any competing system of legal thought. Plaintiffs, for example, argues [sic] that the public trust is antecedent to and thus limits all appropriative water rights, an argument which implies that most appropriative water rights in California were acquired and are presently being used unlawfully. Defendant DWP, on the other hand, argues that the public trust doctrine as to stream waters has been "subsumed" into the appropriative water rights system and, absorbed by that body of law, quietly disappeared; according to DWP, the recipient of a board license enjoys a vested right in perpetuity to take water without concern for the consequences to the trust.

We are unable to accept either position. In our opinion, both the public trust doctrine and the water rights system embody important precepts which make the law more responsive to the diverse needs and interests involved in the planning and allocation of water resources. To embrace one system of thought and reject the other would lead to an unbalanced structure, one which would either decry as a breach of trust appropriations essential to the economic development of this state, or deny any duty to protect or even consider the values promoted by the public trust. Therefore, seeking an accommodation which will make use of the pertinent principles of both the public trust doctrine and the appropriative water rights system, and drawing upon the history of the public trust and the water rights system, the body of judicial precedent, and the views of expert commentators, we reach the following conclusions:

a. The state as sovereign retains continuing supervisory control over its navigable waters and the lands beneath those waters. This principle, fundamental to the
concept of the public trust, applies to rights in flowing waters as well as to rights
in tidelands and lakeshores; it prevents any party from acquiring a vested right to
appropriate water in a manner harmful to the interests protected by the public
trust.

b. As a matter of current and historical necessity, the Legislature, acting directly
or through an authorized agency such as the Water Board, has the power to grant
usufructuary licenses that will permit an appropriator to take water from flowing
streams and use that water in a distant part of the state, even though this taking
does not promote, and may unavoidably harm, the trust uses at the source stream.
The population and economy of this state depend upon the appropriation of vast
quantities of water for uses unrelated to in-stream trust values. California's
Constitution (see art. X, § 2), its statutes (see Wat.Code, §§ 100, 104), decisions
(see, e.g., *Waterford I. Dist. v. Turlock* 1. Dist. (1920) 50 Cal.App. 213, 220, 194 P.
757), and commentators (e.g., Hutchins, The Cal. Law of Water Rights, op. cit.,
supra, p. 11) all emphasize the need to make efficient use of California's limited
water resources: all recognize, at least implicitly, that efficient use requires diverting water from in-stream uses. Now that the economy and population centers of
this state have developed in reliance upon appropriated water, it would be disin-
genuous to hold that such appropriations are and have always been improper to
the extent that they harm public trust uses, and can be justified only upon theories of reliance or estoppel.

c. The state has an affirmative duty to take the public trust into account in the
planning and allocation of water resources, and to protect public trust uses whenever feasible. Just as the history of this state shows that appropriation may be necessary for efficient use of water despite unavoidable harm to public trust values, it
demonstrates that an appropriative water rights system administered without
consideration of the public trust may cause unnecessary and unjustified harm to
trust interests. . . . As a matter of practical necessity the state may have to approve
appropriations despite foreseeable harm to public trust uses. In so doing, however,
the state must bear in mind its duty as trustee to consider the effect of the taking
on the public trust (see *United Plainsmen v. N.D. State Water Con. Commission*
(N.D. 1976) 247 N.W.2d 457, 462–463), and to preserve, so far as consistent with
the public interest, the uses protected by the trust.

Once the state has approved an appropriation, the public trust imposes a duty
of continuing supervision over the taking and use of the appropriated water. In
exercising its sovereign power to allocate water resources in the public interest, the
state is not confined by past allocation decisions which may be incorrect in light
of current knowledge or inconsistent with current needs.

The state accordingly has the power to reconsider allocation decisions even
though those decisions were made after due consideration of their effect on the
public trust. The case for reconsidering a particular decision, however, is even

stronger when that decision failed to weigh and consider public trust uses. In the case before us, the salient fact is that no responsible body has ever determined the impact of diverting the entire flow of the Mono Lake tributaries into the Los Angeles Aqueduct. This is not a case in which the Legislature, the Water Board, or any judicial body has determined that the needs of Los Angeles outweigh the needs of the Mono Basin, that the benefit gained is worth the price. Neither has any responsible body determined whether some lesser taking would better balance the diverse interests. Instead, DWP acquired rights to the entire flow in 1940 from a water board which believed it lacked both the power and the duty to protect the Mono Lake environment, and continues to exercise those rights in apparent disregard for the resulting damage to the scenery, ecology, and human uses of Mono Lake.

It is clear that some responsible body ought to reconsider the allocation of the waters of the Mono Basin. No vested rights bar such reconsideration. We recognize the substantial concerns voiced by Los Angeles—the city's need for water, its reliance upon the 1940 board decision, the cost both in terms of money and environmental impact of obtaining water elsewhere. Such concerns must enter into any allocation decision. We hold only that they do not preclude a reconsideration and reallocation which also takes into account the impact of water diversion on the Mono Lake environment.

...

6. Conclusion.

This has been a long and involved answer to the two questions posed by the federal district court. In summarizing our opinion, we will essay a shorter version of our response.

The federal court inquired first of the interrelationship between the public trust doctrine and the California water rights system, asking whether the "public trust doctrine in this context [is] subsumed in the California water rights system, or . . . function[s] independently of that system? Our answer is "Neither." The public trust doctrine and the appropriative water rights system are parts of an integrated system of water law. The public trust doctrine serves the function in that integrated system of preserving the continuing sovereign power of the state to protect public trust uses, a power which precludes anyone from acquiring a vested right to harm the public trust, and imposes a continuing duty on the state to take such uses into account in allocating water resources.

Restating its question, the federal court stated: "[C]an the plaintiffs challenge the Department's permits and licenses by arguing that those permits and licenses are limited by the public trust doctrine, or must the plaintiffs . . . [argue] that the water diversions and uses authorized thereunder are not 'reasonable or beneficial' as required under the California water rights system?" We reply that plaintiffs can rely on the public trust doctrine in seeking reconsideration of the allocation of the waters of the Mono Basin.

...

This opinion is but one step in the eventual resolution of the Mono Lake controversy. We do not dictate any particular allocation of water. Our objective is to resolve a legal conundrum in which two competing systems of thought—the public trust doctrine and the appropriative water rights system—existed independently of each other, espousing principles which seemingly suggested opposite results. We hope by integrating these two doctrines to clear away the legal barriers which have so far prevented either the Water Board or the courts from taking a new and objective look at the water resources of the Mono Basin. The human and environmental uses of Mono Lake—uses protected by the public trust doctrine—deserve to be taken into account. Such uses should not be destroyed because the state mistakenly thought itself powerless to protect them.

Let a peremptory writ of mandate issue commanding the Superior Court of Alpine County to vacate its judgment in this action and to enter a new judgment consistent with the views stated in this opinion.

[Four judges concurred in this opinion].

Questions, Materials, and Suggestions for Further Study

National Audubon Society v. Department of Water and Power of the City of Los Angeles

Despite what may appear to be the inconclusive nature of the *Audubon* decision, Mono Lake has been protected because of it. One problem with the *Audubon* case may simply arise from the difficulty of illustrating and dealing with a major environmental ideal such as the legal concept of public trust, an extremely abstract notion. As Bernard Barber has noted in *The Logic and Limits of Trust* (New Brunswick, N.J.: Rutgers University Press, 1983), the notion of trust involves faith in the fulfillment of the natural and moral order. Implicit in the idea of holding lands such as tidal wetlands in "public trust" are at least four significant principles; first, that such wetlands have natural functions that should be protected for that reason alone. The modern notion of nature having natural purposes has been discussed recently by many authors. See, for example, Erazim Kohak, *The Embers and the Stars: A Philosophical Inquiry into the Moral Sense of Nature* (Chicago: University of Chicago Press, 1984) and Etienne Gilson, *From Aristotle to Darwin and Back Again* (South Bend, Ind.: Notre Dame University Press, 1984). A second notion implicit in the public trust doctrine is that nature's bounty is to be protected for future generations. Our obligation to future generations is explored in R. I. Sikora and Brian Barry, eds., *Obligations to Future Generations* (Philadelphia: Temple University Press, 1978).

The third principle in the public trust concept that must be recognized is that the resource must be accessible to the public. This notion may appear to conflict with the recent discovery that some common areas—the air, water, and range lands—have been abused precisely because of their open accessibility. But accessibility does not necessarily have to mean overuse: Regulations can be used to preserve these resources while permitting some form of public use. These regulations could, of course, be implemented through the mechanism of state ownership such as we now do through our state park systems, or, as *National Audubon* illustrates, a new kind of ownership of the commons may be envisioned with specific attention to environmental protection. For a discussion of the management of the commons, see Garrett Hardin and John Baden, eds., *Managing the Commons* (Eugene: University of Oregon ERIC Clearinghouse on Education Management, 1977); U.S. National Research Council, *et al.*, *Common Property Resource Management* (Washington, D.C.: National Academy Press, 1986).

Finally, the fourth principle: The public trust concept demands environmental leadership—the notion of trustees of the environment require that there be trustees, and trustees need to be appointed by someone or something. Even if we assume, as many do not, that our current notion of environmentalism should govern the actions of these trustees, the questions of the proper qualifications and of the role of such environmental leaders remain. Are the judges of the courts such leaders? Are environmental lawyers bringing action on behalf of threatened resources for environmental groups the proper trustees? Can public environmental managers be trustees? For a recent discussion of environmental leadership, see Lester W. Milbrath's *Environmentalists: Vanguard for a New Society* (Albany: State University of New York Press, 1984).

Make no mistake: The notion of land held in public trust demands significant changes in our notion of private property, not something our society will undertake lightly. This issue has been discussed in John Clough's *Property: Illusions of Ownership* (Portland, Ore.: Gann, 1984). Despite its vagueness, the Public Trust Doctrine has continued to have a lively and important legal history, especially as applied to coastal areas (see Jack Archer, Donald Connors, Kenneth Laurence, Sarah Columbia, and Robert Bowen, *The Public Trust Doctrine and the Management of America's Coasts* (Boston: University of Massachusetts Press, 1994).

13

Environmental Ideals

Access to Court

Case Study:
Sierra Club v. Morton

Let us assume that you and a friend own houses approximately 3 miles apart and that a cement plant is built between you. Your friend's house is downwind of the plant and continually receives ash, smoke, dust, and vibration. Because of the prevailing winds you, on the contrary, have no dust, no smoke, and no inconvenience. You are absolutely certain, however, that the plant is harming both your friend's health and the health of her children. Your neighbor does not mind the situation. When the plant first began operations she read the *Boomer* decision, brought suit in state court, settled her case before trial for a lump sum that she has invested in tax-free municipal bonds, and stays on. However, you are convinced that the plant is harming her health and that of her children; you even have medical studies that substantiate your position.

What can you do? Very little, under our traditional notions of "standing to sue." Standing is the right of an individual to seek relief in court. The very first requirement faced by a plaintiff seeking legal remedies is that he or she must be seeking relief from something recognized by the court as an injury to the plaintiff's interests. The court has to have some reason to listen. You and I could not go to court to prevent another person from trespassing on our neighbor's land unless we could show that it harmed our interests as well as the neighbor's. The neighbor, by contrast, would automatically have standing in this situation because it is his land.

The traditional requirement for standing—that the plaintiff show some specific injury—made many environmentalists' suits impossible. Certainly the plaintiffs in *Boomer* could claim an injury, as could the Justs and the plaintiff in *Alfaro*. But no

such clear-cut injury exists in *Ethyl*. The question of whether a coalition of loosely related organizations was enough of a "person" to suffer an injury has itself been an
issue in environmental cases. In *Tennessee Valley Authority v. Hill*, 437 U.S. 153 (1978),
the famous "snail darter" case, the plaintiffs were entitled to standing because it was
granted them by the statute: The legislature may grant standing merely by stating that
certain people (in this case citizens) can bring an action in court to enforce or object
to the enforcement of a statute. The Justs received standing from both sources—from
the damage they suffered when the county allegedly "took" their property value as
well as from the statute, which gave standing to an aggrieved party to sue.

For many years, environmental or aesthetic harms were simply not recognized as
the sort of harms that could be remedied in court. But standing has undergone some
radical changes since 1980. The change began when the Supreme Court interpreted
Section 10 of the Administrative Procedures Act to allow a party to appeal a government agency decision upon two showings: first, that the agency action to which the
party was objecting caused it "injury in fact, economic or otherwise," and second, that
the injury the party claimed had been done to it was an injury to an interest "arguably
within the zone of interests to be protected or regulated" by the statute under which
the parties claimed protection (*Association of Data Processing Service Organizations v.
Camp*, 397 U.S. 150, 154 [1970]).

Since *Data Processing*, standing has undergone even more far-ranging changes.
Sierra Club v. Morton is important for two reasons. First, the Supreme Court accepted
without qualm that noneconomic injury could be seen as enough to justify or appeal
an agency decision:

> The complaint alleges that the development "would destroy or otherwise adversely affect
> the scenery, natural and historic objects and wildlife of the park and would impair the en-
> joyment of the park for future generations." We do not question that this type of harm
> may amount to an "injury in fact" sufficient to lay the basis for standing under §10 of the
> APA. Aesthetic and environmental well-being, like economic well-being, are important in-
> gredients of the quality of life in our society. (*Sierra Club v. Morton*, 405 U.S. 727, 734
> [1971])

Strictly speaking, the Sierra Club lost its case, however, because it neglected to allege that its individual members would be harmed by the development—that is, suffer an "injury in fact." The court left the club the option of amending its complaint to
include the allegation. The club did so and was right back in court.

But it is the second reason for *Sierra Club v. Morton*'s importance that makes the
case most interesting. The case is most widely known not for the majority opinion
but for the dissenting opinion by Justice William O. Douglas, which addresses wholly
new aspects to the standing issue. The legal system has always accepted the fact that
in some situations the literal requirements of standing simply cannot be required.
Parents, for example, need to be recognized so they can act on behalf of their minor
children. We must also recognize someone to speak for those who cannot speak for
themselves, such as the mentally incompetent. We do precisely the same for the legal

fictions we create, such as the corporation. The corporation is a legal "person" under our system, with rights and responsibilities like any other person. It can sue or be sued, and its agents can even carry on privileged discussions in its name with its attorneys.

The question addressed by Justice Douglas's dissent in *Sierra Club v. Morton* expands these fictions merely by including Nature. If we recognize corporations, why not forests? Why not simply decide that legal standing for a forest is another legal fiction, grant the forest standing, and allow or appoint some legally competent individuals or organizations to defend its legal rights.

The next step—deciding who gets to define and defend those rights—is the difficult part. The temptation of many environmentalists would be to let the Sierra Club, the Wilderness Society, or the Audubon Society decide when forests need protection and what form that protection should take. But what about the National Association of Manufacturers, the Teamsters Union, or the Building Trades Council? Surely they could mount a strong argument that the purpose of a forest is to be managed and harvested to better accommodate the citizens or consumers who need lumber to house their families.

SIERRA CLUB
v.
MORTON, SECRETARY OF THE INTERIOR, et al.

United States Supreme Court
April 19, 1972
[405 U.S. 727]

Mr. Justice STEWART delivered the opinion of the Court.

I.

The Mineral King Valley is an area of great natural beauty nestled in the Sierra Nevada Mountains in Tulare County, California, adjacent to Sequoia National Park. It has been part of the Sequoia National Forest since 1926, and is designated as a national game refuge by special Act of Congress. Though once the site of extensive mining activity, Mineral King is now used almost exclusively for recreational purposes. Its relative inaccessibility and lack of development have limited the number of visitors each year, and at the same time have preserved the valley's quality as a quasi-wilderness area largely uncluttered by the products of civilization.

The United States Forest Service . . . began in the late 1940's to give consideration to Mineral King as a potential site for recreational development. . . . [T]he

Forest Service published a prospectus in 1965, inviting bids from private developers for the construction and operation of a ski resort that would also serve as a
summer recreation area. The proposal of Walt Disney Enterprises Inc., was chosen . . . and Disney [prepared] a complete master plan for the resort.

The final Disney plan, approved by the Forest Service in January 1969 outlines
a $35 million complex of motels, restaurants, swimming pools, parking lots, and
other structures designed to accommodate 14,000 visitors daily. This complex is
to be constructed on 80 acres of the valley floor under a 30-year use permit from
the Forest Service. Other facilities, including ski lifts, ski trails, a cog-assisted rail-
way, and utility installations, are to be constructed on the mountain slopes and in
other parts of the valley under a revocable special use permit. To provide access to
the resort, the State of California proposes to construct a highway 20 miles in
length. A section of this road would traverse Sequoia National Park, as would a
proposed high-voltage power line needed to provide electricity for the resort.
Both the highway and the power line require the approval of the Department of
the Interior, which is entrusted with the preservation and maintenance of the national parks.

Representatives of the Sierra Club, who favor maintaining Mineral King largely
in its present state, followed the progress of recreational planning for the valley
with the close attention and increasing dismay. They unsuccessfully sought a public hearing on the proposed development in 1965, and in subsequent correspon-
dence with officials of the Forest Service and the Department of the Interior, they
expressed the Club's objections to Disney's plan as a whole and to particular features included in it. In June 1969 the Club filed the present suit in the United
States District Court for the Northern District of California, seeking a declaratory
judgment that various aspects of the proposed development contravene federal
laws and regulations governing the preservation of national parks, forests, and
game refuges, and also seeking preliminary and permanent injunctions restrain-
ing the federal officials involved from granting their approval or issuing permits
in connection with the Mineral King project. The petitioner Sierra Club sued as a
membership corporation with "a special interest in the conservation and the
sound maintenance of the national parks, game refuges and forests of the country," and invoked the judicial-review provisions of the Administrative Procedure
Act, 5 U.S.C. § 701 et seq.

. . .

II.

The first question presented is whether the Sierra Club has alleged facts that entitle it to obtain judicial review of the challenged action. Whether a party has a sufficient stake in an otherwise justiciable controversy to obtain judicial resolution of
that controversy is what has traditionally been referred to as the question of
standing to sue. Where the party does not rely on any specific statute authorizing

invocation of the judicial process, the question of standing depends upon whether the party has alleged such a "personal stake in the outcome of the controversy," *Baker v. Carr,* 369 U.S. 186, 204, as to ensure that "the dispute sought to be adjudicated will be presented in an adversary context and in a form historically viewed as capable of judicial resolution." *Flast v. Cohen,* 392 U.S. 83, 101. Where, however, Congress has authorized public officials to perform certain functions according to law, and has provided by statute for judicial review of those actions under certain circumstances, the inquiry as to standing must begin with a determination of whether the statute in question authorizes review at the behest of the plaintiff.

The Sierra Club relies upon § 10 of the Administrative Procedure Act (APA), 5 U.S.C. § 702, which provides:

> A person suffering legal wrong because of agency action, or adversely affected or aggrieved by agency action within the meaning of a relevant statute, is entitled to judicial review thereof.

Early decisions under this statute interpreted the language as adopting the various formulations of "legal interest" and "legal wrong" then prevailing as constitutional requirements of standing. But, in *Data Processing Service v. Camp,* 397 U.S. 150, and *Barlow v. Collins,* 397 U.S. 159, decided the same day, we held more broadly that persons had standing to obtain judicial review of federal agency action under § 10 of the APA where they had alleged that the challenged action had caused them "injury in fact," and where the alleged injury was to an interest "arguably within the zone of interests to be protected or regulated" by the statutes that the agencies were claimed to have violated.

...

[N]either *Data Processing* nor *Barlow* addressed itself to the question, which has arisen with increasing frequency in federal courts in recent years, as to what must be alleged by persons who claim injury of a noneconomic nature to interests that are widely shared. That question is presented in this case.

III.

The injury alleged by the Sierra Club will be incurred entirely by reason of the change in the uses to which Mineral King will be put, and the attendant change in the aesthetics and ecology of the area. Thus, in referring to the road to be built through Sequoia National Park, the complaint alleged that the development "would destroy or otherwise adversely affect the scenery, natural and historic objects and wildlife of the park and would impair the enjoyment of the park for future generations." We do not question that this type of harm may amount to an "injury in fact" sufficient to lay the bases for standing under §10 of the APA. Aesthetic and environmental well-being, like economic well-being, are important ingredients of the quality of life in our society, and the fact that particular environmental interests are shared by the many rather than the few does not make them less deserving of legal protection through the judicial process. But the "injury in fact" test requires more than an injury to a cognizable interest. It requires that the party seeking review be himself among the injured.

The impact of the proposed changes in the environment of Mineral King will not fall indiscriminately upon every citizen. The alleged injury will be felt directly only by those who use Mineral King and Sequoia National Park, and for whom the aesthetic and recreational values of the area will be lessened by the highway and ski resort. The Sierra Club failed to allege that it or its members would be affected in any of their activities or pastimes by the Disney development. Nowhere in the pleadings or affidavits did the Club state that its members use Mineral King for any purpose, much less that they use it in any way that would be significantly affected by the proposed actions of the respondents.

The Club apparently regarded any allegations of individualized injury as superfluous, on the theory that this was a "public" action involving questions as to the use of natural resources, and that the Club's longstanding concern with and expertise in such matters were sufficient to give it standing as a "representative of the public." This theory reflects a misunderstanding of our cases involving so-called "public actions" in the area of administrative law.

...

The trend of cases arising under the APA and other statutes authorizing judicial review of federal agency action has been toward recognizing that injuries other than economic harm are sufficient to bring a person within the meaning of the statutory language, and toward discarding the notion that an injury that is widely shared is ipso facto not an injury sufficient to provide the basis for judicial review. . . . But broadening the categories of injury that may be alleged in support of standing in a different matter from abandoning the requirement that the party seeking review must himself have suffered an injury.

Some courts have indicated a willingness to take this latter step by conferring standing upon organizations that have demonstrated "an organizational interest in the problem" of environmental or consumer protection. *Environmental Defense Fund v. Hardin,* 138 U.S. App. D. C. 391, 395, 428 F. 2d 1093, 1097. It is clear that an organization whose members are injured may represent those members in a proceeding for judicial review. See, e.g., *NAACP v. Button,* 371 U.S. 415, 428. But a mere "interest in a problem," no matter how longstanding the interest and no matter how qualified the organization is in evaluating the problem, is not sufficient by itself to render the organization "adversely affected" or "aggrieved" within the meaning of the APA. The Sierra Club is a large and long-established organization, with a historic commitment to the cause of protecting our Nation's natural heritage from man's depredations. But if a "special interest" in this subject were enough to entitle the Sierra Club to commence this litigation, there would appear to be no objective basis upon which to disallow a suit by any other bona fide "special interest" organization, however small or short-lived. And if any group with a bona fide "special interest" could initiate such litigation, it is difficult to perceive why any individual citizen with the same bona fide special interest would not also be entitled to do so.

The requirement that a party seeking review must allege facts showing that he is himself adversely affected does not insulate executive action from judicial review, nor does it prevent any public interests from being protected through the judicial process. It does serve as at least a rough attempt to put the decision as to whether review will be sought in the hands of those who have a direct stake in the outcome. That goal would be undermined were we to construe the APA to authorize judicial review at the behest of organizations or individuals who seek to do no more than vindicate their own value preferences through the judicial process. The principle that the Sierra Club would have us establish in this case would do just that.

As we conclude that the Court of Appeals was correct in its holding that the Sierra Club lacked standing to maintain this action, we do not reach any other questions presented in the petition, and we intimate no view on the merits of the complaint. The judgment is Affirmed.

MR. JUSTICE POWELL and MR. JUSTICE REHNQUIST
took no part in the consideration or decision of this case.

MR. JUSTICE DOUGLAS, dissenting.

I share the views of my Brother BLACKMUN and would reverse the judgment below.

The critical question of "standing" would be simplified and also put neatly in focus if we fashioned a federal rule that allowed environmental issues to be litigated before federal agencies or federal courts in the name of the inanimate object about to be despoiled, defaced, or invaded by roads and bulldozers and where injury is the subject of public outrage. Contemporary public concern for protecting nature's ecological equilibrium should lead to the conferral of standing upon environmental objects to sue for their own preservation. See Stone, Should Trees Have Standing?— Toward Legal Rights for Natural Objects, 45 S. Cal. L. Rev. 450 (1972). This suit would therefore be more properly labeled as Mineral King v. Morton.

Inanimate objects are sometimes parties in litigation. A ship has a legal personality, a fiction found useful for maritime purposes. The corporation sole—a creature of ecclesiastical law—is an acceptable adversary and large fortunes ride on its cases. The ordinary corporation is a "person" for purposes of the adjudicatory processes, whether it represents proprietary, spiritual, aesthetic, or charitable causes.

So it should be as respects valleys, alpine meadows, rivers, lakes, estuaries, beaches, ridges, groves of trees, swampland, or even air that feels the destructive pressures of modern technology and modern life. The river, for example, is the living symbol of all the life it sustains or nourishes—fish, aquatic insects, water ouzels, otter, fisher, deer, elk, bear, and all other animals, including man, who are dependent on it or who enjoy it for its sight, its sound, or its life. The river as plaintiff speaks for the ecological unit of life that is part of it. Those people who have a meaningful relation to that body of water—whether it be a fisherman, a canoeist, a zoologist, or a logger—must be able to speak for the values which the river represents and which are threatened with destruction.

I do not know Mineral King. I have never seen it nor traveled it, though I have seen articles describing its proposed "development." . . . The Sierra Club in its complaint alleges that "[o]ne of the principal purposes of the Sierra Club is to protect and conserve the national resources of the Sierra Nevada Mountains." The District Court held that this uncontested allegation made the Sierra Club "sufficiently aggrieved" to have "standing" to sue on behalf of Mineral King.

Mineral King is doubtless like other wonders of the Sierra Nevada such as Tuolumne Meadows and the John Muir Trail. Those who hike it, fish it, hunt it, camp in it, frequent it, or visit it merely to sit in solitude and wonderment are legitimate spokesmen for it, whether they may be few or many. Those who have that intimate relation with the inanimate object about to be injured, polluted, or otherwise despoiled are its legitimate spokesmen.

The Solicitor General, . . . takes a wholly different approach. He considers the problem in terms of "government by the Judiciary." With all respect, the problem is to make certain that the inanimate objects, which are the very core of America's beauty, have spokesmen before they are destroyed. It is, of course, true that most of them are under the control of a federal or state agency. The standards given those agencies are usually expressed in terms of the "public interest." Yet "public interest" has so many differing shades of meaning as to be quite meaningless on the environmental front.

[T]he pressures on agencies for favorable action one way or the other are enormous. The suggestion that Congress can stop action which is undesirable is true in theory; yet even Congress is too remote to give meaningful direction and its machinery is too ponderous to use very often. The federal agencies of which I speak are not venal or corrupt. But they are notoriously under the control of powerful interests who manipulate them through advisory committees, or friendly working relations, or who have that natural affinity with the agency which in time develops between the regulator and the regulated. As early as 1894, Attorney General Olney predicted that regulatory agencies might become "industry-minded." . . .

Years later a court of appeals observed, "the recurring question which has plagued public regulation of industry [is] whether the regulatory agency is unduly oriented toward the interests of the industry it is designed to regulate, rather than the public interest it is designed to protect."

...

The Forest Service—one of the federal agencies behind the scheme to despoil Mineral King—has been notorious for its alignment with lumber companies, although its mandate from Congress directs it to consider the various aspects of multiple use in its supervision of the national forests.

The voice of the inanimate object, therefore, should not be stilled. That does not mean that the judiciary takes over the managerial functions from the federal agency. It merely means that before these priceless bits of Americana (such as a valley, an alpine meadow, a river, or a lake) are forever lost or are so transformed as to be reduced to the eventual rubble of our urban environment, the voice of the existing beneficiaries of these environmental wonders should be heard.

Perhaps they will not win. Perhaps the bulldozers of "progress" will plow under all the aesthetic wonders of this beautiful land. That is not the present condition. The sole question is, who has standing to be heard?

Those who hike the Appalachian Trail into Sunfish Pond, New Jersey, and camp or sleep there, or run the Allagash in Maine, or climb the Guadalupes in West Texas, or who canoe and portage the Quetico Superior in Minnesota, certainly should have standing to defend those natural wonders before courts or agencies, though they live 3,000 miles away. Those who merely are caught up in environmental news or propaganda and flock to defend these waters or areas may be treated differently. That is why these environmental issues should be tendered by the inanimate object itself. Then there will be assurances that all of the forms of life which it represents will stand before the court—the pileated woodpecker as well as the coyote and bear, the lemmings as well as the trout in the streams. Those inarticulate members of the ecological group cannot speak. But those people who have so frequented the place as to know its values and wonders will be able to speak for the entire ecological community.

...

That, as I see it, is the issue of "standing" in the present case and controversy. . . .

MR. JUSTICE BLACKMUN, dissenting.

The Court's opinion is a practical one espousing and adhering to traditional notions of standing as somewhat modernized. . . . If this were an ordinary case, I would join the opinion and the Court's judgment and be quite content.

But this is not ordinary, run-of-the-mill litigation. The case poses—if only we choose to acknowledge and reach them— significant aspects of a wide, growing, and disturbing problem, that is, the Nation's and the world's deteriorating environment with its resulting ecological disturbances. Must our law be so rigid and our procedural concepts so inflexible that we render ourselves helpless when the existing methods and the traditional concepts do not quite fit and do not prove to be entirely adequate for new issues?

The ultimate result of the Court's decision today, I fear, and sadly so, is that the 35.3-million-dollar complex, over 10 times greater than the Forest Service's suggested minimum, will now hastily proceed to completion; that serious opposition to it will recede in discouragement; and that Mineral King, the "area of great natural beauty nestled in the Sierra Nevada Mountains," to use the Court's words, will become defaced, at least in part, and, like so many other areas, will cease to be "uncluttered by the products of civilization."

...

Rather than pursue the course the Court has chosen to take by its affirmance of the judgment of the Court of Appeals, I would adopt one of two alternatives:

1. I would reverse that judgment and, instead, approve the judgment of the District Court which recognized standing in the Sierra Club and granted preliminary relief I would be willing to do this on condition that the Sierra Club forthwith amend its complaint to meet the specifications the Court prescribes for standing. If Sierra Club fails or refuses to take that step, so be it; the case will then collapse. But if it does amend, the merits will be before the trial court once again.

...

2. Alternatively, I would permit an imaginative expansion of our traditional concepts of standing in order to enable an organization such as the Sierra Club, possessed, as it is, of pertinent, bona fide, and well-recognized attributes and purposes in the area of environment, to litigate environmental issues. This incursion upon tradition need not be very extensive. Certainly, it should be no cause for alarm. It is no more progressive than was the decision in Data Processing itself. It need only recognize the interest of one who has a provable, sincere, dedicated, and established status. We need not fear that Pandora's box will be opened or that there will be no limit to the number of those who desire to participate in environmental litigation. The courts will exercise appropriate restraints just as they have exercised them in the past. Who would have suspected 20 years ago that the concepts of standing enunciated in Data Processing and Barlow would be the measure for today? And MR. JUSTICE DOUGLAS, in his eloquent opinion, has imaginatively suggested another means and one, in its own way, with obvious, appropriate, and self-imposed limitations as to standing. As I read what he has written, he makes only one addition to the customary criteria (the existence of a genuine dispute; the assurance of adversariness; and a conviction that the party whose standing is challenged will adequately represent the interests he asserts), that is, that the litigant be one who speaks knowingly for the environmental values he asserts.

I make two passing references:

1. The first relates to the Disney figures presented to us. The complex, the Court notes, will accommodate 14,000 visitors a day (3,100 overnight; some 800 employees; 10 restaurants; 20 ski lifts). The State of California has proposed to build a new road from Hammond to Mineral King. That road, to the extent of 9.2 miles, is to traverse Sequoia National Park. It will have only two lanes, with occasional passing areas, but it will be capable, it is said, of accommodating 700–800 vehicles

per hour and a peak of 1,200 per hour. We are told that the State has agreed not to seek any further improvement in road access through the park.

If we assume that the 14,000 daily visitors come by automobile (rather than by helicopter or bus or other known or unknown means) and that each visiting automobile carries four passengers (an assumption, I am sure, that is far too optimistic), those 14,000 visitors will move in 3,500 vehicles. If we confine their movement (as I think we properly may for this mountain area) to 12 hours out of the daily 24, the 3,500 automobiles will pass any given point on the two-lane road at the rate of about 300 per hour. This amounts to five vehicles per minute, or an average of one every 12 seconds. This frequency is further increased to one every six seconds when the necessary return traffic along that same two-lane road is considered. And this does not include service vehicles and employees' cars. Is this the way we perpetuate the wilderness and its beauty, solitude, and quiet?

2. The second relates to the fairly obvious fact that any resident of the Mineral King area—the real "user"—is an unlikely adversary for this Disney governmental project. He naturally will be inclined to regard the situation as one that should benefit him economically. His fishing or camping or guiding or handyman or general outdoor prowess perhaps will find an early and ready market among the visitors. But that glow of anticipation will be short-lived at best. If he is a true lover of the wilderness—as is likely, or he would not be near Mineral King in the first place—it will not be long before he yearns for the good old days when masses of people—that 14,000 influx per day—and their thus far uncontrollable waste were unknown to Mineral King.

Questions, Materials, and Suggestions for Further Studies

Sierra Club v. Morton

In the introduction to this decision we emphasized that standing is a threshold hurdle over which a prospective plaintiff must leap before his or her case will be heard by a court. The determination of standing suffers from the same defect as many legal descriptions: It has become so ritualized and formulaic—with its two prearranged tests of injury in fact and the zone of interest—that the more significant aspects of the issue are hidden. Justice Douglas's dissent in the Morton case is famous for precisely this reason: It forces us to deal with the underlying logic of the standing question—why do we have it and why is it important?

The standing question raises fundamental issues about the function of the courts in our society and of legal systems in general. Do the courts exist to hear any dispute at all? Or only those disputes involving specific legal rights? If the courts' scope is limited to cases of legal rights, are people with purely moral claims to be denied access to the courts merely because they have suffered their wrong before a law was passed giving that claim legal status? Are there such things as moral rights? If so, where do they come from? Some writers would argue that animals certainly have moral rights and should be accorded legal rights as well. See Peter Singer, *Animal Liberation* (New York: Avon Books, 1977). Other authors, such as Christopher D. Stone, in *Should Trees Have Standing? Toward Legal Rights for Natural Objects* (Los Altos, Calif.: Kaufmann, 1974), would argue that moral and legal rights can be distinguished and that merely because a class of objects might be denied moral rights does not mean that it should also be denied legal rights. Stone also argued that trees and other objects in the environment should have legal rights as, under American Admiralty law, do ships. See also, Roderick Nash, *The Rights of Nature* (Madison: University of Wisconsin Press, 1989).

Even if the discussion is limited to legal rights, the question of standing raises other issues. Should a court recognize threatened injury, that is, injury statistically certain to occur in the future but not yet manifested? Surely the consequence—that a certain percentage of asbestos workers will contract mesothelioma within forty years of exposure—is an injury. However, does it make sense for a court to hear now the claims of an apparently healthy worker who, having been exposed for one month two years ago, may eventually develop the disease? These questions are particularly important in environmental cases in which the manifestation of injuries is often delayed or in which the injury to each individual may be small.

The requirement that one should show injury in fact is necessitated by the adversarial nature of our judicial system. Our courts do not listen to abstract discussions of policy; that is the legislature's job. Instead they listen to specific cases and contingencies, real people arguing on real issues. When their own interests are very much at stake, the parties, through their attorneys, will do a better job of arguing their cases, of digging up facts, and of arguing law. With both sides doing their best, the theory goes, the fact finder (be it judge or jury) will make a more enlightened decision. But we have seen that environmental law regulates risks as well as actual harms. If a citizen claims a right to be protected against a risk, would the resulting case be any the less adversarial?

The approach of relying upon the adversary method to resolve disputes—even environmental disputes—has its attendant problems. Many commentators argue that upholding the adversary ideal is a mistake that will lead to a litigious society (see Judith Shklar, *Legalism: An Essay on Law, Morals and Politics* [Cambridge, Mass.: Harvard University Press, 1964]). Whether the theory that supports the alleged effectiveness of the courts as discoverers of truth is accurate is a different matter. One could ask a number of questions including whether the courts need be the only resolver of real disputes (Jerold S. Auerbach, in *Justice Without Law?* [New York: Oxford University Press, 1983] traced the history of successful alternatives to the court system) and whether in fact courts might do an inadequate job in the absence of any real conflict. A recent work exploring the question of whether courts can conduct reasoned and useful discussions of rights without injury in fact is Joseph Vining's *Legal Identity: The Coming of Age of Public Law* (New Haven: Yale University Press, 1978).

Since *Sierra Club v. Morton* was decided, there have been two related developments headed in two completely different directions. Following Douglas's dissent and Stone's book *Should Trees Have Standing?* there has been an explosion of academic and nature writing urging that the intrinsic values of nature be recognized. The classic book in this field appeared much earlier, Aldo Leopold's *A Sand County Almanac* (New York: Oxford University Press, 1949); additional works by philosophers, historians, and lawyers arguing the same point may be found in the bibliography of this text. In the other direction, an increasingly conservative Supreme Court has narrowed the criteria for securing eligible standing.

What the Supreme Court takes away, the legislature may be able to grant: Many federal and some state environmental statutes now have "citizen suit" provisions that establish a statutory basis for citizens to bring environmental law suits and that grant them automatic standing if they choose to do so. These citizen suit provisions were one result of the late 1960s case *Scenic Hudson Preservation Conference et al. v. Federal Power Commission*, 354 F2d. 608 (1965), in which the court recognized that the standing of citizens to challenge the licensing of a hydroelectric project on the Hudson River was statutory, having been granted under the Federal Power Act.

14

Environmental Ideals

Sustainability and the Wise Use of Public Resources

Case Study:
Intermountain Forest Industry
Association v. Lyng

Just what good is a forest? And just who gets to answer the question? To hikers and campers, a forest is the site of solitude, relaxation, and revitalization. To those who hunt and fish, it is much the same plus the added challenge of pursuing their quarry. To those driving by on the highway or flying overhead in airplanes, it is a magnificent sight rolling on for mile after uninterrupted mile of trees, lakes, mountains, and streams. To those interested in biology, it is the source and support of a seemingly inexhaustible supply of plants, insects, and animals. For all of these, it is a place of solace, grandeur, silent contemplation, even mystery. But there are others. To the miner, oil driller, and forest worker, it is a natural resource, the source of something to be extracted, developed, sold, and on which a profit can be made.

As widely disparate as these two groups may at first seem, they are actually inextricably intertwined: The members of the first group live in houses made of the forest products harvested by the forest workers, drive autos and fly in airplanes powered by the oil extracted by the oil field workers, and use tools and utensils and wear gold and silver jewelry extracted from the mines. And at various times in their lives, the forest workers, oil rig workers, and miners are all hikers, campers, fishers, hunters, and nature lovers. Nature exists both as an entity in itself and as a resource, something that we need and that we exploit. The question we continually come up against is whether we really have to choose, whether we can somehow have our forest and exploit it too.

As is often the case, it is the United States government that acts as gatekeeper, doling out permits and patents to individuals and companies so that they can exploit these resources on public lands. The most publicly visible of these governmental stewards is the U.S. Forest Service, a branch of the Department of Agriculture. Additional governmental rights are sold or auctioned off by the Department of the Interior's Bureau of Land Management and the Energy Department. The Federal Communications Commission even auctions off portions of the radio spectrum. The structures under which these various auctions are held, and the prices paid for the permits or rights, provide inevitable sources of conflict among those with differing, even conflicting, views of the proper function of government and natural resource development. When the Clinton Administration's incoming secretary of the interior, Bruce Babbit, attempted to raise the amount paid by ranchers for grazing rights on public lands, western senators and their constituencies objected so effectively that the proposal—advocated by many environmentalists as a way to cut down on overgrazing and by many conservative economists as an "open market" basis for grazing—was withdrawn.

The federal government is our steward and in some form or other, in fulfilling its stewardship duties, the federal government must at least take into account the wishes and attitudes of all its citizens when it makes decisions about resource development. We see this in the *Intermountain* court's attempt to wrestle with the appropriateness of the internal review mechanisms put in place by the Forest Service. The bottom line is that the land in question is public land, a National Forest for which strict rules and public accountability are demanded.

But what of privately held land? Here we are back into the area covered by zoning, the Justs, and the East Bibb Twiggs landowners, but on a slightly different scale. It is an intriguing question: What duty—if any—is owed by a private landowner (in this case the owner of forest lands) to the wishes of the society as a whole if those wishes run counter to the landowner's own wishes? It is not an idle question. Many vast tracts of land in the United States are owned by private timber companies. Of these, some lands have been harvested once or twice and are currently managed on a sustainable yield basis. Other privately held lands, however, have not been harvested. These forest lands are unique.

Under our system, whether simply to exploit our natural resources, whether to conserve natural resources for future generations, or even whether to preserve Nature, have never been easy questions to answer. As we mentioned in the introduction, the conflict between preservation and exploitation has always been at the heart of our relationship with the land we found when we came to this country. The result of the conflict has been, as it almost always is with the law, a compromise not unlike those we see in zoning: Resource development is zoning writ large. Essentially, we allow private owners to do with their property what they wish, with very few restrictions.

Several years ago, a small timber company in California with almost 200,000 acres of timberlands was in the news as the target of a hostile takeover bid from the

Maxxam Group. Maxxam was interested in Pacific Lumber Company because three-quarters of those holdings (about 150,000 acres) were redwoods and of *those,* fully 57 percent were "old-growth" redwoods. To purchase Pacific, Maxxam borrowed over $750 million through the investment firm of Drexel Burnham, issuing "junk bonds" with interest as high as 12¾ percent. To pay back the creditors and meet its high interest payments, Maxxam began an aggressive cutting program of Pacific Lumber's old-growth holdings, clear-cutting the forest at a previously unheard of rate.

Maxxam's rate of clear-cutting was unheard of by Pacific Lumber or anyone who had been associated with the company for over 100 years. Prior to the takeover, for many in the environmental community, Pacific had been a "model" timber company. Founded in 1869, it had operated for generations on a sustained yield basis. Pacific had also made every attempt to retain its workers through thick and thin in the timber products industry and was widely respected in both the commercial timber and environmental communities. What had changed with the takeover was the company's view of its holdings. Instead of looking at its assets as a "trust," Maxxam evaluated the undeveloped timber holdings in strict dollars-and-cents terms: Factoring this new evaluation into the equation, Maxxam figured that the worth of the company's shares (valued at about $33.00 when the takeover started) was much greater than the shareholders realized. When offered the "real" value for their stock (an additional $7.00 per share), the shareholders sold, and Maxxam took ownership.

And why not? This transaction, and ones like it, brings a number of the conflicting values that we are interested in to the fore. First, although many would identify Pacific Lumber as an "environmentally responsible" company, what, precisely, is wrong with the purchaser's having bought up the shares as it did? Clearly, the shares were, in fact, undervalued in dollar terms (the usual reason one purchases shares is as a financial investment, after all): The company owned a resource, the value of which was not adequately reflected in the value of the shares. How can one fault a shareholder for selling his or her shares in a forest products company to the highest bidder merely because that bidder is another, albeit more aggressive, forest products company? To criticize that transaction would be to say that certain classes of individuals (here, the holders of shares in certain—not all, just certain—companies) should take an economic or a financial loss to benefit others, most of whom don't even know the shareholders exist.

And this discussion leaves out any number of classes of "benefiters" on either side of the transaction. Obviously, the benefiters include not only those who might want redwood lumber but also those who will benefit from the reduced cost accompanying the rapid cutting and sawing. There are also, of course, the loggers and sawmill operators and workers, the truckers, the sales personnel, the finish carpenters, and the real estate agents. The list is endless, and endless on the other side as well. Who suffers? In part, those who suffer overlap with those who benefit. The same loggers who have relied on the company to manage its harvests over the decades will benefit for a while, but not after the supply dries up in five or ten years. Clearly the wildlife suffers, the tourism industry of Northern California suffers, the hunters, hikers, and fishers suffer.

The unusual facts surrounding the Pacific Lumber Company make it a riveting example of the extent to which we allow the exploitation of private lands. Public lands we also see as exploitable, but exploitable within limits. The appropriateness of those limits changes from year to year, generation to generation, political era to political era. The Mining Act of 1872, for example, allows individual prospectors and companies to stake mining claims, take title to property, and pay no royalties to the government for the gold they extract. As recently as 1994, this became a contentious issue when Barrick Mining, a Canadian company, submitted a successful bid of $9,765.00 for gold mining rights to 1,949 acres near Elko, Nevada, containing gold deposits valued at $10 billion. Although there might be some justification for allowing profits to private parties who "develop" the resources from public lands for a "public" benefit, the fact that the company stood to make such vast sums and the public, essentially nothing, raised this particular transaction to a high level of media visibility. Secretary of the Interior Babbitt called it the "biggest gold heist since the days of Butch Cassidy."

This sort of valuing—is the public getting its money's worth for the resource being privately developed?—provides a ready point of attack for those who look to criticize governmental programs. Many environmentalists see farmers, ranchers, and forest service companies as benefiting from huge government subsidies so long as the prices they pay for their irrigation, grazeland, and timber haul roads, respectively, fall short of their true market value. The farmers, ranchers, and forest products businesses who benefit from these subsidies, naturally, don't feel so privileged. To them, the party who is actually subsidized is the consumer, the one whose prices for products are kept low by the very same mechanism.

An approach to natural resources currently advanced by some economists is that we can never run out of resources. At first, this idea may seem counterintuitive, but, on reflection, it does make some sense. We run low on something, its price rises, substitutes are found. Yet, the approach fails to adequately account for what appear to be clear examples of resource overexploitation in the absence of regulations from somewhere. The primary focus of attention and thought in reading *Intermountain* should be on the government as a wise steward who has set certain limits on what it can and cannot do. One final thought to keep in mind in reading *Intermountain*, is just what the extent of the government's responsibilities may be—and to whom (or to what) they extend. In 1996, it is painfully obvious to virtually all Americans that the fisheries of both the Atlantic and Pacific coasts are virtually fished out. The Grand Banks off Newfoundland and New England simply have no fish left and in the Northwest, salmon fishing has been severely restricted. Both of these fisheries were long thought to be virtually inexhaustible. But they weren't. Their past glories now survive as the faintest glimmers, providing a melancholy example of what happens to a "common" resource when it falls outside of effective regulation, whether that regulation is provided by government fiat or the forces of the market.

INTERMOUNTAIN FOREST INDUSTRY ASSOCIATION
and Louisiana Pacific Corporation,
Plaintiffs
v.
Richard E. LYNG,
Secretary, United States Department of Agriculture,
et al.,
Defendants

United States District Court,
D. Wyoming
April 18, 1988
[683 F. Supp. 1330]

BRIMMER, Chief Judge.

. . .

Plaintiffs contend that the defendants are violating a Timber Management Plan ("TMP") prepared by the Bridger-Teton National Forest in 1979. The TMP projects annual timber harvests of approximately 28.4 million board feet ("mmbf"). Approximately one-half of the timber is to be cut in the northern portion of the Bridger-Teton National Forest. This area constitutes the "working circle" of Louisiana Pacific's Dubois, Wyoming sawmill.

On January 6, 1988, the Bridger-Teton National Forest announced planned timber sales for 1988. The announcement projects annual sales of approximately 14.4 mmbf. Less than 6 mmbf is green sawtimber. All of the 7 mmbf offered in the north end of the forest is unsuitable for sawmill operations. Plaintiffs seek a preliminary injunction requiring the United States Forest Service to operate the Bridger-Teton National Forest in accordance with the TMP and to take immediate steps to offer timber for harvesting at levels specified in the TMP. Plaintiffs failed to make a showing sufficient to justify preliminary injunctive relief. Their motion will be denied.

I. Facts

A. The TMP

The Bridger-Teton National Forest is managed under ten Ranger District Multiple Use Plans adopted pursuant to the Multiple-Use Sustained-Yield Act of 1960 ("MUSYA"), 16 U.S.C. §§ 528–531, four unit plans, and several single resource plans. Tr. at 71–76 (testimony of Mr. Stout). Multiple use and unit plans "allocate land and resources for the various multiple uses permitted on the forest and provide direction for the coordination of these uses." TMP, EIS at 1–3. Single resource plans in contrast "are subordinate *1333 to the multiple use or unit plans, [and]

translate the general land management direction they contain into specific guidelines for the management of a particular resource." Id.

The TMP is a single resource plan. Id. It was prepared and adopted in 1979 and
accompanied by an environmental impact statement. The TMP has not been for-
mally amended or revised.

Revisions are planned "as the need arises." A change of plus or minus ten percent in the commercial forest land area or a change of plus or minus in the potential timber yield triggers a review. TMP at 70. Neither change has occurred.

The Secretary of Agriculture affirmed the plan on May 16, 1980. Gov.Ex. 5. The
Secretary cautioned, however, that the Bridger-Teton National Forest "contains
some of the best elk habitat in North America" and that "it is of utmost importance that the Forest Service practice management on this forest which will minimize the impact on the elk habitat to the fullest extent possible consistent with
multiple use management." The Secretary accordingly directed the Forest Service
to consult with the Wyoming Game and Fish Department before permitting any
harvesting under the plan. Finally, the Secretary noted that the TMP must be
"considered an interim plan only." Id.

The TMP enunciates "the overall management direction and objectives for timber management activities" in the Bridger-Teton National Forest. TMP at 66. It
also identifies goals for timber harvesting and establishes guidelines to achieve
those goals. Timber harvest goals are products of the land base suitable for commercial timber harvesting and of timber volumes which can be harvested feasi-
bly—the annual programmable harvest.

1. Commercial Forest Land Base.   The TMP first quantifies the land base available for timber production. The net area of the Bridger-Teton National Forest is
3,400,267 acres. TMP at 12 (Table 3–1). Approximately fifty-five percent, or
1,863,902 acres, is classified as "non-forest" or unproductive forest. The remaining 1,536,365 acres are productive forest. Id.

Productive forest land is classified as "reserved, deferred and commercial." TMP
at 12. "Reserved" land has been withdrawn from timber utilization by statute, regulation or land-use plans approved by the Regional Forester. TMP at 115.
"Deferred" land includes areas identified for study as possible wilderness area.
TMP at 114. Together these two classifications account for 567,261 acres, or approximately thirty-seven percent of the total productive forest land in the Bridger-
Teton National Forest. TMP at 12 (Table 3–1).

The remaining 969,104 acres are classified as "commercial" forest land capable
of producing crops of industrial wood. TMP at 12 (Table 3-1), 114. "Unregulated"
commercial forest (land used as campsites, ranger stations and guard stations, for
example) constitute 12,257 acres of commercial forest which is not managed for
timber production. TMP at 12 (Table 3-1), 117. Nearly fifty-four percent of the
commercial forest is classified as "marginal" land typified by high development
costs and low product value. TMP at 12 (Table 3-1), 114. "Special" lands comprise

251,565 acres of commercial forest land. TMP at 12 (Table 3-1). Standard commercial forest land comprises only 181,928 acres of the Bridger-Teton National Forest, or only five percent of the total forest land area and less than twelve percent of the total commercial forest land in the Bridger-Teton National Forest. Id.

2. Planned Harvest Levels. The TMP also establishes "potential yields and harvest levels." TMP, at i. The potential yield is "the harvest that could be planned on commercial forest land considering the productivity of the land, conventional logging technology, standard cultural treatments, anticipated financing for cultural treatments, and relationships with other resource uses and the environment." TMP at 115. The average annual potential yield for the entire Bridger-Teton National Forest is approximately 81 mmbf. Id. at 43 (Table 6-3). This figure represents the maximum harvest possible under ideal conditions. It assumes economical access to every forested acre, compatibility with other resources, and an existing market for all volumes harvested. Declaration of Brian Stout at para. 8.

The potential yield is the sum of three components: standard, special and marginal. The standard component is the harvest that:

> (1) can and should be produced through intensive management on standard acres . . . ; (2) has a reasonable probability of demand and/or funding under the accessibility and economic conditions projected for the plan period; and (3) can be harvested with adequate protection of the Forest resources under standard provisions of the timber sale contract.

TMP at 36, 116. Of the 81 mmbf average annual potential yield, only 21 mmbf falls within the standard component. Id. at 43 (Table 6-3). Salvage timber (cutting designed to utilize scattered dead and down trees) constitutes 3.6 mmbf of the standard component. Id. at 116, 43 (Table 6-3).

The second element of the annual average potential yield is the special component. Areas requiring special treatment of the timber resource are included in this component. Id. at 116. The main purposes of the special component are to promote quality elk hunting and aesthetics. Tr. at 245–46 (testimony of Mr. Baker). The special component is approximately 8 mmbf of the average annual potential yield. TMP at 43 (Table 6-3).

The marginal component makes up nearly two-thirds (51.5 mmbf) of the average annual yield. This component is typified by excessive development cost, low product value or resource protection constraints. Id. at 114. Harvests in these areas require special funding, and offerings have a low probability of being accepted by prospective purchasers. Id. at 36.

The annual programmed allowable harvest more accurately estimates potential timber harvests. Declaration of Brian Stout at para. 9. The programmed allowable harvest is based on current demand, funding, silvicultural practice and multiple use considerations. TMP at 47. The programmed harvest for fiscal year 1979 was approximately 27 mmbf. Id. at 48.

The total ten year timber sales program for the standard and special components is 302.51 mmbf. Id. at 68 (Table 9-1). The program projects an annual harvest of approximately 28 mmbf. Id.; see also Supplemental Affidavit of James S. Riley, para. 9. Approximately 14 mmbf is programmed for sale within the working circle of the Dubois sawmill (the Pinedale, Gros Ventre and Buffalo Ranger Districts). TMP at 68 (Table 9-1). Salvage timber constitutes roughly 4.3 mmbf of the total annual harvest. Id. The ten year timber sales program lists "timber sales volume objectives by fiscal year and Ranger District." Id. at 67 (emphasis added). The TMP refers to this projection as "annual target volumes." Id.

B. Actual Timber Volumes Offered

On January 6, 1988, the Forest Service announced timber sales scheduled in the Bridger-Teton National Forest during the period from October 1, 1987 to March 31, 1988. The announcement also identifies tentative harvest levels for April 1, 1988 until September 30, 1988. Annual sales of approximately 14.4 mmbf are planned. Less than 6 mmbf is green sawtimber.

From 1978 through 1987, annual timber offerings averaged approximately 24 to 26 mmbf. Gov.Ex. 11. Volumes fluctuated substantially. Until 1982 the volumes offered were below the amounts targeted in the TMP. Tr. at 252 (testimony of Mr. Baker). In 1982 and 1983, offerings considerably exceeded planned harvest levels but declined in 1985. Volumes offered in 1986 and 1987 again exceeded planned harvest levels, in part because the Forest Service offered 12.1 mmbf to make up for three sales which had previously been deferred for further study. Tr. at 121 (testimony of Mr. Stout).

Previous clearcutting, existing topography and soil conditions, elk migration routes and information revealed by site-specific analyses constrain timber harvests in the northern Bridger-Teton National Forest. Timber harvesting concentrated heavily on this end of the forest for the last 20 to 25 years. More opportunities for harvesting now exist in the southern end of the forest. Id. at 106. Clearcutting has been especially heavy within Louisiana Pacific's working circle. Gov.Ex. 6; Tr. at 203–204 (testimony of Mr. Baker). A substantial portion of the remaining land is designated wilderness area. See Gov.Ex. 1 (map of Wyoming wilderness areas). Many of the prime timber stands in the northern half of the Bridger-Teton National Forest are depleted. More careful study and analysis must be undertaken before offering the remaining areas for logging. Tr. at 102 (testimony of Mr. Stout). The first constraint on logging in the Bridger-Teton National Forest is a comparative shortage of commercially desirable stands of timber.

Topography also affects harvest levels. Many of the flatter sites in the northern end of the forest have been harvested. Compare Gov.Ex. 6 with Gov.Ex. 7. The remaining stands may be uneconomical to harvest because of steep slopes and poor soil conditions. Tr. at 100–101 (testimony of Mr. Stout).

The need for elk habitat further limits timber harvesting. Elk migration routes converge in this area. Studies of migration patterns in 1950 and 1980 show ever-narrowing elk migration routes through the Bridger-Teton National Forest. The animals are being forced into the corridor between Yellowstone and Grand Teton National Parks. Gov.Ex. 8. Some evidence connects diminished elk habitat with timber harvesting. Compare Gov.Ex. 6 with Gov.Ex. 8. See also Tr. at 98–99, 103–106.

The TMP was prepared without site-specific data. Tr. at 194–96. Studies of specific stands of timber often reveal that harvesting those stands is impossible.

Announced timber sales in the Bridger-Teton National Forest did not, as plaintiffs contend, "disappear." An analysis of sales from 1978 through 1987 shows a total of 173 sale names. Nine sales are under study. Sixty-five were offered and sold. Sixteen were sold under different names. Seven sales generated no bids. Three sales offered under different names produced no bids. Nineteen were cancelled because of insufficient volume, inaccessibility or other economic reasons. Two were cancelled due to right-of-way problems. Six sales were withdrawn because the stands were located in wilderness or wilderness study areas. Another six sales were deferred because of conflicts with other resources. Forty sales were deferred pending further analysis. Gov.Ex. 10; tr. at 112–18 (testimony of Mr. Stout). In the late 1970's and early 1980's Louisiana Pacific processed 600,000 to one million board feet. The company now processes 1.9 to 2.2 mmbf annually. Tr. at 222 (testimony of Mr. Baker). Louisiana Pacific processed more timber in recent years than ever before. Gov.Ex. 20.

C. The Relationship Between Louisiana Pacific and the Bridger-Teton National Forest

At the time of the hearing, Louisiana Pacific had not decided to close the Dubois sawmill. The sawmill does not depend entirely upon timber from the Bridger-Teton National Forest. Tr. at 227, 232 (testimony of Mr. Baker). Louisiana Pacific's average purchases from the Bridger-Teton National Forest over the last ten years have been 10 to 11 mmbf per year. Gov.Ex. 20; Tr. at 232–33. Louisiana Pacific has reached out 150 to 250 miles to purchase timber. Tr. at 212. The company has not analyzed how far it can economically haul timber to the Dubois sawmill, other than by appraising individual timber sales. Id. at 225.

Louisiana Pacific was outbid on two sales in the Bridger-Teton National Forest and two sales in the Shoshone National Forest. The sales in the Bridger-Teton National Forest were the North Fish Creek sale and the North Piney Bench sale. Tr. at 209. The North Fish Creek sale was an important timber sale close to the Dubois mill. The timber was sold at a sealed bid auction. A firm from Afton, Wyoming outbid Louisiana Pacific. Afton is approximately 200 miles from the North Fish Creek site. Tr. at 210, 227. The North Piney Bench sale was on the fringe of Louisiana Pacific's working circle. Tr. at 211.

The sawmill was marginally profitable when operated at a level of 16 mmbf per year. The sawmill was more profitable when it processed 21 mmbf per year. Tr. at

229–30. Profitable operations could be conducted at slightly less than 21 mmbf per year. Tr. at 230. Louisiana Pacific sawed less than 21 mmbf in 1976, 1978, 1983 and 1986 yet earned profits in each of those years. Compare Gov.Ex. 20, 17 with Gov.Ex. 18.

Periods of losses and closures at Louisiana Pacific's Dubois and Riverton mills correspond to the inflationary cycle and construction declines of the late 1970's. Gov.Ex. 20; Tr. at 219. Present market conditions are different from those which led to the closures in the early 1980's. Tr. at 220.

The normal logging season is from the last two weeks in June until the middle of March. If timber sales were offered that did not require road construction, Louisiana Pacific could harvest the timber within a few weeks after purchasing the timber. It would take longer if roads have to be built. Tr. at 216–17.

II. Standard for Preliminary Injunctive Relief

[The court analyzes the reasons for granting a preliminary Injunction, pointing out that it is an "extraordinary remedy" to be granted only in very limited circumstances. The first portion of the court's analysis, the possibility of irreparable harm, is omitted in this excerpt.]

A. *Irreparable Harm*

...

B. *Probable Success on the Merits*

Plaintiffs' eventual success on the merits is insufficiently likely to justify preliminary injunctive relief. Planned timber harvest levels for 1988 comply with all applicable statutes and regulations.

Plaintiffs argue first that the Forest Service is violating the Organic Administration Act ("Organic Act") of June 4, 1987, 16 U.S.C. §§ 473–482, 551, the Multiple Use Sustained Yield Act of 1960 (MUSYA), 16 U.S.C. § 528–531, and Forest Service regulations promulgated at 36 C.F.R. § 221.3 by failing to manage the Bridger-Teton National Forest in a manner assuring a continuous supply of timber. This contention lacks merit.

The Organic Act provides that "[n]o national forest shall be established, except to improve and protect the forest within the boundaries, or for the purpose of securing favorable conditions of water flows, and to furnish a continuous supply of timber for the use and necessity of citizens of the United States." 16 U.S.C. § 475. The Act envisioned only two purposes for the national forests: conserving water flows and furnishing continuous supplies of timber. *United States v. New Mexico,* 438 U.S. 696, 707, 98 S.Ct. 3012, 3017, 57 L.Ed.2d 1052 (1978).

In this case, an annual average of 24 to 26 mmbf of timber was harvested in the Bridger-Teton National Forest from 1978 to 1987. Gov.Ex. 11. Louisiana Pacific itself purchased an average of 10 mmbf to 11 mmbf annually. Tr. at 232–33 (testimony of Mr. Baker). The evidence shows that the Bridger-Teton National Forest has produced a continuous supply of timber since 1978. The forest will produce "continuous" supplies of timber at harvest levels planned for 1988.

Arguing that the Organic Act requires the Forest Service to manage national forests primarily for the production of timber and for the protection of watershed ignores the Multiple-Use Sustained-Yield Act of 1960, 16 U.S.C. §§ 528–531. MUSYA substantially broadened the purposes of the national forests to include "recreation, range, timber, watershed and wildlife and fish purposes." 16 U.S.C. § 528; *United States v. New Mexico,* 438 U.S. at 713, 98 S.Ct. at 3020. These purposes are, however, "supplemental to, but not in derogation of, the purposes for which the national forests were established as set forth in the [Organic Act]." 16 U.S.C. § 528.

The Act directs the Secretary of Agriculture to administer all national forests on a multiple-use and sustained-yield basis. 16 U.S.C. § 529. Multiple use is defined as:

> . . . the management of all of the various renewable surface resources of the national forests so that they are utilized in the combination that will best meet the needs of the American people; making the most judicious use of the land for some or all of these resources . . . over areas large enough to provide sufficient latitude for periodic adjustments in use to conform to changing needs and conditions; that some land will be used for less than all of the resources; and harmonious and coordinated management of the various resources, each with the other, without impairment of the productivity of the land, with consideration being given to the relative values of the various resources, *and not necessarily the combination of uses that will give the greatest dollar return or the greatest unit output.* 16 U.S.C. § 531(a) (emphasis added).

Multiple-use sustained-yield administration must consider the relative values of all resources within the national forests. 16 U.S.C. § 529.

MUSYA itself rebuts plaintiffs' assertion that the national forests must be managed primarily for economic reasons. Although MUSYA does not repeal the Organic Act, Congress envisioned the domination of non-timber uses in certain forests. H.REP.NO. 1551, 86th Cong., 2nd Sess. (1960), reprinted in 1960 U.S.Code Cong. & Admin.News 2377, 2379. The Act gives range, recreation, and wildlife an equal footing with timber production. *Sierra Club v. Hardin,* 325 F.Supp. 99, 123 (D.Alaska 1971), rev'd on other grounds sub nom., *Sierra Club v. Butz,* 3 E.L.R. 20293 (9th Cir.1973); *National Wildlife Fed'n v. United States Forest Serv.,* 592 F.Supp. 931 (D.Or.1984), appeal dismissed, 801 F.2d 360 (9th Cir.1986).

The National Forest Management Act of 1976 ("NFMA"), 16 U.S.C. §§ 1600–1614, tied the broad discretion to sell timber granted by the Organic Act, 16 U.S.C. § 476, to the multiple use concept. Congress provided that:

> [f]or the purpose of achieving the policies set forth in the Multiple-Use Sustained-Yield Act of 1960, and the Forest and Rangelands Renewable Resource Planning Act of 1974 the Secretary of Agriculture, under such rules and regulations as he may prescribe, *may sell,* at not less than appraised value, trees, portions of trees, or forest

products located on National Forest System lands. 16 U.S.C. § 472a (emphasis added).

Plaintiffs' argument that the Forest Service has violated the Organic Act is specious. First, the Bridger-Teton National Forest has produced and will produce a continuous supply of timber. Second, the Organic Act does not require the Forest Service to manage national forests solely to furnish timber. The Organic Act delegated to the Secretary of Agriculture the discretion whether or not to sell timber. 16 U.S.C. § 476; *Hi-Ridge Lumber Co. v. United States*, 443 F.2d 452, 455 (9th Cir.1971); *Parker v. United States*, 307 F.Supp. 685, 688 (D.Colo.1969). NFMA modifies the Organic Act by providing that the Secretary "may sell" timber located on national forest land. 16 U.S.C. § 472a(a). Finally, MUSYA establishes additional purposes for the national forests and expressly directs that all uses be considered, not necessarily those producing the greatest dollar return or the greatest unit output. 16 U.S.C. § 531(a). There is no principled basis for plaintiffs' assertion that the national forests must be managed primarily to produce economic benefits.

. . .

The Court concludes that the defendants complied with all applicable statutes and regulations. Accordingly, plaintiffs' eventual success on the merits is insufficiently likely to warrant the issuance of a preliminary injunction.

C. Balance of Hardships

The balance of hardships favors the Forest Service. Plaintiffs argue that they will suffer permanent injury if the injunction does not issue and the Dubois sawmill closes. The mill has closed many times and, despite judicial attempts to intervene, is likely to close again.

Substantial harm would result from granting plaintiffs the relief they request. The Forest Service will be forced to divert personnel and resources from preparation of the forest plan required by NFMA and to cut back services in the Bridger-Teton National Forest. Tr. at 190 (testimony of Mr. Stout). Tourism, recreation, ranchers, and small loggers will be harmed. Finally, increased timber harvesting may have unforeseen environmental effects. This damage tips the balance of equities in favor of the Forest Service. *Amoco Prod. Co. v. Village of Gambell*,—U.S. —, 107 S.Ct. 1396, 1404, 94 L.Ed.2d 542 (1987). Court-ordered timber harvests could cause more harm than closure of the mill.

D. Injury to the Public Interest

The public interest will be harmed if an injunction issues. That interest is better served by following existing forest management practices. Issuing the injunction, in contrast, would upset the careful structure of forest planning crafted by Congress.

Congress wanted decisions affecting the national forests to consider all forest resources. Congress delegated to the Forest Service discretion to balance the use of these resources. 16 U.S.C. § 1600(1), (2), (6). Ordering the Forest Service to make timber available for harvest without considering all relevant factors would frustrate the intent of Congress.

Accepting the plaintiffs' position would have the anomalous result of reducing public participation in the forest planning process. Needed resources would be diverted from completion of the forest management plan. Substantial harm would result with no corresponding assurance of helping the plaintiffs. In all likelihood, sufficient volumes of timber cannot be harvested in sufficient time to prevent temporary closure of the Dubois mill. Issuing the preliminary injunction would be a futile act and merely delay the forest management plan. The forest planning process is an appropriate forum to begin resolving the conflicts over the Bridger-Teton National Forest. The public interest is better served by permitting that process to go forward.

III. Conclusion

The Court finds that the plaintiffs failed to establish irreparable harm and a probability of success on the merits with sufficient certainty to justify issuing a preliminary injunction. The Court also finds that the balance of hardships favors the Forest Service and that issuing the injunction would palpably injure the public interest. It is therefore

ORDERED that the plaintiffs' motion for a preliminary injunction be, and the same hereby is, denied.

Questions, Materials, and Suggestions for Further Study

Intermountain Forest Industry Association v. Lyng

Conservation, as exemplified in the case, is the husbanding of resources for future generations. (References to books discussing our obligations to future generations are cited in the study questions following the *Tanner* case.) At the turn of the twentieth century, the conservation of resources became a major political issue. For a history of the conservation movement, see Joseph Petulla, *American Environmental History: The Exploitation and Conservation of Natural Resources* (San Francisco: Boyd and Frazier Publishing Co., 1977).

A book that looks at alternative conservation strategies is Kimon Valaskakis, P. S. Sindell and J. G. Smith's *The Selective Conserver Society*, vol. 1 (Montreal: Gamma, University of Montreal/McGill University, 1977). An economic approach to conservation, one of the alternatives, is outlined in S. V. Ciriacy-Wantrup's *Resource Conservation: Economics and Policies* (Berkeley: University of California Press, Division of Agricultural Sciences, Agricultural Experiment Station, 1968). Recycling—the reuse of residuals in mining, in manufacturing, or in consumption—is examined in Martin Pawley's *Building for Tomorrow: Putting Waste to Work* (San Francisco: Sierra Club Books, 1982), and Thomas Dutton, *Recycling Solid Waste* (Westport, Conn.: Quorum Books, 1993). An engineering perspective on recycling is offered by Allan F. Barton in *Resource Recovery and Recycling* (New York: Wiley, 1979).

Conservation raises the question of whether we can limit our demand for the goods that generate residuals. Two excellent studies of consumption are Mary Douglas and Baron Isherwood's *World of Goods: Toward an Anthropology of Consumption* (New York: Norton, 1979, reprinted in 1982) and Eugene Linden's *Affluence and Discontent: The Anatomy of Consumer Societies* (New York: Viking Press, 1979). The limiting of consumption is closely allied to the idea of a "no growth" economy, explored in Herman E. Daly's *Toward a Steady-State Economy* (New York: Freeman, 1973).

The conservancy movement was stimulated by a public concern over the exhaustion of resources. Recent economists have demonstrated that this concern may not be warranted. As a resource becomes scarce, its price rises, and substitutes enter the market (See Harold Barnett and Chandler Morse, *Scarcity and Growth: The Economics of Natural Resource Availability* [Baltimore: Johns Hopkins University Press, 1963]).

The early approach to conservation concentrated upon one or another resource: forests, soils, metals, coal, and so on. Critics pointed out that such a concentration failed to consider the impact of overuse of one resource upon the entire ecosystem. As a consequence a new, admittedly vague idea, "sustainability," has arisen. The notion is that a development should be sustainable, yielding a stream of benefits that more than compensates for any environmental harms, including the initial and continuing use of resources. The political statement of the sustainability ideal is set forth in the World Commission on Environment and Development's *Our Common Future* (Oxford: Oxford University Press, 1987). Economists have sought to refine the idea in Charles Perring's *Economy and Environment: A Theoretical Essay on the Interdependence of Economics and Environmental Systems* (Cambridge: Cambridge University Press, 1987). The definitive legal treatment of sustainability is Celia Campbell-Mohn, ed., *Environmental Law: From Resources to Recovery* (St. Paul: West Publishing Co., 1993).

Conservation may also be viewed as part of the broader religious tradition of stewardship and the cultural traditions of thrift. For a discussion of the former, see John Passmore's *Man's Responsibility for Nature: Ecological Problems and Western Traditions* (New York: Charles Scribner & Sons, 1974); for a discussion of the importance of forests in culture, see Robert Payne Harrison, *Forests, the Shadow of Civilization* (Chicago: University of Chicago Press, 1992); for a discussion of the culture of thrift, see David Shi's *The Simple Life: Plain Living and High Thinking in American Culture* (Oxford: Oxford University Press, 1985).

Conclusion

The equitable application of law and legal principles to our current and future environmental problems is the one indispensable requirement if we are to clean up our environment and arrive at an environmentally just society. Although the legal system is central to any resolution of these problems, in some ways that system itself is inadequate to the task. A society's laws grow by accretion; irritations are smoothed over by laws, compromises, and limitations on individual behavior that enable us to carry on our everyday business and protect society from physical dangers that could harm its health and the social discord that could tear it apart. Labor law, public utilities regulation, securities regulation, contract law, property, and estates are some of the more traditional areas of law, both statutory and judge made, which reflect systematic compromises that enable us to live in harmony. Environmental law, whether embodied in antipollution statutes, complex regulations, or recent judge-made common-law decisions, makes another layer, one more protective coating that has become incorporated into the general body of law.

The ways in which environmental law differs from other types, however, account for its unique importance. Unlike securities regulation, for example, environmental law serves to protect basic health; unlike labor law, it is not restricted to workplaces, factories, industries, or work-related activities. Environmental law encompasses the entire cycle of production from mining to transportation to manufacturing to consumption to waste disposal. It applies to almost the entire range of our society's output of goods and services; almost all productive activity originates in natural resource development or results in some form of waste, which must be disposed of in an ecologically sound manner. Environmental law regulates the behavior of individuals hundreds of miles apart to protect their well-being. At this writing, more than fifteen years have passed since we created the topic of environmental news; yet in one form or another the subject remains a staple of daily newspapers. Far from being a passing fad, environmental issues are debated in Congress or the mass media almost weekly. Opinion polls time and again indicate the enduring importance of environmental issues to the general public. Environmental coverage has already become as much a staple of our news as the daily business report. And well it might: The health of the economy, the health of the people, and the health of the environment go hand in hand.

Specific issues of concern, of course, will change as older problems are rectified and newer ones are recognized. Acid rain, global warming, and hazardous waste disposal are today's issues; they promise to be supplanted by concerns such as indoor pollution and the disposal of radioactive wastes and by broad-scale questions about the relative advantages of the large-scale preservation of entire ecosystems.

Although the specific issues will change, the approaches to these issues will remain those reflected in the leading decisions we have chosen for this casebook. The questions will remain the same: Do we compensate those who suffer loss from environmental change? If so, what form does that compensation take? How do we extract payment from those who have gained from the suffering of others? How do we control the entrenched bureaucracies and the technologies that promise so much in order to ensure that they deliver on their promises and not simply leave us with more damage and uncertainty? Finally, perhaps the ultimate question with which our society must wrestle as it confronts continual change: How do we hold on to our traditional legal concepts—relics of an agrarian England—and adapt them to a world of nuclear waste and bioengineering without making them unrecognizable?

As we have attempted to illustrate in this casebook, even in our brave new world our legal—ultimately ethical—decisions will remain the same ones that human beings have had to confront since before nuclear physics, before the Constitution, even before English or Greek civilization. We face the same problems as does every society striving to be just, and we deal with them in variations of the same ways as did our predecessors in civilizations that did not yet understand the mechanics of rainfall. The decisions in this casebook reflect the process whereby nonexpert judges have arrived at these decisions on the basis of norms with which we are all familiar. By reading the cases carefully, we come to appreciate how difficult these claims are.

Along with an awareness of the ethical dimensions of our legal problems and an appreciation of how those ethical questions arise in environmental law, the authors hope that the reader will also gain an appreciation of the complexity of motives, both those of the society and those of individuals. In the 1970s, environmentalists were fond of quoting Walt Kelly's comic strip character Pogo: "We have met the enemy and he is us"—perplexing, even humbling, but all too true. We all contribute to the pollution we decry by demanding the products that generate it at prices that make totally clean production impossible. Business people are working to make money, and without adequate profit they will go out of business. If the purchasing public refuses to pay for a pollution-free product yet insists that the cost does not reflect the cost of clean production, the manufacturer may shut down the factory, putting people out of work and shifting the cost of maintaining them to the same buying public—this time in the form of higher taxes for unemployment payments.

Pollution and its cleanup both involve costs. Our only option as a society is to decide what form that cost will take. If we insist on our cars, our stereos, our televisions, toasters, microwaves, and computers, we must either include the cost of cleanup in the final product by paying more for it, or we must make the payments elsewhere, in health, higher taxes, or the quality of life. In trying to find our way through these thickets, we must remember that if no one's motives are pure, no one's motives are totally corrupt either. The enemy *is* us, after all, and now we must determine some way to set matters right.

Chronology of Cases

The beginning of the modern environmental movement is reflected in the *Scenic Hudson Preservation Conference v. Federal Power Commission,* 1965. The first awareness of environmental issues is evident in this case. Its initial focus was citizens' aesthetic concerns, but this subject was soon broadened to include concern about ecological impacts.

With the adoption of the first major pieces of environmental legislation new legal problems arose in the courts. In the *Boomer v. Atlantic Cement Company* case in 1970, the old common law can be seen struggling with the new environmental statutes. Perhaps the peak of environmental fervor is best reflected in the three 1972 cases: *Just v. Marinette County,* in which a judge asserted that property did not include the right to develop natural land; *Sierra Club v. Morton,* in which a dissenting judge argued that natural objects have legal standing; and *Tanner v. Armco Steel Corporation,* in which the plaintiffs sought to establish a constitutional right to a decent environment. Through the mid-1970s the environmental movement became institutionalized. In the cases of this era the courts were struggling with the very real problems of assessing the environmental risks in *du Pont v. Train,* 1977.

The cases of the 1980s have a different tone. Rather than enthusiastically supporting the environmental ideals that were common in the 1970s, the cases of the 1980s express sober second thoughts about the new environmental legal regime. Thus, in *National Audubon Society v. Department of Water and Power of the City of Los Angeles,* 1983, the court used the public trust doctrine to second-guess already established environmental policies. These cases also present a deepening of our awareness of what it means to "protect the environment." For example, in *Palila v. Hawaii,* 1988, we discovered that our commitment to protect species involved a possibly massive effort to protect their habitats as well. In *Sierra Club v. Lyng,* we discovered the paradoxes inherent in attempting to identify "wilderness areas" and keep them "untouched." Finally, *East Bibb Twiggs Neighborhood Association v. Macon-Bibb County Planning and Zoning Commission,* brought out the always unspoken, frequently ignored, racial equity issues underlying our land-use and environmental protection efforts. The most recent decisions reveal different and new dimensions of environmental problems and solutions. The international dimension is displayed in *Dow Chemical v. Alfaro,* 1990, and *Guo Chun Di v. Carroll,* 1994. New approaches to environmental controls through consumer labeling is the subject of *Nicolle-Wagner v. Deukmejian,* 1991.

Future editions of *Green Justice* will see cases arising out of new regulatory efforts now "on the drawing board": the use of multimedia (that is, air, soil, and water) regulation, ecosystem management, corporate auditing, and pollution prevention. All of these noble efforts will eventually end up in conflicts, in the courts, and in the mix going to make up *Green Justice.*

This progression described here—from the first glimmerings of environmental consciousness to full-blown enthusiasm, followed by the painful efforts to translate environmental ideals into law, to a culmination in a period of skeptical second-guessing—is too pat to reflect the complicated reality of history. But in its rough outlines it does reflect the experience of the courts as they attempt to deal with the crises brought on by the environmental decade.

Glossary

Adduce. To present, bring forward, offer, or introduce. Used particularly with reference to evidence.

Adjourn. To postpone the action of a convened court or legislative body until a specified time or indefinitely.

Adjudicate. To settle a legal controversy by the exercise of judicial authority.

Adjudication. The formal giving or pronouncing of a judgment or decree; entry of a decree by a court in respect to the parties in a case.

Administrative agency. A governmental body charged with administering and implementing particular legislation.

Administrative law. Body of law created by administrative agencies in the form of rules, regulations, orders, and decisions.

Administrative procedure. Methods and processes of administrative agencies regarding the resolution of a controversy, as distinguished from judicial procedure, which applies to courts.

Administrative remedy. Nonjudicial remedy provided by an agency, board, commission, or the like. In most instances all administrative remedies must have been exhausted before a court will take jurisdiction of a case.

Affirm. In the practice of appellate courts, to declare that a judgment, decree, or order is valid and right and must stand as rendered.

Amendment. An alteration by modification, deletion, or addition. The correction of an error committed in any process, pleading, or proceeding at law, or in equity, which is done either as a matter of course or by the consent of parties or upon motion to the court in which the proceeding is pending.

Ancillary. Aiding, auxiliary, or subordinate; describing a proceeding attendant upon or aiding another proceeding considered as principal.

Ancillary jurisdiction. Power of a court to adjudicate and determine matters incidental to the exercise of its primary jurisdiction in an action.

Appeal. To resort to superior (e.g., appellate) court to review the decision of an inferior (e.g., trial) court or administrative agency.

Appellant. The party who takes an appeal from one court or jurisdiction to another; the one who appeals a court decision.

Appellate court. A court having authority to review and decide a case appeal.

Appellee. The party against whom an appeal is taken, or the party who has an interest adverse to setting aside or recovering a prior judgment. See *respondent*.

Aver. In pleading, to allege or assert positively; to admit something.

Bona fide. In or with good faith; honest, open, and sincere; without deceit or fraud; in the attitude of trust and confidence.

Burden of proof. In the law of evidence, the necessity or duty of affirmatively proving a fact or facts in dispute on an issue raised between the parties in a case.

Case. A judicial proceeding for the determination of a controversy between parties wherein rights are enforced or protected or wrongs are prevented or redressed.

Common law. Those principles and rules of action, relating to the government and security of persons and property, that derive authority solely from usages and customs of immemorial antiquity, or from the judgments and decrees of the courts recognizing, affirming, and enforcing such usages and customs.

Complaint. The pleading, or document, that sets forth a claim for relief in a legal controversy.

Concur. To agree. In the practice of appellate courts, a concurring opinion is one filed by a judge or justice, in which he or she agrees with the conclusions or the result of another opinion filed in the case (which may be either the opinion of the court or a dissenting opinion) though the judge states separately his or her views of the case or the reasons for so concurring.

Contract. An agreement between two or more parties that creates an obligation to do or not to do a particular thing.

Court. An organ of the judicial branch of the government whose functions are the application of the laws to controversies brought before it and the public administration of justice.

Cross-examination. The examination or questioning of a witness at a trial or hearing by a party other than the direct or original examiner, upon a matter within the scope of the direct or original examination of the witness.

Default. The omission or failure to perform a contractual or legal duty.

Default judgment. A judgment against a party that is made when he or she has failed to plead (answer) or otherwise defend against a judgment for relief.

Defendant. The person defending or denying; the party against whom relief or recovery is sought in a case or the accused in a criminal case.

Dissent. The explicit disagreement of one or more judges of a court with the decision passed by the majority upon a case before them. In such event the nonconcurring judge is "dissenting." A dissent may or may not be accompanied by reasons for such dissent.

Due process of law. A course of legal proceedings following those rules and principles that have been established in the U.S. systems of jurisprudence for the enforcement and protection of private rights. The concept of due process of law, as it is embodied in the Fifth Amendment, demands that a law shall not be unreasonable, arbitrary, or capricious and that the means that a law shall not be unreasonable, arbitrary, or capricious and that the means selected shall have a reasonable and substantial relation to the object being sought.

Easement. A right of the owner of one parcel of land, by reason of such ownership, to use the land of another for some purpose not inconsistent with a general property right of the owner.

Eminent domain. The right to take private property for public use by the state, federal government, municipalities, and private persons or corporations authorized to exercise functions of public character under the Fifth Amendment to the U.S. Constitution.

Enabling clause. That portion of a statute or constitution that gives to governmental officials the right to put the law or statute into effect and to enforce it.

Equal protection of the law. The constitutional guarantee, under the Fourteenth Amendment to the U.S. Constitution, that no person or class of persons shall be denied the same protection of the laws enjoyed by other persons or other classes in like circumstances in their lives, liberty, and property and in their pursuit of happiness.

Equitable. Just; conformable to the principles of justice and right.

Equitable relief. That type of relief sought in a court with equity powers, as in the case of a party seeking an injunction or specific performance instead of money damages.

Equity. Justice administered according to fairness as contrasted with the strictly formulated rules of common law. Such justice is based on a system of rules and principles that originated in England as an alternative to the harsh rules of common law and that were based on what was fair in a particular situation.

Error. A mistaken judgment or incorrect belief as to the existence or effect of matters of fact, or a false or mistaken conception or application of the law to the facts in a case.

Estoppel. A legal bar by which a party is prevented by his or her own acts from claiming a right to the detriment of another party, who was entitled to rely on such conduct and has acted accordingly.

Evidence. Testimony of witnesses, writings, material objects, or other things presented at a trial that are offered to prove the existence or nonexistence of a fact.

Exclusionary zoning. Any form of zoning ordinance that tends to exclude specific classes of persons or businesses from a particular district or area.

Ex parte. A judicial proceeding, order, injunction, and so on that is taken or granted at the insistence and for the benefit of one party only, and without notice to, or contestation by, any person adversely interested.

Expedient. Suitable and appropriate for the accomplishment of a specified object.

Ex post facto. After the fact; by an act or fact occurring after some previous act or fact and relating to it.

Good faith. An honest intention to abstain from taking any unconscientious advantage of another, even through technicalities of law, together with absence of all information, notice, or benefit or belief of facts that render a transaction unconscientious.

Injunction. A prohibitive, equitable remedy issued or granted by a court directed to a defendant in an action, forbidding that defendant to do some act that he or she is threatening or attempting to commit because such act is unjust or injurious to the plaintiff and cannot be redressed by an action at law.

Injury. Any wrong or damage done to another, either in his or her person, rights, reputation, or property.

Interdiction. Under civil law, a judicial decree by which a person is deprived of the exercise of his or her civil rights.

Judgment. A court of law's last word in a judicial controversy; the court's final determination of the rights of the parties upon matters submitted to it in an action.

Judicial review. A form of appeal from an administrative body to the courts for review of either the findings of fact or of law or of both; an appeal.

Jurisdiction. The authority by which courts and judicial officers take cognizance of and decide cases.

Jury. A body of persons selected from the citizens of a particular district and invested with power to present or indict a person for a public offense or to try a question of fact.

Justiciable. Appropriate for court review.

Laches. A failure to do something that should be done or to claim or enforce a right at a proper time; operates as a bar to bringing a law suit.

Legislation. The act of giving or enacting laws using legislative power through the legislative process in contrast to court-made laws.

Legislative intent. The legislative history revealing the purpose of the law, which is examined when a court attempts to construe or interpret an ambiguous or inconsistent statute.

Legislature. The department, assembly, or body of persons that makes statutory laws for a state or nation.

Liability. Condition of being actually or potentially subject to an obligation; condition of being responsible for a possible or actual loss, penalty, evil, expense, or burden; a duty to perform an act immediately or in the future.

Majority opinion. The opinion of an appellate court in which the majority of its members join.

Master plan. The omnibus plan of a city or town for housing, industry, and recreational facilities and their impact on environmental factors; used in land-use control law, zoning, and urban redevelopment.

Mitigation. Alleviation, reduction, abatement, or diminution of a penalty or punishment imposed by law.

Motion. An application made to a court or judge to obtain a rule or order directing some act to be done in favor of the applicant. It is usually made within the framework of an existing action or proceeding and is ordinarily, but not always, made with notice to the other party.

Negative averment. An allegation of some substantive fact that, although negative in form, is really affirmative in substance, and that the party alleging the fact must prove; opposed to the simple denial of an affirmative allegation.

Negligence. The failure to use such care as a reasonably prudent and careful person would use under similar circumstances.

Opinion. The statement by a judge or course of the decision reached in regard to a case tried or argued before it, expounding the law as applied to the case and detailing the reasons upon which the judgment is based.

Order. A mandate, command, or direction authoritatively or officially given by a court.

Ordinance. A law or statute that is an enactment of the legislative body of a municipal corporation (city or town).

Pendent jurisdiction. The concept whereby a federal district court, in examining a federal law claim properly before it, may also at its discretion proceed to examine a related state law claim when both claims arise out of a common nucleus of operative facts.

Petition. A formal, written application to a court requesting judicial action on a certain matter.

Petitioner. One who presents a petition to a court, officer, or legislative body.

Plain meaning rule. A rule of statutory interpretation whereby a court, in defining or interpreting a certain word, phrase, or segment of a statute relevant to the case at hand, will give deference to the face value of that word.

Plaintiff. A person who brings an action; the party who complains or sues in a civil action and is so named on the court record.

Plat. A map of a town, section, or subdivision showing the location and boundaries of individual parcels of land subdivided into lots, with streets, alleys, and easements; usually drawn to scale.

Plead. To deliver in a formal manner the defendant's answer to the plaintiff's declaration or complaint or to the indictment.

Pleadings. The formal allegations by the parties of their respective claims and defenses in a case.

Police power. The power of the state to place restraints on the personal freedom and property rights of persons for the protection of the public safety, health, and morals or the promotion of the public convenience and general prosperity. The police power is subject to limitations of the federal and state constitutions and especially to the requirement of due process.

Possession. That condition of facts under which one can exercise power over a corporeal thing or piece of property at his or her pleasure to the exclusion of all other persons.

Precedent. The application, by courts attempting to decide cases, of rules and principles established in prior cases that are close in facts or legal principles to the case under consideration.

Preponderance of evidence. Body of evidence that as a whole shows that the fact sought to be proved is more probable than not.

Prima facie. On first appearance; used to describe a fact presumed to be true unless disproved by evidence to the contrary.

Proffer. To offer or tender, as the production of a document and offer of the same in evidence.

Property. Ownership; the unrestricted and exclusive right to a thing; the right to dispose of a thing in every legal way, to possess it, to use it, and to exclude everyone else from interfering with it.

Reasonable. Not immoderate or excessive; rational, honest, equitable, fair, suitable, tolerable.

Reasonable man doctrine. The standard that one must observe to avoid liability for negligence; the standard of the average, reasonable man under all the circumstances, including the foreseeability of harm to one such as the plaintiff.

Relevant. Bearing on or pertinent; a fact is relevant to another fact when the existence of one, taken alone or in connection with the other fact, renders existence of the other certain or more probable.

Remand. To send, by an appellate court, a case back to the same court out of which it came for the purpose of having some further action taken on it there.

Respondent. The party who answers a complaint or the party who contends against an appeal (the appellee).

Settlement. An adjustment or agreement between persons concerning their dealings or difficulties.

Special use permit. A permit that allows a certain piece of property to not conform to the relevant zoning ordinance affecting that property.

Spot zoning. Zoning that singles out an area for treatment different from that of similar surrounding land and that cannot be justified on the bases of health, safety, morals, or general welfare of the community and that is not in accordance with a comprehensive plan.

Standing to sue. A party's status resulting because he or she is found to have a sufficient stake in an otherwise justifiable controversy to obtain judicial resolution of that controversy.

Stare decisis. A policy that requires courts to abide by or to adhere to rules of previous cases in deciding new ones.

Statute. A particular law enacted and established by the will of the legislative department of government.

Statutory construction. A judicial function required when a statute is invoked and different interpretations are in contention.

Subdivision. The division of a lot, tract, or parcel of land into two or more lots, tracts, parcels, or other divisions for sale or development.

Summary judgment. A ruling, permitted by Federal Rule of Civil Procedure 56, made by the judge in a civil action in response to a party's request that the court declare that party victor regarding any issue in the case about which there is no dispute over facts. Essentially, the party asks the judge to say that he or she prevails as a matter of law. Similar rules can be found at the state level.

Supreme court. The highest appellate court or the court of last resort in the federal court system and in most state systems.

Sustain. To affirm or approve, as when an appellate court upholds the decision of a lower court.

Taking. The deprivation of an individual's right to use or possess some piece of property. A taking has occurred when the entity with power of eminent domain substantially deprives an owner of use and enjoyment of his or her property without compensation.

Ultra vires. Beyond the scope of the powers of a corporation or governmental agency as defined by its charter, laws of state of incorporation, or enabling legislation.

Variance. An authorization to a property owner to depart from literal requirements of zoning regulations in utilizing his or her property where strict enforcement of the zoning regulations would cause undue hardship for the property owner.

Verdict. The definitive answer given by the jury to the court concerning the matters of fact committed to the jury for deliberation and determination.

Zoning. The division of a city by a legislative regulation (ordinance) into districts, and the prescription and application in each district of regulations on the structural and architectural designs of buildings and of regulations on the uses to which buildings within designated districts may be put.

Bibliography for Public Policy, the Environment, and the Law

Contents

About This Bibliography

This bibliography is designed to be read in the approximate order presented in the table of contents, although the fifth through the ninth categories can be read in any order. The last category, Environment, provides readings on specific environmental issues and contains mostly new readings (3–4 years old). The first nine categories contain both new and old readings that represent the major themes and works in each subject. The authors welcome suggestions for additional works or topics.

The bibliography was compiled primarily through the dedication and hard work of Mary B. Keeler. We would like to express our sincere appreciation to Ms. Keeler for her creativity, thoroughness, and enthusiasm.

1. Overviews

Brown, Lester. *World Watch Reader on Global Environmental Issues*. New York: Norton, 1991.

Brundtland Commission. *Our Common Future: World Commission on Environment and Development*. New York: Oxford University Press, 1987.

Clark, Mary E. *Ariadne's Thread*. New York: St. Martin's Press, 1989.

Commoner, Barry. *Making Peace with the Planet*. New York: Pantheon, 1990.

Gore, Al. *Earth in the Balance: Ecology and the Human Spirit*. Boston: Houghton Mifflin, 1992.

IUCN, UNEP, and WWF, eds. *Caring for the Earth: A Strategy for Sustainable Living*. London: Earthscan, 1991.

Matthews, Jessica Tuchman, ed. *Preserving the Global Environment: The Challenge of Shared Leadership*. New York: Norton, 1991.

McKibben, Bill. *The End of Nature*. New York: Random House, 1989.

Miller, Alan S. *Gaia Connections: An Introduction to Ecology, Ecoethics, and Economics*. Savage, Md.: Rowman & Littlefield Publishers, Inc., 1991.

Organization for Economic Cooperation and Development. *State of the Environment*. Paris: OECD Publications and Information Centre, 1991.

Piel, Gerard. *Only One World: Our Own to Make and Keep*. New York: Freeman and Co., 1992.

Silver, Cheryl, with Ruth DeFries, eds. *One Earth, One Future: Our Changing Global Environment*. Washington, D.C.: National Academy Press, 1990.

Willers, Bill. *Learning to Listen to the Land*. Washington, D.C.: Island Press, 1991.

2. Classics

Abbey, Edward. *Desert Solitaire: A Season in the Wilderness*. New York: Ballantine, 1968.

Berry, Wendell. *Unsettling of America: Culture and Agriculture*. San Francisco: Sierra Club Books, 1977.

Carson, Rachel. *Silent Spring*. New York: Houghton Mifflin, 1962.

Commoner, Barry. *The Closing Circle: Nature, Man, and Technology,* New York: Knopf, 1971.

Crevecoeur, J. Hector Saint John. *Letters from an American Farmer*. New York: Dutton, 1957.

Cronon, William. *Changes in the Land: Indians, Colonists, and the Ecology of New England*. New York: Hill and Wang, 1983.

Darwin, Charles. *Origin of the Species*. New York: Macmillan, 1962.

de Chardin, Pierre Teilhard. *The Phenomenon of Man*. New York: Harper & Row, 1959.

Douglas, William O. *A Wilderness Bill of Rights*. Boston: Little, Brown and Co., 1965.

Dubos, Rene. *Man Adapting*. New Haven: Yale University Press, 1965.

Ehrenfeld, David W. *The Arrogance of Humanism*. New York: Oxford University Press, 1978.

Fanon, Frantz. *The Wretched of the Earth*. New York: Grove, 1968.

Halpern, D., ed. *On Nature, Landscape and Natural History*. San Francisco: North Point, 1986.

Jackson, J. B. *Landscapes*. Amherst: University of Massachusetts Press, 1970.

Jacobs, Jane. *The Death and Life of Great American Cities*. New York: Random House, 1961.

Kuhn, Thomas S. *The Structure of Scientific Revolutions*. 2d ed. Chicago: University of Chicago Press, 1970.

Leopold, Aldo. *A Sand County Almanac*. New York: Oxford University Press, 1949.

Lovejoy, Arthur. *The Great Chain of Being: A Study of History as an Idea*. Cambridge, Mass.: Harvard University Press, 1936.

Lovelock, James. *Gaia: A New Look at Life on Earth*. New York: Oxford University Press, 1979.

Malthus, Thomas. *An Essay on the Principle of Population*. London: Penguin, 1970.

Marsh, George Perkins. *Man and Nature*. Cambridge, Mass.: Harvard University Press, 1965.

McPhee, John. *Encounters with the Archdruid*. New York: Farrar Straus & Giroux, 1971.

Muir, John. *Yosemite*. San Francisco: Sierra Club Books, 1988.

Nash, Roderick. *Wilderness and the American Mind*. New Haven: Yale University Press, 1972.

Nearing, Helen, and Scott Nearing. *Living the Good Life: Half a Century of Homesteading*. New York: Schocken Books, 1970.

Schumacher, E. F. *Small is Beautiful: Economics as if People Mattered*. New York: Harper & Row, 1973.

Stone, Christopher. *Should Trees Have Standing? Toward Legal Rights for Natural Objects*. Los Altos, Calif.: Kaufman, 1974.

Teal, John, and Mildred Teal. *Life and Death of the Salt Marsh*. New York: Ballantine, 1974.

Thoreau, Henry David. *Walden*. New York: MacMillan, 1962.

3. History

Barzun, Jacques. *Darwin, Marx, Wagner: Critique of a Heritage*. Chicago: University of Chicago Press, 1981.

Bramwell, Anna. *Ecology in the 20th Century*. New Haven: Yale University Press, 1989.

Cronon, William. *Nature's Metropolis: Chicago and the Great West*. New York: Norton, 1991.

Crosby, Alfred. *Ecological Imperialism: The Biological Expansion of Europe 900–1900*. New York: Cambridge University Press, 1986.

Gilson, Etienne. *From Aristotle to Darwin and Back Again*. Notre Dame, Ind.: University of Notre Dame Press, 1984.

Glacken, Clarence. *Traces on the Rhodian Shore: Nature and Culture in Western Thought from Ancient Times to the End of the Eighteenth Century*. Berkeley: University of California Press, 1967.

Hays, Samuel. *Beauty, Health and Permanence*. New York: Cambridge University Press, 1987.

Luten, Daniel. *Progress Against Growth*. New York: Guilford, 1986.

Maas, Arthur. *Muddy Waters: The Army Engineers and the Nation's Rivers*. Cambridge, Mass.: Harvard University Press, 1951.

Marx, Leo. *The Machine in the Garden: Technology and the Pastoral Idea in America*. New York: Oxford University Press, 1964.

Mayr, Ernst. *The Growth of Biological Thought: Diversity, Evolution, and Inheritance*. Cambridge, Mass.: Harvard University Press/Belknap, 1982.

Merchant, Carolyn. *The Death of Nature: Women, Ecology, and the Scientific Revolution*. New York: Harper & Row, 1980.

_____. *Ecological Revolutions: Nature, Gender, and Science in New England*. Chapel Hill: University of N.C. Press, 1989.

Mumford, Lewis. *The Culture of Cities*. New York: Harcourt Brace Jovanovich, 1970.

Nash, Roderick. *The Rights of Nature: A History of Environmental Ethics*. Madison: University of Wisconsin Press, 1989.

Oelschlaeger, Max. *The Idea of Wilderness: From Prehistory to the Age of Ecology*. New Haven and London: Yale University Press, 1991.

Olson, Paul. *The Struggle for the Land: Indigenous Insight and Industrial Empire in the Semiarid World*. Hanover: University of New England Press, 1990.

Petulla, Joseph M. *American Environmentalism: Values, Tactics, Priorities*. College Station: Texas A&M University Press, 1980.

Pinchot, Gifford. *Breaking New Ground*. Washington, D.C.: Island Press, 1974.

Runte, Alfred. *National Parks: The American Experience*. Lincoln: Nebraska University Press, 1987.

Schaffer, Daniel, ed. *Two Centuries of American Planning*. Baltimore: Johns Hopkins University Press, nd.

Shi, David. *The Simple Life: Plain Living and High Thinking in American Culture*. Oxford: Oxford University Press, 1985.

Stilgoe, John. *Common Landscape in America*. New Haven: Yale University Press, 1982.

Strauss, Leo. *Natural Right and History*. Chicago: University of Chicago Press, 1965.

Thomas, Keith. *Man and the Natural World: History of Modern Sensibility*. New York: Pantheon Books, 1983.

Worster, Donald. *Nature's Economy: A History of Ecological Ideas*. San Francisco: Sierra Club Books, 1977.

_____. *Rivers of Empire: Water, Aridity, and the Growth of the American West*. New York: Pantheon, 1985.

_____. *The Ends of the Earth; Perspectives on Modern Environmental History*. New York: Cambridge University Press, 1988.

4. Ethics/Philosophy

Barbour, Ian G. *Technology, Environment and Human Values*. New York: Praeger, 1980.

Bateson, Gregory. *Steps to an Ecology of Mind: Collected Essays in Anthropology*. New York: Ballantine, 1972.

Berry, Thomas. *Dream of the Earth*. San Francisco: Sierra Club Books, 1988.

Bormann, F. Herbert, and Stephen Kellert, ed. *Ecology, Economics, Ethics: The Broken Circle*. New Haven: Yale University Press, 1991.

Callicott, J. B. *Companion to A Sand County Almanac: Interpretive and Critical Essays*. Madison: University of Wisconsin Press, 1987.

Callicott, J. B., ed. *Nature in Asian Traditions of Thought: Environmental Philosophy*. Albany: State University of New York Press, 1989.

Clark, Stephen, R. L. *The Moral Status of Animals*. New York: Oxford University Press, 1977.

Devall, Bill. *Simple in Means, Rich in Ends*. Salt Lake City: Peregrine Smith, 1988.

Devall, Bill, and George Sessions. *Deep Ecology: Living as if Nature Mattered*. Salt Lake City: Peregrine Smith, 1985.

Fox, Warwick. *Toward a Transpersonal Ecology: Developing New Foundations for Environmentalism*. Boston: Shambhala, 1990.

Hanson, Philip P., ed. *Environmental Ethics: Philosophical and Policy Perspectives*. Burnaby, B.C.: Simon Fraser University, 1986.

Hardin, Garrett. *Exploring New Ethics for Survival*. New York: Viking, 1968.

Hull, David. *Philosophy of Biological Science*. Englewood Cliffs, N.J.: Prentice-Hall, 1974.

Johnson, Lawrence. *A Morally Deep World: An Essay on Moral Significance and Environmental Ethics*. Cambridge: Cambridge University Press, 1991.

Jonas, Hans. *The Phenomenon of Life: Toward a Philosophical Biology*. New York: Harper & Row, 1966.

MacIntyre, Alasdair. *A Short History of Ethics*. New York: Collier Books, 1966.

Mayr, Ernst. *Toward a New Philosophy of Biology: Observations of an Evolutionist*. Cambridge, Mass.: Harvard University Press, 1988.

Mighetto, Lisa. *Wild Animals and American Environmental Ethics*. Tucson: University of Arizona Press, 1991.

Naess, Arne. *Ecology, Community and Lifestyle: Outline of an Ecosophy*. Cambridge: Cambridge University Press, 1989.

Ornstein, R., and P. Ehrlich. *New World New Mind, A Brilliantly Original Guide to Changing the Way We Think About the World*. New York: Simon and Schuster, 1990.

Passmore, John. *Man's Responsibility for Nature: Ecological Problems and Western Traditions*. New York: Charles Scribner & Sons, 1974.

Regan, Tom. *All That Dwell Within*. Berkeley: University of California Press, 1982.

Rolston, Holmes, III. *Environmental Ethics: Duties to and Values in the Natural World*. Philadelphia: Temple University Press, 1987.

Sikora, R. I., and Brian Barry, eds. *Obligations to Future Generations*. Philadelphia: Temple University Press, 1978.

Singer, Peter. *Animal Liberation*. 2d ed. New York: Random House, 1990.

Stone, Christopher. *Earth and Other Ethics: The Case for Moral Pluralism*. New York: Harper & Row, 1987.

Taylor, Paul W. *Respect for Nature: A Theory of Environmental Ethics*. Princeton: Princeton University Press, 1986.

Thompson, Dennis. *Political Ethics and Public Office*. Cambridge, Mass.: Harvard University Press, 1984.

Wilson, Edward O. *Biophilia: The Human Bond with Other Species*. Cambridge, Mass.: Harvard University Press, 1984.

Young, John. *Sustaining the Earth*. Cambridge, Mass.: Harvard University Press, 1990.

5. Policy

Bookchin, Murray. *The Ecology of Freedom*. Palo Alto, Calif.: Cheshire, 1982.

Caldwell, Lynton. *Between Two Worlds: Science, the Environmental Movement and Policy Choice*. Cambridge: Cambridge University Press, 1990.

Dryzek, John. *Rational Ecology: Environment and Political Economy*. Oxford: Basil Blackwell, 1987.

Finin, W., and G. Smith, eds. *The Morality of Scarcity*. Baton Rouge: Louisiana State University Press, 1979.

Gorz, Andre. *Ecology as Politics*. Translated by Patsy Vigderman and Jonathan Cloud. Boston: South End Press, 1980.

Haefele, Edwin T. *Representative Government and Environmental Management*. Baltimore: Johns Hopkins University Press, 1974.

Johnson, Warren. *Muddling Toward Frugality*. San Francisco: Sierra Club Press, 1978.

Kassiola, Joel Jay. *The Death of Industrial Civilization*. Albany: State University of New York Press, 1990.

Landy, Marc, Marc Roberts, and Stephen Thomas. *The Environmental Protection Agency: Asking the Wrong Questions*. New York: Oxford University Press, 1990.

Lester, James P., ed. *Environmental Politics and Policy*. Durham, N.C.: Duke University Press, 1989.

Meadows, Donella H., Dennis L. Meadows, and Jorgen Randers. *Beyond the Limits: Confronting Global Collapse Envisioning a Sustainable Future*. Post Mills, Vt.: Chelsea Green Publishing Co., 1992.

Neustadt, Richard, and Ernest May. *Thinking in Time: The Uses of History for Decision Makers*. New York: Free Press, 1986.

Ophuls, William. *The Politics of Scarcity*. San Francisco: Freeman, 1977.

Paehlke, Robert. *Environmentalism and the Future of Progressive Politics*. New Haven: Yale University Press, 1988.

Portney, Paul, ed. *Public Policies for Environmental Protection*. Washington, D.C.: Resources for the Future, 1990.

Sagoff, Mark. *The Economy of the Earth: Philosopy, Law and the Environment*. Cambridge: Cambridge University Press, 1988.

Simon, Julian. *The Ultimate Resource*. Princeton: Princeton University Press, 1982.

Unger, Roberto. *Knowledge and Politics*. New York: Free Press, 1975.

Winner, Landgon. *The Whale and the Reactor*. Chicago: University of Chicago, 1986.

6. Ecology

Begon, M., J. L. Harper, and C. R. Townsend. *Ecology: Individuals, Populations, and Communities*. 2d ed. Boston: Blackwell Scientific Publications, 1990.

Blum, Harold. *Times's Arrow and Evolution*. Princeton: Princeton University Press, 1968.

Botkin, Daniel. *Discordant Harmonies: A New Ecology for the Twenty-First Century*. New York: Oxford University Press, 1990.

Darlington, P. J. Jr. *Evolution for Naturalists: The Simple Principles and Complex Reality*. New York: Wiley, 1980.

Dobzansky, T. *Genetics and the Origin of Species*. New York: Columbia University Press, 1951.

Ehrlich, Anne, and Paul Ehrlich. *Extinction.* New York: Random House, 1980.

Elton, C. S. *The Ecology of Invasions by Animals and Plants.* New York: Methuen, 1977.

Gould, Stephen Jay. *Panda's Thumb.* New York: Norton, 1980.

Hutchinson, G. E. *An Introduction to Population Ecology.* New Haven: Yale University Press, 1978.

Lovelock, James. *Healing Gaia: A Practical Medicine for the Planet.* New York: Harmony Books, 1991.

Margalef, R. *Perspectives in Ecological Theory.* Chicago: University of Chicago Press, 1968.

Mayr, Ernst. *Systematics and the Origin of Species.* New York: Columbia University Press, 1982.

Miller, G. Tyler. *Living in the Environment.* 6th ed. Belmont, Calif.: Wentworth, 1990.

Norton, Byron. *Why Preserve Natural Variety?* Princeton: Princeton University Press, 1987.

Odum, Eugene P. *Ecology: The Link Between the Natural and Social Sciences.* New York: Holt, Rinehart & Winston, 1975.

ReVelle, P., and C. ReVelle. *The Environment: Issues and Choices for Society.* 3d ed. Boston: Jones & Bartlett, 1988.

Richards, P. W. *The Tropical Rain Forest: An Ecological Study.* New York: Cambridge University Press, 1952.

Thompson, D'Arcy Wentworth. *On Growth and Form.* New York: Cambridge University Press, 1952.

Watson, James D. *Molecular Biology of the Gene.* Menlo Park, Calif.: Benjamin Cummings, 1976.

7. Economics

Anderson, Frederick et al., eds. *Environmental Improvement Through Economic Incentives.* Baltimore: Johns Hopkins University Press, 1977.

Barnett, Harold J., and Chandler Morse. *Scarcity and Growth: The Economics of Natural Resource Availability.* Baltimore: Johns Hopkins University Press, 1963.

Baumol, William. *The Theory of Environmental Policy.* 2d ed. New York: Cambridge University Press, 1988.

Brunner, D., W. Miller, and N. Stockholm, eds. *Corporations and the Environment: How Should Decisions be Made?* Palo Alto, Calif.: Stanford University Press, 1981.

Calabresi, Guido. *The Costs of Accidents: A Legal and Economic Analysis.* New Haven: Yale University Press, 1970.

Daly, Herman E. *Toward a Steady-State Economy .* New York: Freeman, 1973.

_____. *Steady-State Economics.* 2d ed. Washington, D.C.: Island Press, 1991.

Daly, Herman E., and John B. Cobb, Jr. *For the Common Good.* Boston: Beacon Press, 1989.

Dixon, John A., and Paul B. Sherman. *Economics of Protected Areas: A New Look at Benefits and Costs.* Washington, D.C.: Island Press, 1990.

Hirsch, Fred. *Social Limits to Growth.* Cambridge, Mass.: Harvard University Press, 1976.

Leiss, William. *The Limits to Satisfaction: An Essay on the Problem of Needs and Commodities.* Buffalo, N.Y.: University of Toronto Press, 1976.

McNeely, J. *Economics and Biological Diversity.* Gland, Switzerland: IUCN, 1988.

Mishan, E. J. *Cost Benefit Analysis.* New York: Praeger, 1976.

Nichols, Albert. *Targeting Economic Incentives for Environmental Protection.* Cambridge, Mass.: MIT University Press, 1984.

Reese, Craig. *Deregulation and Environmental Quality: The Use of Tax Policy to Control Pollution in North America and Western Europe*. Westport,Conn.: Quorum, 1983.

Schelling, Thomas, ed. *Incentives for Environmental Protection*. Cambridge, Mass.: MIT University Press, 1983.

Thurow, Lester C. *The Zero-Sum Society: Distribution and the Possibilities for Economic Change*. New York: Basic Books, 1980.

Tietenberg, T. *Emissions Trading: An Exercise in Reforming Pollution Policy*. Washington, D.C.: Resources for the Future, 1985.

8. Planning

Altshuler, Alan. *The City Planning Process: A Political Analysis*. Ithaca: Cornell University Press, 1969.

Babcock, Richard. *The Zoning Game: Municipal Practices and Policies*. Madison: University of Wisconsin Press, 1966.

Delafons, John. *Land Use Controls in the United States*. Cambridge, Mass.: MIT University Press, 1969.

Fischel, William. *The Economics of Zoning Laws: A Property Rights Approach to American Land-Use Controls*. Baltimore: Johns Hopkins University Press, 1985.

Friedman, John. *Planning in the Public Domain: From Knowledge to Action*. Princeton: Princeton University Press, 1987.

Geisler, C., and F. Popper. *Land Reform American Style*. Totowa, N.J.: Rowman, 1985.

Getzels, Judith, and Charles Thurow, eds. *Rural and Small Town Planning*. Chicago: American Planners Association Press, 1980.

Hall, Peter G. *Great Planning Disasters*. Berkeley: University of California Press, 1982.

Jackson, Richard. *Land Use in America*. New York: Wiley, 1981.

Mandelker, Daniel. *Environment and Equity: A Regulation Challenge*. New York: McGraw Hill, 1981.

McHarg, Ian L. *Design with Nature*. Garden City, N.Y.: Doubleday/Natural History Press, 1971.

Ortolano, Leonard. *Environmental Planning and Decision Making*. New York: Wiley, 1984.

Rudel, Thomas K. *Situations and Strategies in American Land-Use Planning*. Cambridge: Cambridge University Press, 1989.

Todd, Nancy, and John Todd. *Bioshelters, Ocean Arks, City Farming: Ecology as the Basis of Design*. San Francisco: Sierra Club Press, 1984.

Whyte, William Hollingsworth. *The Last Landscape*. Garden City, N.Y.: Doubleday, 1970.

9. Legal

Auerbach, Jerold S. *Justice Without Law?* New York: Oxford University Press, 1983.

Brodeur, Paul. *Restitution*. Boston: Northeastern University Press, 1985.

Friedman, Lawrence Meir. *A History of American Law*. New York: Simon & Schuster, 1973.

_____. *The Legal System: A Social Science Perspective*. New York: Russell Sage, 1975.

Fuller, Lon. *The Morality of Law*. New Haven: Yale University Press, 1969.

Gaskins, Richard. *Environmental Accidents: Personal Injury and Public Responsibility*. Philadelphia: Temple University Press, 1989.

Gruter, M., and P. Bohannan, eds. *Law, Biology, and Culture: The Evolution of Law*. Santa Barbara, Calif.: Ross-Erikson, 1983.

Hart, H. L., and Tony Honore. *Causation in Law*. 2d ed. New York: Oxford University Press, 1985.

Hayek, Fredrich A. *The Constitution of Liberty*. Chicago: University of Chicago Press, 1960.

Huber, Peter. *Liability: The Legal Revolution and its Consequences*. New York: Basic Books, 1988.

Jenkins, Iredell. *Social Order and the Limits of Law*. Princeton: Princeton University Press, 1980.

Lieberman, Jethro K. *The Litigious Society*. New York: Basic Books, 1981.

Rawls, John. *A Theory of Justice*. Cambridge, Mass.: Harvard University Press, 1971.

Rescher, Nicholas. *Distributive Justice: A Constructive Critique of the Utilitarian Theory of Distribution*. Lanham, Md.: University Press of America, 1966, reprinted in 1982.

Russell, Clifford S., W. Harrington, and W. Vaughan. *Enforcing Pollution Control Laws*. Washington, D.C.: Resources for the Future, 1986.

Schellenberg, James A. *The Science of Conflict*. New York: Oxford University Press, 1982.

Schneider, Jan. *World Public Order of the Environment: Towards an International Ecological Law and Organization*. Toronto: University of Toronto Press, 1979.

Shklar, Judith. *Legalism: An Essay on Law, Morals and Politics*. Cambridge, Mass.: Harvard University Press, 1964.

Unger, Roberto Mangabeira. *Law in Modern Society*. New York: Free Press, 1976.

Vining, J. *Legal Identity: The Coming of Age of Public Law*. New Haven: Yale University Press, 1978.

Wenz, Peter. *Environmental Justice*. Albany: State University of New York Press, 1988.

White, G. Edward. *Tort Law in America*. New York: Oxford University Press, 1980.

10. Environment

Agriculture

Antle, John. *Pesticide Policy, Production Risk, and Producer Welfare: An Econometric Approach to Applied Welfare Economics*. Washington, D.C.: Resources for the Future, 1988.

Conford, Philip, ed. *The Organic Tradition. An Anthology of Writings on Organic Farming 1900–1950*. Biddeford, Maine: Green Books, 1988.

Fowler, Cathy, and Pat Mooney. *Shattering: Food, Politics, and the Loss of Genetic Diversity*. Tucson: University of Arizona, 1990.

Goodman, David, and Michael Redclift. *Refashioning Nature: Food, Energy, and Culture*. London: Routledge, 1991.

Jackson, Wes. *Altars of Unhewn Stone: Science and Earth*. San Francisco: North Point Press, 1987.

Jackson, Wes, Wendell Berry, and B. Colman, eds. *Meeting the Expectations of the Land: Essays in Sustainable Agriculture and Stewardship*. San Francisco: North Point Press, 1984.

Kenney, M. *Biotechnology: The University-Industrial Complex*. New Haven: Yale University Press, 1989.

Little, Charles. *Green Fields Forever: The Conservation Tillage Revolution in America*. Washington, D.C.: Island Press, 1987.

Nabhan, Gary. *Enduring Seeds: Native American Agriculture and Wild Plant Conservation.* San Francisco: North Point Press, 1989.

National Resources Council, ed. *Alternative Agriculture; Committee on the Role of Alternative Farming Methods in Modern Production Agriculture.* Washington, D.C.: National Academy Press, 1989.

Opie, John. *The Law of the Land: 200 Years of American Farmland Policy.* Lincoln: University of Nebraska, 1987.

Soule, Judith, and Jon Piper. *Farming in Nature's Image.* Washington, D.C.: Island Press, 1992.

Strange, Marty. *Family Farming: A New Economic Vision.* Lincoln: University of Nebraska, 1988.

Tompkins, Peter, and Christine Bird. *Secrets of the Soil.* New York: Harpers & Row, 1989.

World Commission on Environment and Development, ed. *Food 2000, Global Policies.* London: Zed Books, 1987.

World Resources Insitute. *Paying the Farm Bill: U.S. Agricultural Policy and the Transition to Sustainable Agriculture.* Washington, D.C.: World Resources Institute, 1991.

Atmosphere

Abrahamson, Dean Edwin. *The Challenge of Global Warming.* Washington, D.C.: Island Press, 1989.

Benedick, R. E. *Greenhouse Warming: Negotiating a Global Regime.* Washington,D.C.: World Resources Institute, 1991.

Bridgeman, Howard. *Global Air Pollution: Problems for the 1990s.* London: Belhaven Press, 1990.

Churchhill, Robin, and David Freestone, eds. *International Law and Global Climate Change.* London: Graham & Trotman, 1992.

Cohen, Richard E. *Washington at Work: Back Rooms and Clean Air.* New York: Macmillan, 1992.

Cross, Frank. *Legal Responses to Indoor Air Pollution.* Westport: Quorum, 1990.

Dornbusch, Rudiger, and James M. Poterba, eds. *Global Warming: Economic Policy Responses.* Cambridge, Mass.: MIT Press, 1991.

Feldman, David. *Managing Global Climate Change Through International Cooperation.* Oak Ridge, Tenn.: Oak Ridge National Laboratory, 1990.

Firor, John. *The Changing Atmosphere.* New Haven: Yale University Press, 1990.

Grubb, Michael. *The Greenhouse Effect: Negotiating Targets.* London: Royal Institute of International Affairs, 1989.

MacKenzie, James J., and Mohamed T. El-Ashry. *Air Pollution's Toll on Forest and Crops.* New Haven: Yale University Press, 1989.

Meyers, Norman. *Deforestation Rates in Tropical Forests and Their Climatic Implications.* London: Friends of the Earth, 1989.

Oppenheimer, Michael, and Robert Boyle. *Dead Heat.* New York: Basic Books, 1990.

Schneider, Stephen H. *Global Warming: Are We Entering the Greenhouse Century?* San Francisco: Sierra Club Books, 1989.

World Resources Institute and Francesca Lyman. *The Greenhouse Trap: What We're Doing to the Atmosphere and How We Can Slow Global Warming.* Boston: Beacon Press, 1990.

Biodiversity/Animals

Collard, Andre. *Rape of the Wild: Man's Violence Against Animals and the Earth.* Bloomington: Indiana University Press, 1989.

Decker, Daniel J., ed. *Challenges in the Conservation of Biological Resources: A Practioner's Guide.* Boulder: Westview, 1991.

Ehrlich, Anne, and Paul Ehrlich. *Extinction.* New York: Random House, 1980.

Eldredge, Niles, ed. *Systematics, Ecology and the Biodiversity Crisis.* New York: Columbia University Press, 1991.

Kohm, Kathryn. *Balancing on the Brink of Extinction: The Endangered Species Act.* Washington, D.C.: Island Press, 1991.

Margulis, Lynn, ed. *Environmental Evolution.* Cambridge, Mass.: MIT Press, 1992.

McNeely, Jeffrey A. *Economics and Biological Diversity: Developing and Using Economic Incentives to Conserve Biological Resources.* Gland, Switzerland: IUCN, 1988.

Natural Research Council. *Animals as Sentinels of Environmental Health Hazards.* Washington, D.C.: National Academy Press, 1991.

Oldfield, M., and J. Alcorn. *Biodiversity: Culture, Conservation and Ecodevelopment.* Boulder: Westview, 1991.

Reisner, Marc. *Game Wars: The Undercover Pursuit of Wildlife Poachers.* New York: Viking, 1991.

Tober, James A. *Wildlife and the Public Interest: Nonprofit Organizations and the Federal Wildlife Policy.* New York: Praeger, 1989.

Tobin, Richard J. *The Expendable Future: U.S. Politics and the Protection of Biological Diversity.* Durham, N.C.: Duke University Press, 1990.

Woodwell, George, ed. *Earth in Transition: Patterns and Processes of Biotic Impoverishment.* Cambridge: Cambridge University Press, 1990.

WRI, ICUN, and UNEP, eds. *Global Biodiversity Strategy.* Washington, D.C.: World Resources Institute, 1992.

Decisionmaking

Chechile, Richard, and Susan Carlisle. *Environmental Decisionmaking: A Multidisciplinary Perspective.* (Editor: Tufts Center) New York: Van Nostrand Reinhold, 1991.

Clarke, Lee. *Acceptable Risk? Making Decisions in a Toxic Environment.* Berkeley: University of California, 1989.

Glickman, Theodore, and Michael Gough, eds. *Readings in Risk.* Washington, D.C.: Resources for the Future, 1990.

Graham, John, Laura Green, and Marc Roberts. *In Search of Safety: Chemicals and Cancer Risk.* Cambridge, Mass.: Harvard University Press, 1988.

Hadden, Susan. *A Citizen's Right to Know: Risk Communication and Public Policy.* Boulder: Westview, 1989.

Shrader-Frechette, K. S. *Risk and Rationality: Philosophical Foundations for Populist Reforms.* Berkeley: University of California Press, 1991.

Development

Anderson, Terry, and Donald Leal. *Free Market Environmentalism.* Boulder: Westview Press, 1991.

Cairncross, Francis. *Costing the Earth: The Challenge for Governments.* Boston: Harvard Business School Press, 1992.

Costanza, R. *Ecological Economics: The Science and Management of Sustainability.* New York: Columbia University Press, 1991.

Cross, Frank. *Environmentally Induced Cancer and the Law: Risks, Regulation and Victim Compensation.* New York: Quorum Books, 1989.

Darmstadter, Joel, ed. *Global Development and the Environment*. Washington, D.C.: Resources for the Future.

Leonard, H. Jeffrey. *Pollution and the Struggle for the World Product: Multinational Corporations: Environment and International Competitive Advantage*. Cambridge, Engl. And New York: Cambridge University Press, 1988.

Lofgren, Don J. *Dangerous Premises: An Insider's View of OHSA Enforcement*. Ithaca: Cornell University Press, 1989.

Morrison, Catherine. *Managing Environmental Affairs: Corporate Practices in the U.S., Canada, and Europe*. New York: Conference Board, 1991.

Pearce, David, and R. K. Turner. *Economics of Natural Resources and the Environment*. Baltimore: Johns Hopkins University Press, 1990.

Pearson, Charles, ed. *Multinational Corporations, Environment and the Third World: Business Matters*. Durham, N.C.: Duke University Press, 1987.

Peet, John. *Energy and the Ecological Economies of Susutainability*. Washington, D.C.: Island Press, 1992.

Schmidheiny, Stephen. *Changing Course—Global Business Perspective on Development and the Environment*. Cambridge, Mass.: MIT, 1991.

Energy

Bedford, Henry F. *Seabrook Station: Citizen Politics and Nuclear Power*. Amherst: University of Massachusetts Press, 1990.

Chernousenko, V. M. *Chernobyl Insight from the Inside*. Berlin: Springer Verlag, 1991.

Coraeub, Ralph. *The Pelkau Effect: Nuclear Radiation, People and Trees*. New York: Four Walls Eight Windows, nd.

Dowlatabdi, Hadi, and Michael Tomans. *Technology, Options for Electricity Generation: Economic and Environmental Factors* . Washington, D.C.: Resources for the Future, 1992.

Kosmo, Mark. *Money To Burn? The High Cost of Energy Subsidies*. Washington, D.C.: World Resources Institute, 1987.

Krause, Florentine. *Energy Policy in the Greenhouse*. New York: John Wiley, 1992.

Leggett, J., ed. *Global Warming: The Greenpeace Report*. New York: Oxford University Press, 1990.

Lemco, J. *Tensions at the Border: Energy and Environmental Concerns in Canada*. New York: Praeger, 1992.

McCutcheon, Sean. *Electric Rivers: The Story of the James Bay Project*. Montreal: Black Rose Books, 1991.

Medvedev, Grigori. *The Truth About Chernobyl*. New York: Basic Books, 1991.

Morone, Joseph, and Edward Woodhouse. *The Demise of Nuclear Energy?* New Haven: Yale University Press, 1989.

Peet, J. *Energy and the Ecological Economics of Sustainability*. Washington, D.C.: Island Press, 1992.

Tester, Jefferson W., ed. *Energy and the Environment in the 21st Century*. Cambridge, Mass.: MIT Press, 1991.

Forests

Cowell, Adrian. *The Decade of Destruction: The Crusade to Save the Amazon Rain Forest*. New York: Anchor, 1990.

Dietrich, William. *The Final Forest: The Battle for the Last Great Trees of the Pacific Northwest*. New York: Simon & Schuster, 1992.

Gradwohl, Judith, and Russell Greenberg. *Saving the Tropical Forests*. Washington, D.C.: Island Press, 1988.

Head, Suzanne, and Robert Heinzman, ed. *Lessons of the Rainforest*. San Francisco: Sierra Club Books, 1990.

Jacobs, Marius. *The Tropical Rain Forest: A First Encounter*. New York: Springer-Verlag, 1988.

Kelly, David, and Gary Bransch. *Secrets of the Old Growth Forest*. Salt Lake City: Peregrine Smith, 1988.

Maser, Chris. *The Redesigned Forest*. San Pedro: R & E Miles, 1988.

_____. *Forest Primeval; The Natural History of an Ancient Forest*. San Francisco: Sierra Club Books, 1989.

Miller, Kenton, and Laura Tangley. *Trees of Life: Saving Tropical Forests and their Biological Wealth*. Boston: Beacon Press, 1991.

Norse, Eliott. *Ancient Forests of the Pacific Northwest*. Washington D.C.: Island Press, 1990.

Perlin, Noel. *A Forest Journey: The Role of Wood in the Development of Civilization*. New York: Norton & Co., 1989.

Repetto, Robert, and Malcolm Gillis, eds. *Public Policies and the Misuse of Forest Resources*. New York: Cambridge University Press, 1988.

Richards, J. F., and R. P. Tucker. *World Deforestation in the 20th Century*. Durham, N.C.: Duke University Press, 1988.

Sampson, R. Neil, and D. Hair, eds. *Natural Resources for the 21st Century*. Washington, D.C.: Island Press, 1990.

Thoreau, Henry David. *The Maine Woods*. Princeton: Princeton University Press, 1972.

International

Akerman, Nordal, ed. *Maintaining a Satisfactory Environment: An Agenda for International Environmental Policy*. Boulder: Westview, 1990.

Caldwell, Lynton. *International Environmental Policy: Emergence and Dimensions*. 2d ed. Durham, N.C.: Duke University Press, 1991.

Carroll, John E., ed. *International Environmental Diplomacy: The Management and Resolution of Transfrontier Environmental Problems*. New York: Cambridge University Press, 1988.

Engel, J. Ronald, and Joan Gibb Engel, eds. *Ethics of Environment and Development*. Tucson: University of Arizona, 1990.

Falk, Richard. *Explorations at the Edge of Time: The Prospects for World Order*. Philadelphia: Temple University Press, 1992.

Gosovic, Branislav. *Quest for World Environmental Cooperation*. London: Routledge, 1991.

Haigh, Nigel, and Frances Irwin. *Integrated Pollution Control in Europe and North America*. Washington, D.C.: Conservation Foundation, 1990.

Johnson, Stanley P., and Guy Corcelle. *The Environmental Policy of the European Communities*. London: Graham & Trotman, 1989.

MacNeill, Jim, Pieter Winsemius, and Taizo Yakushiji. *Beyond Interdependence: The Meshing of the World's Economy and the Earth's Ecology*. New York: Oxford University Press, 1991.

Mikesell, Raymond. *International Banks and the Environment: From Growth to Sustainability*. San Francisco: Sierra Club Books, 1992.

Neuhold, Lang, and Zemanek. *Environmental Protection and International Law*. London: Graham and Trotman, 1991.

Plant, Glen. *Environmental Protection and the Law of War*. New York: Belhaven Publishers, 1992.

Pryde, Philip R. *Environmental Management in the Soviet Union*. Cambridge: Cambridge University Press, 1991.

Rehbinder, E., and R. Stewart. *Environmental Protection Policy: Legal Integration in the U.S. and the E.C.* Berlin and New York: Walter de Gruyter, 1985.

Rush, James. *The Last Tree: Reclaiming the Environment of Tropical Asia*. New York: Asia Society (Westview), 1991.

Sand, Peter H. *Lessons Learned in Global Environmental Governance*. Washington, D.C.: World Resources Institute, 1990.

Triggs, Gillian D., ed. *The Antarctic Treaty Regime: Law, Environment and Resources*. Cambridge: Cambridge University Press, 1987.

Weiss, Edith Brown. *In Fairness to Future Generations: International Law, Common Patrimony and Intergenerational Equity*. Dobbs Ferry, N.Y.: Transnational Publishers, 1989.

Natural Resources

Andresen, Steinar, and Willy Ostreng, eds. *International Resource Management: The Role of Science and Politics*. London: Belhaven Press, 1989.

Berger, John, J. *Environmental Restoration: Science and Strategies for Restoring the Earth*. Washington, D.C.: Island Press, 1990.

Collins, Beryl, and Emily Russell. *Protecting the New Jersey Pinelands*. New Brunswick, N.J.: Rutgers, 1988.

Dysart, Ben, and Marion Clawson. *Public Interest in the Use of Private Lands*. New York: Praeger, 1989.

Frome, Michael. *Regreening the National Parks*. Tucson: University of Arizona Press, 1992.

Gates, Paul W. *Land and Law in California: Essays on Land Policies*. Ames: Iowa State University Press, 1991.

Hage, Wayne. *Storm over Rangelands: Private Rights in Federal Lands*. Bellevue, Wash.: Free Enterprise, 1990.

Henning, D., and W. Mangun. *Managing the Environmental Crisis: Incorporating Competing Values in Natural Resources Management*. Durham, N.C.: Duke University Press, 1989.

Ledec, George. *Wildlands: Their Protection and Management in Economic Development*. Washington, D.C.: World Bank, 1988.

Mantell, Michael A. *Managing National Park System Resources: A Handbook on Legal Duties, Opportunities, and Tools*. Washington, D.C.: Conservation Foundation, 1990.

Rothman, Hal. *Preserving Different Pasts: the American National Monuments*. Urbana: University of Illinois, 1989.

Savory, Allan. *Holistic Resource Management*. Washington, D.C.: Island Press, 1988.

Shater, Craig L. *Nature Preserves, Island Theory and Conservation Practice*. Washington, D.C.: Smithsonian, 1990.

Stokes, S., and National Trust for Historic Preservation. *Saving America's Countryside: A Guide to Rural Conservation*. Baltimore: Johns Hopkins University Press, 1989.

Taylor, C. J. *Negotiating the Past: The Making of Canada's National Historic Parks and Sites*. Montreal: McGill University Press, 1990.

Wallach, Bret. *At Odds with Progress: Americans and Conservation*. Tucson: University of Arizona Press, 1991.

Wilkinson, Charles F. *The Eagle Bird: Mapping a New West*. New York: Pantheon Books, 1992.

Politics

Dankelman, Irene, and Joan Davidson. *Women and the Environment in the Third World*. London: Earthscan, 1988.

Day, Daniel. *The Environmental Wars: Reports from the Front Lines*. New York: St. Martin's, 1989.

Diamond, Irene, and Gloria F. Orenstein. *Reweaving the World: The Emergence of Ecofeminism*. San Francisco: Sierra Club Books, 1990.

Manes, Christopher. *Green Rage: Radical Environmentalism and the Unmaking of Civilization*. Boston: Little, Brown and Co., 1990.

Plant, Judith, ed. *Healing the Wounds: The Promise of Ecofeminism*. Philadelphia: New Society Publishers, 1989.

Porter, Gareth, and Janet Brown. *Global Environmental Politics*. Boulder: Westview Press, 1991.

Rifkin, Jeremy, and Carol Grunewald Rifkin. *Voting Green*. New York: Doubleday, 1992.

Scarce, Rik. *Eco-Warriors: Understanding the Radical Environmental Movement*. Chicago: Noble Press, 1990.

Urban

Frieden, B., and Lynne Sagalyn. *Downtown, Inc.: How America Builds Cities*. Cambridge, Mass.: MIT Press, 1989.

Gordon, David. *Green Cities: Ecologically Sound Approaches to Urban Space*. Montreal: Black Rose Books, 1990.

Hall, Peter. *Cities of Tomorrow: An Intellectual History of Urban Planning and Design in the 20th Century*. Cambridge: Basil Blackwell, 1988.

Hiss, Tony. *The Experience of Place*. New York: Knopf, 1990.

Robinson, James C. *Toil and Toxics: Workplace Struggles and Political Strategies for Occupational Health*. Berkeley: University of California Press, 1991.

Stren, Richard, Rodney White, and Joseph Whitney, eds. *Sustainable Cities: Urbanization and the Environment in International Perspective*. Boulder: Westview Press, 1991.

Wilson, William H. *The City Beautiful Movement*. Baltimore: Johns Hopkins University Press, 1989.

Wastes

Batstone, Roger, James Smith, Jr., and David Wilson, eds. *The Safe Disposal of Hazardous Wastes: The Special Needs and Problems of Developing Countries*. Washington, D.C.: World Bank, 1989.

Bullard, R. *Dumping in Dixie: Race, Class, and Environmental Quality*. Boulder: Westview, 1991.

Denison, Richard A., and John Ruston. *Recycling & Incineration: Evaluating the Choices*. Washington, D.C.: Environmental Defense Fund, Island Press, 1990.

Gourlay, K. A. *World of Waste: Dilemmas of Industrial Development*. London: Zed Books, 1992.

Mazmanian, Daniel, and David Morell. *Beyond Superfailure: America's Toxic Policy for the 1990s*. Boulder: Westview, 1992.

Office of Technology Assessment. *Facing America's Trash: What's Next for Municipal Solid Waste?* New York: Van Nostrand Reinhold, 1989.

Rebowich, Donald J. *Dangerous Ground: The World of Hazardous Waste Crime.* New Brunswick: Transaction Publishers, 1992.

Schwartz, Seymour, and Wendy Pratt. *Hazardous Waste from Small Generators.* Washington, D.C.: Island Press, 1990.

Water

Clarke, R. *Water: The International Crisis.* London: Earthscan, 1991.

Committee on Western Water Management, ed. *Water Transfers in the West.* Washington, D.C.: National Academy Press, 1992.

Glassner, Martin Ira. *Neptune's Domain: A Political Geography of the Sea.* New York: Unwin Hyman, 1990.

Haar, Charles, ed. *Of Judges, Politics, and Flounders: Perspectives on the Cleaning up of Boston Harbor.* Cambridge, Mass.: Lincoln Land Institute, 1986.

Haas, Peter. *Saving the Mediterranean: The Politics of International Environmental Cooperation.* New York: Columbia University Press, 1990.

Henrichsen, Don. *Our Common Seas: Coast in Crisis.* London: Earthscan (in association with UNEP), 1990.

Hundley, Norris, Jr. *The Great Thirst: California and Water, 1770s–1990s.* Berkeley: University of California Press, 1992.

Littlehales, Bates, and William A. Niering. *Wetlands of North America.* Charlottesville, Va.: Thomasson-Grant, 1991.

Matthieson, Peter. *Men's Lives: The Surfmen and Baymen of the South Fork.* New York: Random House, 1986.

Palmer, Tim. *Endangered Rivers and the Conservation Movement.* Berkeley: University of California Press, 1986.

Sand, Peter H., ed. *Marine Environmental Law in the UN Environment Program.* London: Tycooly Publishing, 1988.

About the Book and Authors

Do trees have legal rights? What risks to the environment should we legally try to control or prevent? In this updated edition of *Green Justice,* the authors further explore the interrelationship between the legal system and the environment, using key environmental law cases (over half of which are new selections) on such topics as Superfund and biodiversity—and that are as recent as 1990. The authors' liberal arts approach leads to a wide spectrum of related topics: the history of the common law, the political science of administrative agencies, our obligation to future generations, and the ecology of species extinction.

With the help of explanatory introductions, study questions, and references to relevant literature, students are challenged to determine for themselves how the cases should have been decided and how they link up to broader issues. This accessible text is ideal for undergraduate courses in environmental law and environmental policy as well as non-law graduate courses in planning or public administration.

Thomas More Hoban, a New Hampshire attorney, also serves as environmental consultant to several major manufacturing corporations. Richard Oliver Brooks was founding director of the Environmental Law Center and is professor of law at the Vermont Law School.

Index